COURAGE

COURAGE

The Testimony of a Cancer Patient

Barbara Creaturo

Introduction by Helen Gurley Brown
Afterword by Ezra M. Greenspan, M.D.

Pantheon Books 🏛 New York

Library of Congress Cataloging-in-Publication Data
Creaturo, Barbara.
Courage: the testimony of a cancer patient / by Barbara
Creaturo.
p.   cm.
ISBN 0-394-58077-X
1. Creaturo, Barbara—Health.   2. Ovaries—Cancer—
Patients—New York—Biography.   I. Title.
RC280.O8C73   1991
362.1'9699465—dc20   90-7884

Book Design by Fearn Cutler
Manufactured in the United States of America
First Edition

CONTENTS

For my mother, my father, and Hugh

The three who got me through

PREFACE

The story you are about to read is a very personal story, a story of pain and of fearful struggle. It is the story of those I love, and who love me, of middle-of-the night dreads and glorious dawns of hope. Of life honored and praised.

But this is also the story of my medical odyssey. It tells how I made my way through a labyrinth of often uncommunicative and sometimes uncaring doctors in order to find the best treatment available to a person with my malignancy. Mine was a rigorous and confusing journey, for the best treatment, in my case found at the cutting edge of science, can be murderously elusive. The ordinary physician can't direct you to it; given how far medical practice typically lags behind the frontiers carved out by research, he probably doesn't even know it exists. What he will recommend, and what most cancer patients in this country get, isn't the best, but rather the standard treatment. And when the patient's survival chances are poor—under fifty percent—standard treatment just isn't good enough.

I found the most advanced treatment, but in my search for it,

I was perilously, frighteningly alone. I had no guide, no one to hold my hand. Though sick and dispirited, I read, researched, and made aggressive use of the telephone. The information I turned up was baffling, complex, and often contradictory. I made the best sense of this information that I could, I made my own decisions, difficult though they sometimes were.

Someday it may be your life or the life of someone you love that is on the line. And when and if such an occasion arises, I submit that your best chance may well be to do as I did. Not to accept passively the recommendations of the first doctor that you see, but to make an energetic and wholehearted effort to investigate all available treatments, to educate yourself, and to become your own most impassioned and informed advocate.

Isn't this a great deal to expect from a person already in considerable emotional and physical distress? Shouldn't the doctor you consult *know* what medicine to prescribe? Yes, and again, yes. Unfortunately, the medical community does not yet offer the cancer patient the quality of care he or she may need. Those who would survive must approach this community aggressively; and stubbornly, persistenly *wrest* from it the best and timeliest therapies.

The battle to find and receive these life-saving treatments is not an easy one. But the prize to be won—a victory over cancer, your life and health restored—is precious indeed.

INTRODUCTION

by Helen Gurley Brown

Everyone thinks his friends are extraordinary and, of course, they *are*. They love you, you love them, you understand each other other and can talk yourselves into the next day, the next year, the next *century* when you are together. Never mind that some of these people—including *you*—are about as extra-ordinary as *popcorn!* I feel/think Barbara Ann Creaturo *was* extraordinary—and I doubt any of her friends would disagree if "extraordinary" means there isn't anybody else remotely like this person (though, of course, they don't actually make *any* two people alike). She was gifted.

Barbara Ann came to *Cosmo* in her mid-twenties, beautiful in a wild-gypsy kind of way. We used her as a model in some of our fashion pages, and we are very fussy about models. Through the years she became a superb editor, one of two or three I felt I could never get the magazine out without and, mercifully—except for temporary periods—didn't have to, until she left us just a few weeks ago. She could take the limpest manuscript and, if it had a *message* but just wasn't saying it very well, take it apart, put it back together, and make it shimmer. Any great editor can do that, but Barbara Ann had no peer. She worked so swiftly and effortlessly—for her it was no big deal. She never missed a deadline. She also wrote. Some of her articles, single-girl life being her specialty—she never married—were the best *Cosmo* ever published. Her article ideas for *others* were outstanding—sophisticated, noncliché, inspiring. I marveled that she could keep producing them in such volume year after year. Her classical education (Northwestern, Vassar, Harvard), wedded to her imagination and understanding of women, were a winning combo for us, to put it mildly. She was the soul of *Cosmo*.

May I tell you a few personal things about her? She loved men and was usually involved in a volatile relationship, which sometimes needed sorting out, though she had the same companion for the past fifteen years. Early on I enjoyed helping sort. She listened. You meant to go to her office to talk about *her* or a work project, and first thing you knew you were babbling about a terrible party you'd been to, or an incipient wisdom tooth extraction, or *possibly* a promising writer. She, mesmerized by the story she'd lured *you* to tell. Jealousy and envy were unknown to her. You could have just been made a Nobel Laureate, won the New York lottery, or been asked by Mel Gibson to run away to Tahiti; her response would have been, "but that's fabulous!" And she'd mean it. God knows she was loyal. One of her assistants, an aspiring opera singer, was not seen by co-workers for weeks one year. "Involved in family problems," Barbara would explain. What she was involved in was *auditions,* but Barbara did her own typing and manned the phones to give the kid a chance. "Generous" she invented. I once gave her a feather boa she fancied. Three weeks later, to the day, vacationing in the Galapagos Islands, she turned it over to a native who also fancied it. Next morning she decided to get the boa back because "that was what you would want me to do, Helen, right?" Right, but her first instinct was the authentic one—to share, bestow, make happy. Her temper, sometimes directed at me, was *not* a thing of beauty. I would get hell for some "unassailable" reason, next day she would come to my office to announce she had decided to forgive me and keep me a while longer. Quel relief! I never felt I could manage without her. We would embrace, and she would plant a kiss on the top of my head since I only came up to her chin. She never gave up trying to teach me to swim . . . properly. After each splashing and near-drowning—she was planning *another* outing for us the year she died—she would declare, vexedly, "There is just no *reason* you can't get the *hang* of this. You *aren't* a klutz."

Four years ago, at an editors' lunch at a Japanese restaurant, she came late, complaining of a stomachache. Her doctor had told her it was nothing, but she still hurt. Our health editor, Mallen de Santis, urged her to see another doctor, which she did. The diagnosis, after much testing: ovarian cancer. I helped her obtain the services of one of New York's top cancer surgeons. Not a charming man . . . she despised him, but recognized his skill. After surgery he told me they "hadn't been able to get it all. No way we could, without getting too close to vital organs." She didn't know, but his prediction was that she wouldn't survive. *He* didn't know Barbara Ann. She did survive—for four turbulent, pain-filled, adventurous (*dark* adventures) years as she fought her tyrant. She fought so well that several times the cancer seemed to have been vanquished, and she would return to the office to resume editing. Then something would go wrong again, and it was back to the hospital or clinic, frequently one she had not been to before, to resume her monumental struggle against the disease (you'll be reading about these procedures in the following pages). After each new bout of surgery or other treatment she would not only hope but *believe* it had worked. They were Not Going to Take Her . . . Never! Part of her struggle to write this book was because its completion meant to her ultimate victory over cancer. Finished book. Finished cancer. If her book got written, she had won. It got written, though the writing—and *living*—required titanic effort. She repudiated anything, including pain, that could come between her and victory. She never signed a will; that would have been an admission that she was going to die. She refused last rites, not only because she wasn't religious, but last rites meant for *sure* she was not going to be here. Her parents were devout, however, and brought in a priest an hour or two before the very end. Asked what she would like to hear, she told him she didn't have a clue. "Surprise me!"

Barbara Ann's indomitable spirit reveals itself in every page of her book. I think you will be moved by it. I glory in the years I spent with her

December 1990

EDITOR'S NOTE

The names and identifying details of many of the
people in this book, including those of nearly all
the doctors, technicians, nurses, and other medical
practitioners, have been changed, as have the
names of the hospitals with which they are associated.

COURAGE

DISCOVERY

November 1986

The day has been hectic; nothing unusual in that, at the office of *Cosmopolitan*. All day the phones ring—writers in need of assignments, writers with work in hand unsure of how to proceed, writers wondering, it's been three weeks, are you buying my piece or what? Public relations people keep calling; they're pushing a gourmet chocolate truffle, yet another trivia game, a spandex swimming-suit dress. A new movie is being screened; can I come? A new performer, very hot, is just in town; will I lunch?

Friends call too, and editors from other magazines, and we fiddle with calendars, setting dates two months in advance, which one or the other of us will often cancel the week or day before, pushing the date into yet the next month. We are all so busy! The Boss drops in, and I drop everything to "chat" about whatever aspect of office or personal life is bewildering or disturbing her. The art department is late, or somebody in copy is impossible, or she just hasn't the energy to fly to Houston for a speech. I listen, advise, console. But when coworkers come by to gossip, I let them sprawl for five minutes, then issue the standard office cry— I'd love to talk, I really would, I'll stop around later, but now I've got to *work*.

Amid the chaos, I grab precious quiet moments to smooth the irregular logic and syntax of "What Everybody's Doing About Sex in the Age of AIDS" or to write a blurb for the next month's novel: "Stunning Sabrina had vaulted to the top in the music world, bottomed *out* in love. . . ." No time to wonder if I mightn't be making more of my life—writing a novel, or more of a "contribution"—teaching adult illiterates to read. I've been in harness for so many years, I just trot.

I'm not thinking about my symptoms. The bloating in my midsection that's caused the scale to jump several pounds, the mild stomachache, the pressure when I pee. I've been to the doctor. "No cancer," he said, not that I'd been thinking about that. I'm marvelously healthy, bionic practically, and anyway I'm not the type. Maybe I'm pregnant. That's what I'm hoping for—a late first child, a "miracle baby." Other women have pulled it off; why not me?

Instead of lunch I run to my swimming club—fifty fast lengths, a quick shower, towel-dry the hair and take a taxi back to the office. I can manage it all in under an hour and a half, and the oxygen rush makes me feel marvelous. Then after work, drinks and an omelette with a writer/friend who wonders if she should stay on in Manhattan—the freelance writer's life is no piece of cake, she reminds me—or take a teaching job in Montana. I tell her, go teach.

I'm home by ten, and usually it's my habit to stretch out with a brandy (or two—I've got to watch that, I tell myself), read a little, watch TV, phone my brother in Hawaii. I'm never in bed before midnight. But that night, that Wednesday night, that last night of my old life, that beginning of a new and treacherous epoch in my personal history, I crawl right into bed, exhausted.

I sleep. And I dream. I dream that a great pyramid of light is shining upon the world. I am moving out of the light into a dim shadow place.

I dream another dream. This time I am to be put to death. The method is to be by sword. I will be pierced in the *left* side; this detail of the dream is very clear.

Next day I do not think at all about these dreams. But I do make an early call to the doctor I've been seeing, saying, "John, you must squeeze me in." The doctor has become a friend. He finds time for me at three.

A dozen or so pregnant women are waiting to see John—he is quite handsome, there's no shortage of women wanting him to deliver their babies—but they are all kept waiting. He sees me right away. "John," I say—and the words that come next surprise me; I hadn't planned them—"John, I want a sonogram. There's something wrong with my ovaries."

To humor me, he pulls strings, gets me an immediate appointment a few blocks away with a Dr. Weissman, who has the hardware for state-of-the-art ultrasound. John, who thinks that nothing much is wrong with me—he's wedded to the unlikely diagnosis of endometriosis—says that Weissman will talk to me after the test.

In the sonogram room a technician smears lotion on my swollen stomach—this will be cold she warns—then runs two probes over my chilly flesh. Pictures flash on a television screen beside the bed on which I lie and her attention goes back and forth, first the screen, then my abdomen, as she moves the probes this way and that. Afterward, I wait a little for the plates to be developed and to see Weissman. I do not like the expression on his face. I do not like it when he says, "I think you should discuss the results of the test with Dr. Frederickson," and sends me away.

When I leave Weissman's office it is just after five and there's not a taxi in sight. I walk, briskly through the noisy rush-hour twilight back to the office. From the Upper East Side to Fifty-Seventh Street and Broadway. A longish walk; I am not thinking too much about the sonogram. I am thinking about work left to do, calls to make, and the manicurist who will arrive at 5:45 to do my nails. I don't want to be late.

I dial John's number with my left hand, while Denise, the manicurist, pushes back the cuticles of my right hand. John comes to the phone right away. He sounds nervous. There is a mass around my left ovary. My *left* ovary. My dream death. There are several possible explanations for this. It might be endometriosis, or a benign mass—or—there is a possibility of a malignancy. I yank my hand away from Denise to note what he's saying on a scrap of memo paper. Denise lowers her eyes as I recite back the possibilities. "And it's possible," I say, "that there's a malignancy."

I stay calm. It is only a "possible" malignancy. I do not, however, have the patience to wait forty-five minutes for three coats of Sugar 'n Spice polish to take their own good time to dry. I tell Denise that tonight I'll just settle for clear polish.

I have a dinner date that night with a good office buddy, Diane Baroni, and I can see no purpose to be served by canceling. We proceed to a fancyish Italian place on Fifty-Fifth, where I am unable to eat more than a bite or two of my fettucini with smoked salmon in cream sauce. That's another of my symptoms, sluggish appetite. I show Diane an essay I have written—about how I hid my new mink coat from my maid for three months because I felt guilty about her poverty and my prosperity. I hope to place it in the "Hers" column in the *New York Times*. She finds the essay very good, which pleases me no end.

I am still not focusing strongly on the "possible malignancy," though over brandy, Diane and I determine that I should see Dr. Smithson at the Medical Institute as soon as possible. Whatever is wrong with me, it is clearly not to be treated by John.

I do not tell Diane about my dream-death. I do not tell her that somewhere in me more deeply buried than the tumor, more inaccessible than my already afflicted bowels, I know I have cancer.

. . .

The next day, Marie—the "woman who helps me with my apartment," as I so carefully call her, avoiding "maid" and "cleaning woman" because they sound demeaning—arrives at ten. I live in two rooms, one large and handsome, the main parlor of a formerly distinguished West Side brownstone, the other small, dreary, originally a maid's annex. Tight quarters.

In this small space, and in this circumstance, it is excruciating to be with Marie. I am in the bedroom, calling, arranging, while Marie mops and sweeps and dusts the rest of the place. I hear her humming and occasionally sending up a message to the Lord. "Jesus, be with me. Your will is mine, sweet master." Marie, half-blind, a sharecropper's daughter, first pregnant at fourteen—there are reasons for her piety.

Since I have two separate lines, the living room phone sometimes rings while I am engaged in the bedroom. Marie answers these calls much too loudly and formally, sounding like the principal housekeeper in a large suburban estate. "Ms. Creaturo's resi-*dence!"* her voice fairly shrieks. I lose track of what I am saying and jotting down on memo paper, as she calls me to the phone in a nervous high-pitched voice. It is always somebody I don't need to talk to. A representative from MCI offering a new phone service. A writer who missed me at the office and wants to know if Monday's lunch is still on. The constant interruptions madden and confuse me. This is bedlam.

Marie is confused and frightened by the atmosphere here, which is charged, electric. So am I. This will be the last time, after over ten years of service, that she will come to me. My soon to be deranged schedule won't accommodate her weekly visits, and then poor health prevents her from working. We don't know this. And though we are very fond of each other, we will fail to say our proper good-byes.

I call a friend to tell her I need to speak to Harry, her gynecologist husband, a partner in Smithson's practice, right away. I need an immediate appointment, and Harry will be able to arrange that. I call the radiologist, because I must bring the pictures of my abdomen to Smithson. He is out, but his assistant believes they are with John. I call John and am endlessly put on hold. Finally I connect. John has the pictures. I phone *Cosmo* to ask that the pictures be messengered from John's office to my house.

The living room phone rings with a call I must take. Parker, my assistant, is on the line saying Helen Brown needs an immediate opinion on an article: do we buy "A New Look at the Uncommitted Man" or not? Marie is sweeping up within inches of my bare feet, still humming. I call Helen to tell her I am having some medical difficulties—no details—and must be out for a few days. Her "not to worry, dear," seems tinged with irritation. I suspect she thinks I am playing truant. I am never sick.

Finally, I reach Harry. I tell him what I have been told by Frederickson, that I have a mass and "ascites." I mispronounce "ascites," but he corrects me and adds that in such cases, "the presumption is cancer."

"The presumption is cancer." To presume, to make a presumption. What does that *mean?* Aren't presumptions often false? "A false presumption"—that's a phrase you come across all the time, isn't it? Or is it a "faulty assumption." I am an editor. I should know how a presumption differs from an assumption and to what degree each suggests a certainty. But his words so rattle me that I do not ask for clarification.

Marie cleans, the phone rings, my mind reels. "The presumption is cancer." Harry has arranged an early-morning appointment with Smithson.

"The presumption is cancer." Such brutal words, delivered in so neutral a tone, with no explanation and no expression of sympathy. I find myself disliking Harry. But maybe I just hate the messenger.

The presumption is cancer.

. . .

Smithson's presence soothes. He is sixtyish, comfortably overweight, benign in manner. Diane has said, "he's like a saint," and there is about him a priestly quality. I can imagine him in the listening chair of a confessional, calm in the face of ghastly sins, steady through daily confrontation with the caprices and venalities of the flesh.

I have brought him Weissman's plates, which he quickly reviews, then listens to me recite my symptoms. The pressure I feel when urinating is "like when you have cystitis," I say hopefully. He doesn't bite. Then I explain, eyes lowered, as I might lower them in the confessional, that I had an episode of unusually vigorous sex just before my symptoms made their first appearance. Couldn't that be the cause, I prompt. Smithson thinks not. His eyes go flat, expressionless. Doesn't the man blink? Then, too, I took half a bottle of diet formula, lured by those sexy commercials, when I first began putting on weight. Perhaps that contributed to the bloating. I am reaching. The radiologist has already identified "ascites," and I've the feeling that, whatever this "ascites" may be, it is not caused by sex or by diet formula. It is caused by cancer.

Smithson suggests we move to the examining room, where he reaches inside me fore and aft. The pelvics I'd had with John earlier had been excruciatingly painful, but I've been gobbling the Motrin he prescribed like jellybeans. The examination hardly hurts at all. I tell him how much being examined hurt before and how it doesn't anymore. Couldn't that be construed as a sign that whatever has been troubling me is abating? Couldn't it? Smithson nods, acknowledging that possibility.

Back again in the consulting room, Smithson tells me there is a strong possibility I have an "ovarian malignancy." He does not say the word. He does not say "cancer." What is needed, he suggests, are tests, and I should be admitted to the hospital for them right away.

And if I have a "malignancy"—I, too, avoid the word "cancer"—what happens then? In that case, Smithson explains, I must have a radical hysterectomy. Everything goes. Womb, ovaries—all that makes me womanly. Trashed in some pathologist's waste bin. "I cannot tell you how much I *don't* want a hysterectomy," I tell Smithson fiercely. I explain about the late baby, the hoped-for miracle child. Whatever thoughts Smithson may have on this subject he keeps to himself.

So far, apart from doctors, only Diane and Denise the manicurist, know of my possible danger. The time has come to make a wider disclosure. The first person who must be told is Hugh, my on-and-off companion—companion, not husband—of over ten years. Our history has been bumpy. We've broken up, come together, broken apart again. Now we are in a half-together, half-apart stage. It would be difficult to construct a more ambiguous situation.

Hugh lives in our house in the Catskills, attempting to launch an antique business. The place is overrun with beveled mirrors and *armoires*. I live in the Seventy-Sixth Street brownstone, plugged into the speedy world of deadlines, expense-account lunches, publicity parties, and the like five days a week. On weekends, we are together, as a rule, in the country, where we make love, whether we're in the mood or not.

We have put ourselves in the hands of Destiny. If I become pregnant, we will marry and work through our problems some way or another. If not, I don't know what alternate fate Hugh imagines for himself, but my own mind holds an exploding kaleidoscope of possibilities. Although childless, I will learn to live more peaceably with Hugh. Some other man will fall wildly in love with me. I will shed my attachment to Hugh and come to revel in the joys of solitude. I will become a late-blooming *femme fatale* and have many marvelous affairs. I will finally write a novel, become famous and rich, and my life will be abrim with unheard-of possibilities.

It is all in the hands of Destiny. Of course, it had never occurred to me that what threatens me now is what Destiny—that bitch!—might decree.

I call Hugh. Quickly and unemotionally, I tell him that I have seen several doctors about the symptoms that have been bothering me and that cancer is suspected. I cannot come to the country over the weekend because I will be in the Medical Institute for tests.

Hugh's response is prompt and as prosaic as my own announcement of the news. He will drive to town right away and be with me in the hospital. There are no outpourings of sympathy and concern, and I do not miss them. I am already racing flat-out emotionally, haven't anything to spare. I do not want to cry and be soothed. Nor do I want to deal with calming his fears. I am *busy*. Inside, the drumbeat rolls and it signals danger, danger, danger and death. Run, girl, run.

What I do, of course, is to plan and to shop. Must dash down to Shakespeare and Company and buy a book or two—I'll be in the hospital several days. Got to get to the Town Shop for a decent nightgown and robe—usually I sleep in tattered T-shirts—oh, and slippers, too. I haven't owned a pair of slippers in years. A carton of cigarettes. They've *got* to let me smoke. And brandy, just a pint, contraband in hospitals, I'm sure, but I'll wrap it in my nightgown. The patient as smuggler, pirate, brigadier.

I run my errands and rush home where I wash and condition my hair, carefully shave legs and underarms, rub myself all over with moisturizer, pluck my brows, check my makeup kit. As if preparing for a new lover. For a new life. Certainly not for death.

And then I down as much brandy as I can hold, swallow ten milligrams of Valium, and stagger, drunk and drugged, to bed.

. . .

Hugh and I are soon parted at the Medical Institute, where, in the waiting lounge, I am summoned for preliminary tests. An electrocardiogram—is the ticker normal? I ask the pretty black technician. She smiles and says yes. Blood tests. And, frighteningly for me since I'm a smoker, a chest X-ray. I haven't had one in years and I'm terrified it will show lung cancer. The fear that I have an ovarian malignancy recedes as soon as I set my chin on the steel rim of the X-ray machine, eclipsed by that other, even blacker dread.

My room is on the Babies floor. An irony. Just where I might have been if I'd conceived the miracle child. Smithson is chief of gynecology at the Institute, not primarily a cancer doctor, not an oncologist. Everybody on the Babies floor is, or soon will be, cradling an infant. Except for me.

Among the books I've brought along are Penny Budoff's *No More Hot Flashes and Other Good News,* a reliable gynecological handbook, and the *Merck Manual,* 15th edition. Years of editing stories about women's reproductive ailments have familiarized me with both books, particularly the *Merck's.* You find it on every woman's magazine editor's shelf, sandwiched between the dictionary and *Roget's Thesaurus.*

Over and over again, I read the sections of both books devoted to ovarian cancer. I very nearly commit them to memory. I am looking for evidence that I do not have the disease. I do not find much. Still, I mark in red ink whatever reassures me.

Penny Budoff points out that ovarian cancer is rare. Just eighteen thousand women diagnosed every year. I do the arithmetic.

With the female population at the over one hundred twenty-four million mark, that means that just about one in a hundred get ovarian cancer. So far, my luck, though uneven, hasn't been nearly bad enough to warrant my getting so uncommon and so deadly a disease.

I am not, I find out, in the risk group. That must mean something. Though doctors should be on the lookout for ovarian cancer in all women over forty, the incidence of the disease doesn't peak until age eighty. I am forty-three. Too young. I am too young for this disease.

Ovarian cancers are most common in women with female family members who have also succumbed. Cancer hardly ever occurs in my family. My Italian immigrant grandparents had, between them, fifteen children, and only one of these, a maternal uncle, got caught. By colon cancer. In his sixties. My brother and slew of cousins—I must have fifty—are all clean. I haven't the right family background for this disease.

Ovarian cancer occurs with greatest frequency in women with no children, or no more than two children—too bad about that one—but on the other hand, women who've taken oral contraceptives are considered protected from the disease. My ovaries were on vacation for the ten years I was on the pill. Not so tired out from releasing all those eggs that they'd give up and get cancer. Plenty of pep in them still. My reproductive organs are too lively for this disease.

I can't know at this point that in the course of treatment, almost every ovarian cancer patient I will meet—women in their twenties and thirties, women with a flock of children, women with no family history of cancer—will be outside the risk group, which, evidently, has been poorly defined. Right now I take comfort in knowing that *it is most unlikely that I should get this disease.*

Except. Except . . . I have the symptoms. The classic symptoms. All of them. Bloating, distention, vague abdominal discomfort, feeling of fullness after even a slight meal, frequent urination—you can read the *Merck's* forward and backward, as I very nearly have by now, and not find this cluster of symptoms any place but in the chapter on ovarian cancer. I call my brother in Hawaii. "I have all the symptoms, Tony, all of them." I whisper into the phone, "I think I have The Disease."

Harry pays me a courtesy call. I am very smart in black silk pajamas, a black-and-white, kimono-style robe. I have on purple eyeshadow, vivid orange lipstick. My long, dark-brown hair is brushed and shining. It is very important, I feel, to look well for your doctors. "The bloating seems to be going down," I tell him, almost believing it. My hands are constantly at my middle, assessing my girth. Is it greater or lesser than it was yesterday? Two days ago? It seems to me my stomach has shrunk a little, or at least that the distension isn't as firm as before. "Wouldn't that be a good sign?" I ask sweetly. "Oh, yes," says Harry, who smiles and makes a notation on my chart.

My chart. I badly want a look at that chart. The way at school you yearned impatiently to see inside the bundle of report cards, bound by a thick, red, rubber band, that sat so tantalizingly on the teacher's desk. Or wanted a peek inside the file that contained the results of your SAT scores. Or to look at the first page of the blue book, where the grade was marked. Yours always came with maddening slowness, as the professor distributed the lot, book by book.

I have my opportunities. Though I feel quite bouncy, it is a hospital rule that patients be conveyed from test to test in a wheelchair. My chart is plopped on my lap as I'm rolled along. I open it up and read, ignoring admonishments from the attendants. "You're not supposed to be looking at that!" I feel like a delinquent schoolgirl, defying teacher's orders. Mostly, the attendants are too excruciatingly bored to take action. Only one of them is aggressive enough to reach down and snatch my chart away from me.

But the trips back and forth to my room are short, my sleuthing time abbreviated. Besides I am confused by the illegibility of the handwriting and the unfamiliar medical vocabulary. What I manage to read is unenlightening. "Patient admitted November third . . . ovarian neoplasm suspected . . . IVP scheduled . . ." The Chart does nothing to satisfy my curiosity or soothe my distress.

Up to this point, my body has lived a charmed life. I have always been very pleased to give my medical history—no diabetes, no heart condition, no menstrual irregularities, no this, no that, no the other. I am without stain. Except for a tonsillectomy when I was four—memories of a dark room, a terrible soreness in the knife-scraped throat, much ice cream—I have never before been hospitalized. Spared even the indignities of pregnancy and childbirth, I am inviolate.

All that will end soon. My body will be abused most disgracefully. My veins will collapse from the jab of countless needles, my abdomen be invaded repeatedly by the knife, awesome poisons will be sent surging through my bloodstream and pumped into my belly. But, I get ahead of myself.

For now, the first violation is a barium enema scheduled for the next day, and I am frightened by the prospect of this event. I am instructed to eat or drink nothing after midnight, but it is going on one A.M., and I can't sleep. The night nurse is tiny and Irish, with a heavy brogue. I confide in her. "I'm not supposed to drink anything after midnight," I say, but it's not *that* far after, and . . . they think I might have cancer . . ."

I whisper the word. "Aaaagh," sighs the night nurse consolingly.

"I can't sleep, but I think a drop of brandy might help," I plead.

"Just a little tiddle you're used to, is it?" asks the nurse. What luck that she's Irish! "Ummm," I lie, planning to down a substantial half-glass of Fundador.

"Well, let me ask the intern on duty." The little nurse reappears after a short absence. "The intern can't authorize it," she says, "but I don't believe he thinks it would hurt if you had your wee drop. And good luck to you."

Overcome by her kindness, I pour myself two shots of brandy, drink them down fast, and am soon asleep.

. . .

The next morning I snatch stolen looks at The Chart as I am wheeled to the barium enema room; there The Chart is taken from me, and I turn to the *Best Short Stories of 1986*. Or try to. I should tell you that I am a reader, given not just to long, juicy reads, though I don't despise these, but to the more discrete enjoyments of short, aesthetically balanced exercises in prose. I am in love with the sounds of sentences—crisp, surgical sentences, long, rolling sentences that swell like waves. I have been a fan of sinewy, barely-plotted stories where what you actually read is the subtext, the story beneath the story, given to the imaginative reader to divine.

Yet, as I wait for the barium enema room to disgorge whatever victim it currently holds and to engulf me, I find the *Best Short Stories of 1986* curiously unsatisfying. Why, I'm wondering, did these people bother *writing* these stories? They're not *about* anything! The objections of a philistine; but right now, as I wait for the barium to be pushed through my anus and up into my intestines coiled secretly within me, my objections don't seem philistine to me at all. Real life has hijacked me. I have no patience for literary style.

Finally, the door opens. I am wheeled into the barium enema room, where three technicians, two white women and a black man, smile at me as enthusiastically as a frat-house crew during rush week. I look at the cot onto which I'm to be placed, and at the black box, full of gadgetry, suspended above it, which, presumably, will transfer images of my snakelike insides onto film.

"Couldn't we be all girls?" I ask the smiling crew.

"Oh no," says one of the women. "You'll want Bob. Really you will. He takes the fastest pictures."

"Tell you what," says Bob, who is short, powerfully built,

good-looking. "I'll leave till you're all set up." I smile my thanks for this gallantry.

And so my hospital gown is opened, the lubricated tip of the enema bag inserted, and, as the barium whooshes up inside me, back comes Bob, who is a demon with the black box and who takes his pictures—fast, very fast—as I'm instructed to hang on, to tighten my sphincter, to hold in the oceans of barium until views of my colon and small intestine are well recorded for my doctor's perusal. Afterward, clutching my hospital gown around me, I skip to the john in my paper, hospital-issued slippers and release the chalky barium—it pours out like the contents of a milk jug—and then Bob is wheeling me back.

"Hell of a job you've got," I tell him.

"You said it. One more year and I'm lighting out. See that guy we just passed?"

I look back at a man, very thin, who is about to take my place in the barium enema room.

"Know what he's got?"

"Um-uhm."

"The big A, man."

"The big A?"

"AIDS, man, AIDS."

I try to pick up reading the *Best Short Stories of 1986,* but they seem to me even more precious, more removed from life—and from death—than before.

· · ·

More tests are scheduled; besides the barium enema, there is an IVP. A contrast dye drips into the vein of my arm as the technician takes pictures of my bladder and urinary tract. And I have another sonogram, this one administered by one of life's lucky few, a man who has found his exactly-right vocation. The diminutive technician, whose transducer skates across my belly as he manically adjusts the knobs and dials of his ultrasound TV, appears to be having the time of his life. It's as if he's playing a complex and wonderfully engrossing video game.

"Ascites," I say, "do you see ascites?" By now I know "ascites" simply means fluid. When accompanied by a mass, however, this ascites is usually poison-fluid, swimming with malignant cells.

"Ah yes, ascites. Much ascites," says the sonogram man. He sounds delighted.

Hugh visits for several hours each day. I try to coax him to sit at the bottom of my bed and hold my hand, but he can manage this for only a few moments at a time. Mostly he restlessly paces the room and adjoining corridor, frequently disappearing into the lounge down the hall to smoke a cigar. "You're no good at hand-holding," I complain. "What happens if I'm really sick?"

But Hugh doesn't believe I'm really sick. I am the strong one in this relationship—he gets into scrapes, I bail him out. This pattern will not accommodate a Barbara who is stricken by disease, no longer alert or powerful enough to pilot our shaky craft.

As I yearn for comfort and get little enough of it, I feel the prick of a potentially paralyzing fear. If I am ill, I will be abandoned. Hugh will fail to find the resources, material or psychological, to care for me. I am wrong about this, thank God, but it will be some time before Hugh really registers the *impact* of this disease. And until he does, I will be emotionally on my own.

After the tests are finished, Smithson visits me, a visit I'd looked forward to, imagining what the doctor would say. He'd tell me I wasn't nearly as sick as they'd feared, that no surgery was needed, no cancer waited to be rooted out. I could go back home and take up my life.

Indeed, Smithson lingers in my doorway, as if ready to jump and run. He says my kidneys seem fine, there's nothing wrong with colon or intestines. Yes, yes . . . this is very like what I'd expected. But, Smithson continues, I should have this operation as soon as possible. They have found nothing to contradict the presumption of a malignancy. The only way to know with certainty is to perform a laparotomy, an exploratory surgery. He reminds me of the talk we had in his office. If it's cancer, everything goes; if not, only the diseased ovary must come out.

19

Oh, but this isn't good news, this isn't good news at all. I open my carefully made-up eyes widely and stare, with beseeching intent, at Smithson. I am hoping he will say something more, something better, something *else.*

But all he says is this: "Look, it isn't any fun for us, telling people, I mean. It really isn't."

"What are the chances it's malignant?" I ask. "Fifty-fifty?" I draw a blank. "Sixty-forty?" I suggest, revising my estimate downward. So begins my long obsession with percentages. "More like seventy-thirty, I'm afraid," says Smithson, "but you never know about these things." He tells me of an operation he performed just last week. The woman had a tumor, ascites, bloating, yet her condition was benign.

Smithson explains I can stay in the Medical Institute and have the surgery directly if I choose, though I must be moved from the Babies floor to an oncology ward. "Some women find that upsetting," he says apologetically. Well, yes, upsetting—so it might well be. An oncology ward is hardly the place for a girl like me.

I am tempted. I form attachments easily, and everybody at the Medical Institute has been very kind to me. I will be with Bob, with the agreeable Irish night nurse. That will be nice.

But wait, what am I thinking? I may have *cancer.* I will need *the best of care.* Smithson isn't an oncologist, the Medical Institute not an institution known for bold or imaginative cancer treatment.

"Perhaps I'll think it over a few days," I say. "I can always come back, can't I?"

"Yes, of course, but don't take too long deciding. You need this operation right away."

I do not dally, nor do I cry. Instead, I call Hugh asking him to pick me up and pack my things. Odd, how I'm not even tempted to tears. Nor will I be—at least not often—in the difficult months to come. Only a few torrents and almost no self-pity. I would have imagined myself, had I ever foreseen this situation, awash in both.

One cannot predict one's behavior in a predicament like this. The curtain rises—on what? Melodrama? Tragedy? I don't know what to call this piece of theater which has begun to unfold around me. The curtain rises and one acts in ways nobody, least of all oneself, would have thought to predict.

· · ·

It's just a week since the "presumption" of cancer was established and I'm on the phone to Helen Brown. "You know I'm not one to ask for personal favors," I say, "but this is life-or-death important. I want the best surgeon in New York, and I've no idea who that would be. And I want to see him right away. They'll know 'across the street' "—that's how we in editorial refer to management's executive offices—"and they'll be able to get him for me."

"Honey, whatever it is you need, you know you've got it," says Helen, without hesitation. Our professional association has been long, our mutual loyalty deep. I have, of course, briefed her —by now Helen knows, though she has nearly as much trouble believing it as I do—that I probably have cancer.

A few hours later, the appropriate calls have been made and the appointment set. Don Lawson, a top-notch surgeon at Community Hospital will see me the next day. According to management, he's the best, no doubt about it. The brass knows these things somehow. Whenever one of their number falls ill, the others close ranks, arranging top-of-the-line treatment with the finest medical talent. They are fortunate men—wealthy, powerful—and would live forever if they could. Through Helen I've tapped into their club.

Diane Baroni will come along. Though Hugh has offered to see Lawson with me, he's expressed a certain manly reticence— my problem embarrasses him I think—that I'm pleased to indulge. I want another woman's intuitive judgment of the man who'll operate on me.

After the physical examination, Diane and I move into Lawson's office. The surgeon's face is sallow, with a pinched look, and he is built like a pear. Not a prepossessing-looking man.

Lawson talks, as I sit facing him, scribbling, schoolgirl-like, into my notebook. The information he passes along is technical and it confuses me. At the time of surgery there will be a "cytoscopy," followed by multiple biopsies. I don't understand "cytoscopy." The only other possibility, aside from cancer, is an "ovarian fibroma with Meigs syndrome." "Fibroma?" "Meigs syndrome?" Suddenly, I'm brought up short by a word I do understand. "Castration," Lawson is saying, "Castration" is what happens to me if there is a malignancy. The word is medically correct. That's how doctors describe the surgical excision of a woman's ovaries.

Throughout this recitation, Lawson takes a hearty, business-like tone—he sounds like a successful entrepreneur discussing a merger. I'm stung. What we are talking about here is the removal of precious parts of me. What we are talking about here is my life.

The phrases float by me—"germ cells," "epithelial cancer." I'm baffled and I'm panicky. All I understand is that I may need a hysterectomy, may be "castrated," and I'm so focused on this loss I barely note it when Lawson explains that if a malignancy is found, I'll need six to twelve months of chemotherapy. One catastrophe at a time, if you please.

"And if it's not cancer?" I ask. How extensive, then, must surgery be?

"As long as it's not cancer, I'm flexible," says Lawson grandly. All he'll take is the diseased ovary. His estimate of the chances that I have the disease? Sixty-forty. Ten percentage points better than Smithson gave me. Numbers, numbers! How they are coming to preoccupy me.

My hopes refuse to die. I tell Lawson about the unusually vigorous sex I had just before my symptoms appeared. Could that have any relevance? "Only if it was good," says Don Lawson, with a har-hardy-har and a slap at his knee.

And how soon must I make my decision?

Lawson consults his calendar in the manner of a man far too

busy for his own good. I'm given to understand he'll make time for me, though it will hardly be easy—he has speaking obligations in distant cities, a crowded calendar of surgeries. I'm left thinking this man of top-notch reputation will be lost to me unless I commit myself right away. And yet I hesitate. His manner troubles me. I say I'll call as soon as I've made up my mind.

"What did you think?" I ask Diane, when we hit the corridor.

Well frankly, Diane isn't sure I'll be entirely comfortable with him. My friend doesn't speak ill of anyone easily. "He's awful, isn't he," I say.

"He does seem rather unpleasant," Diane agrees. "But maybe that's the way cancer surgeons are."

"Jesus, I hope not," I say.

· · ·

At the entrance to Community Hospital, Hugh waits curbside, at the wheel of our Toyota. Diane and I slip into the car. "Where to?" asks Hugh. "A bar, any bar," I answer promptly, knowing for once exactly what I want. "Diane, you come too!" "Of course," Diane is one of life's great comforters, sweet, maternal, very smart. The best hand-holder in town.

Though it's mid-November we are still having spectacular autumn weather. The city is obliquely lit, the clouds cast shifting shadows, and when we move out from under them, it's into a sweet, penetrating, golden light. It's an October sky, October light. I try to shield my eyes and heart from the beauty of the day which reminds me painfully of how much I cherish life. "It's so beautiful" I say. "I can't stand it being so beautiful." I wish it were dull and bleak, the warmth and brightness already leeched from the world, as it properly should be by this time in November.

We find a bar of the type I particularly like. Dark and Irish with pubby food—chops, knockwurst and sauerkraut, great fatty chunks of pastrami—served cafeteria style. You fill up your tray, then move along to green formica tables, no tablecloth, no amenities. I toy with a plate of stew—by this time I can't eat at all—

and drink four beers. I do not want to budge from the bar, which seems to me as secure as a fortress. Nothing really bad can possibly happen to a girl who is downing a few beers at the Shamrock. Besides, it is dark and seasonless inside this place; no need to be confronted with the sense of summer's brilliance slipping into eclipse. There isn't a window here to admit a hint of our lovely, heartbreaking weather.

We drink our beers, hash over my visit to Lawson, and conclude there must be a better man for me. Somehow, we will find him.

. . .

It's not without embarrassment that I tell Helen how much I disliked Lawson, but she is graciousness itself, saying she'll check with a friend, a prominent thoracic surgeon, to see if she can turn up somebody else equally good. I call John, who is himself not without embarrassment over having so spectacularly misdiagnosed my case, to ask who else in New York has a reputation to rival that of Don Lawson.

John gives me several names. The two top men are unavailable. The first is in Paris for the month, and the second is no longer taking new patients. John has also mentioned two younger men, with reputations in the making: Carl Whiting of Montgomery Hospital, and Henry Jeffries, junior to Lawson at Community Hospital but thought to be enormously talented. I make appointments with both men and wait for my parents to arrive.

I'd called my mother and father from the Medical Institute, apprising them of the situation, but insisting all was well—I'd be okay, I didn't need them. But now they'll be put off no longer. They've booked a flight and are on their way.

My parents have no fondness for Hugh. They've been trying to pry us apart for years, and, at times when the relationship was at its most rickety, have very nearly succeeded. Hugh's here-and-there career appalls them. For their talented firstborn and only daughter, they'd had in mind an ambassador. I'm afraid they'll use this illness, or even the prospect of an illness, to further their ardently-held hopes that we would separate. It's an issue with which I'd prefer not to become engaged right now.

Go out and buy a new suit, I urge Hugh. But something gorgeous. Something expensive. If Hugh can't become the ambassador of my parents' fantasies, I'll have him look the part, at least. Right now, Hugh's wardrobe consists of jeans, bulky sweaters, down vests—suitable for bidding at auction barns, but not for stepping out in New York City. Hugh thinks I'm ridiculous, but off he goes, returning with an elegantly tailored suit in bankers' blue, pink silk shirt, skinny eggshell tie. Tall and well-built, Hugh carries himself with distinction, and in his new suit, he looks as if the roughest labor he's ever done is to pluck a glass of champagne from a silver tray.

By this time, the phone has begun to ring and will hardly pause all week. Friends wondering how I am. It quite amazes me, since I myself have called practically no one, how fast the word has spread. News travels quickly in small-town Manhattan where, within milliseconds, everybody has heard about everybody else's momentous events—lurid illnesses included—and has immediately transformed them into the stuff of gossip. Here, no less than in some sleepy rural hamlet, the grapevine is immediately abuzz with word of one's neighbors travails. Did you hear? Did you hear? Did you hear that Barbara Creaturo may have *cancer?*

It's becoming a little overheated, this drama of mine. The phone rings and rings. My panicked parents are about to set down on a runway at Kennedy. Old friends—some of whom I haven't seen for years—call, offering help and comfort. Jennifer will send her limo around when I need to see doctors.

And so it is that for the rest of that week, we come to travel from doctor to doctor by caravan. My middlewestern Mother and Father, though trim and handsome, look dull as wrens sitting beside Jennifer, gaudy in her gypsy silks, mountains of fur, high-heeled snakeskin boots. Hugh, blue-suited when we met my parents at the airport—that didn't go half-badly, I think—is back in jeans and down vests. I sit in the back of the car, chain smoking, clutching my belly, talking little, glad of the limo's tinted windows that dim my view of the still lively light. Quietly, I'm losing my grip on reality.

All this has the quality of a dream. Or nightmare. Anyway, it is a well-provisioned nightmare, with cheese and juices and whiskey in a fridge at the back of the car—the occasional shot of bourbon helps calm my nerves.

Silently, the limo cruises the streets of Manhattan. How surprised onlookers would be if they could hear the hubbub we're raising within. Everybody is talking a mile a minute, about how I don't have cancer, it's just not possible, a benign tumor is what it must be. They are talking over each other; they are talking all at once; the effect is practically choral.

It's almost *jolly* inside that car. I feel as if I'm on some odd sort of holiday. Cars to fetch me, and no office to go to, and dinners out—the driver and the limo are often ours in the evening as well. Nobody feels sane or ordered enough to cook. The money is flying around as if all of us, and not just Jennifer, are rich beyond restriction.

I think I was better off nursing my beers at the Shamrock, with just Hugh and Diane for company. But there is no slowing the action now. We are hurtling through New York in a Lincoln Continental limousine, talking and laughing like partiers on a spree. Given all this noise and mock-hilarity, it's easy to forget that our purpose is grave—we must find the doctor who will help me save my life.

. . .

The caravan arrives at Carl Whiting's office. I go in first for the initial consultation and physical exam, while my retinue sits anxiously in the waiting room. Later the doctor will address us as a group. That's standard procedure. Cancer doctors routinely deal with the patients' anxious loved ones; I doubt it's their favorite part of the job.

I've dressed carefully. I'm wearing a longish, vividly patterned silk dress—turquoise flowers on a field of taupe—with an uneven scalloped hem that falls about my calves in pretty folds. It's a romantic effort. Over my arm, I carry the $18,000 mink I have borrowed from Jennifer. I'm desperate to look like a woman of substance and sophistication.

My poise collapses the moment I see Whiting. He has a like-able, funny-looking face—red-cheeked and nearly bald, with twinkling myopic eyes. No smoothie, this Whiting, he looks like a street-kid made good.

"I'm losing it, Doc," I say, before I've even taken a seat. "I'm really losing it. I'm running all over town trying to find somebody to tell me I don't have cancer."

I rattle off my symptoms. "Cancer, right?"

"You'll know for sure after the operation, but, yes, that's what your symptoms strongly suggest," says Dr. Whiting.

"I'm not sure I can handle this," I say.

Whiting feels my distress sharply. Are the surgeon's eyes filling with tears? It would seem so. His voice grows ragged with emotion as he begins to talk about death, not the cancer-death I've begun to fear, but the sudden, casual deaths of war. He's talking about Vietnam. Most of those who died were young, he says. Just as I am young. There's no forgetting them, no matter how hard you try. Anyway, no decent person would choose ever to forget.

Did the doctor lose a brother there, a friend? Or perhaps Whiting served as a surgeon in Vietnam. He's about the right age for that. Are memories of torn-apart bodies in faraway jungles tough to shake? Do the patients his skills can't save prod haunting memories of those lost or maimed on the jammed-together operating tables of the war?

So now the two of us are losing it, doctor and patient alike, struck with grief over the prospect of untimely suffering and early death. I come to him with cancer, he talks to me of war. Apparently, he's had no small experience of both. Somehow this doesn't seem in the least inappropriate. On the contrary, it makes a bond. I want to reach out and take his hand—for courage. Whiting is evidently no stranger to the battlefield. Me, I'm just a raw recruit.

27

Almost as an afterthought he examines me. Yes, cancer, that's certainly the likelihood. I've been remiss about my annual check-ups, I confess. Years went by when I didn't see a gynecologist. Have I, through my own carelessness, contributed to this catastrophe?

"You could have spent your life in a gynecologist's office," Whiting says, "and have found yourself in exactly the same fix." It's in the nature of this disease, which in my small but growing collection of cancer books is uniformly referred to as "the deadliest of all gynecological cancers," to show no symptoms and thereby to evade detection until dangerously far advanced. Since ovarian tumors are smooth and plaquelike, they can be of substantial size and still not be noted during the standard pelvic exam. A pap smear doesn't show the disease either, unless the endometrium is affected, which is rare. This is why, in spite of the tiny number of women afflicted, deaths due to ovarian malignancies exceed the toll taken by cervical and endometrial cancers combined. There was no way, barring having had regular sonograms —not yet part of the average gynecologist's routine exam—I could have kept myself safe from this uncommon, uncommonly dangerous predicament.

I go to fetch the gang of four, who are pretending to thumb through magazines in the doctor's waiting room. Immediately, they overwhelm Whiting with questions that are hardly questions at all, but rather pleas for reassurance. How likely is the cancer? How curable? I'm nothing like the average patient, they all assure him. My mother boasts of my excellent health, product of her dedicated maternal care. My father brags about my genes, his contribution—his mother lived well into her nineties, his brothers and sisters are all paragons of health and longevity. Jennifer testifies to my hardness of spirit, and Hugh emphatically agrees—they just don't come more robust than me. Even if it *were* to be cancer, a prospect none of them is ready to accept, I'll come through as easily as if I had a head cold.

Whiting raises his hands, palms front, as if to quiet an auditorium of unruly school kids. Cancer isn't a head cold, and nobody, however marvelous their genes or health or attitude, is exempt from its lethal threat. The doctor is doing his best to quell the crazed optimism of my parents, lover, friend, and how I thank him for it! If only they were to hush, to take my hand, to murmur, poor baby, poor dear, how awful this must be for you. That would be soothing. Instead, I am rattled by their boisterous assertions that, however substantial the evidence to the contrary, I am going to be fine, just fine.

"She's the one who's going to have to go through all this," Whiting continues. "It's going to be quite some time, a year— maybe longer—before she can be sure she's going to live." If ever, is what he doesn't add. Silently, I complete the thought.

"Nobody knows whether or not they're going to survive," asserts Jennifer, displaying a metaphysical bent. "Any one of us could go out on the street after leaving this office and be run down by a car!"

"That's very different," says Whiting, sounding tired. He's heard this one before. "You can speculate about dying, but that's not the same as living with a disease you know can kill you. She has to come to terms with that, and it's not going to be easy. There are patients who survive their cancer and succumb to something else. Ulcers. A bad heart."

I'm glad Whiting has pointed out the differences between living with cancer and toying with thoughts of your own mortality as you watch the traffic race by, or look up at a construction site, the precariously balanced beams and concrete blocks, and idly think, suppose something were to slip. Because the little chill that passes through you then is nothing like the dread that comes from knowing that you carry within you the seeds of your own destruction. And that you cannot predict whether the surgeries and other radical therapies to which you'll be obliged to submit will crush these seeds to a harmless dust, or whether they will flower, in spite of killing knives and chemicals, and consume you in what writer Philip Roth has referred to as the "hairless, seventy-eight-pound death."

In the months to come, I will hear that stale observation—that survival is assured to none of us—again and again. That my predicament isn't really so different from that of everybody else. And I will pretend, quite reasonably, to agree. Instead of exploding in anger, saying you try it, you see what having cancer is like, you who are subject to only the most theoretical of fears and feel quite safely wrapped in your own good health, your snug presumption of invincibility.

Jennifer plunges brashly ahead, taking full charge of my case. "How soon," she asks, "can you operate?" Whiting regrets to say that he's booked until Thanksgiving, and then, following the long holiday weekend, has surgeries scheduled for another full week. I should have the operation sooner than that. "Couldn't you come in Thanksgiving and do it then?" demands Jennifer. I'm appalled she has the nerve to suggest the doctor give up his holiday. "I suppose I could," says Whiting mildly, "but Thanksgiving weekend isn't the optimal time for surgery. Most of the hospital staff is off."

I begin to rise from my chair, signaling that we should leave. I want to get out of here before Jennifer says or does something else to try the surgeon's patience. There are warm handshakes all around. Carl Whiting has made a hit.

Whiting has been as sympathetic as Lawson was abrasive. I would be pleased to have him for my surgeon. But he hasn't time; the operation must be performed right away. Still, as we leave, I feel better for the visit. I'm glad to have met so compassionate a physician, glad, too, that he's made an attempt to show the others that to be *with* me in this, to give intelligent support, they must acknowledge that cancer is the likelihood and death a possibility.

· · ·

I've had a stroke of luck. David Beck has been persuaded to see me. An old friend, Joyce, has heard about my problems; as a longtime patient of Beck's she's interceded with him on my behalf.

"He's a genius, there's nobody like him, you can't *know* how

30

good this doctor is," Joyce tells me on the phone, in her rich, throaty voice.

I doubt that Joyce's charms have been lost on Beck. I'd bet she's one of his favorites. Most probably that has had some bearing on how quickly my appointment has been arranged.

The caravan sets off with hopes pitched high. Not only is Beck one of the city's most gifted gynecological surgeons, he has also figured prominently in the research on ovarian malignancies. One of the first physicians to chart the dangers of this cryptic disease, he has helped develop the treatments in use against it, and has worked on a vaccine which may some day serve as both preventative and cure. Beck is known, respectfully, as "the father of ovarian cancer," though, as Jennifer quips, he could hardly wish to claim paternity to so disagreeable a disease.

Beck's office, several blocks west of hospital row, is cheerful. As I sit in this comfortable, inviting place, I'm suddenly not sure —no, not sure at all—that this cancer is such an inevitability. If anybody can liberate me from my fears it is Beck, and all at once I'm optimistic.

My name is called. Beck has a manner calculated to inspire confidence: gentle and measured, accessible albeit reserved.

The surgeon asks about my symptoms and takes my medical history. When I tell him about my long use of oral contraceptives, he says, "Well, that should have protected your ovaries," and my heart surges with hope. I don't have it! I'm *protected*—protected by that little dialpack I hid so assiduously from my mother as soon as I became sexually active at age nineteen.

We retire to the examining room. By now I'm something of a connoisseur of pelvic exams—I've had my heels in stirrups on and off for weeks—and Beck's hands are so sure I barely feel them. His touch is as smooth as cream. Back in his office, I am hopeful, relaxed.

Not for long.

Beck tells me he is certain I have the disease. How certain? Ninety-nine percent, no, one hundred percent if I want the truth.

He hasn't a doubt. "I'd say you're stage III, though there's a chance, thin as an eyelash, that you might be stage II."

I know a little about staging from my reading. Stage III means the cancer is far advanced, spread from the reproductive organs through the peritonium, and resistant to cure. The frail balloon of my hopes collapses.

"You can't be sure. You're not God!" I say.

Beck agrees he's not.

"It's *possible* I don't have cancer."

The surgeon remains silent.

What follows is a wrangle about the extent of surgery, in the unlikely event that I don't have a malignancy. Beck insists, cancer or no cancer—"though I don't think you need worry about that" —that he must perform a radical hysterectomy. "But *why?*" I passionately object. "Because it's good medicine," is all the surgeon will say. We go back and forth for a little while, neither of us budging from our position. I am unwilling to consent to the full surgery until it's been established that I have a malignancy. He won't operate unless I agree to the hysterectomy, even if my tumor is benign. We're at a stalemate.

"How in God's name did I *get* this thing," I ask.

"If I knew the answer to that," says Beck mildly, "I'd win the Nobel prize."

"I hate to subject you to this," I say, "but I'm afraid it's time you met the eternally optimistic brigade." I go back to the waiting room, returning with my parents, Hugh, and Jennifer in tow.

Even their invincible high spirits are quickly quashed in the face of Beck's unshakable certainty. The hurricane rush of questions and objections I'd anticipated subsides to a desultory swell. I tell Beck I'll call by day's end to give him my decision. He nods. Then he looks at me keenly, shifts his glance to the others, and volunteers a few short sentences none of us is likely to forget. "Don't worry about her. She'll come through this. She's going to be okay."

It is as if an oracle has spoken. At that moment, we're all of us certain that Beck is blessed with the gift of prophecy.

That evening I call, and I beg, and I plead. But Beck will not consent to the less radical surgery, even in the absence of a malignancy. I'm strongly inclined to believe he's right about the cancer, but the man *could* be mistaken. I'd never forgive myself or him if I were to be deprived of my chance at the late-life child, the miracle baby, because of an unnecessary hysterectomy. Reluctantly, I decline Beck's services but ask him whether, if I should have cancer, he'd be willing to take over my postsurgical care, directing the chemotherapy. Perhaps, says the surgeon, but his possible involvement will depend on how he feels about the pathology.

Why is Beck so inflexible about the extent of surgery? Medically, his is a minority view, rarely held by doctors of his prominence. Perhaps Beck, as physician-warrior, has been too often bested by this disease. He's come to know the ovary most intimately, not as the source of life, but as a guileful, treacherous adversary. Why grant the devil a potential advantage when you can instead invade and destroy his hiding place?

· · ·

So it is that, after seeing these men in a single frantic, frightening week, I find myself back where I started, at Community Hospital, this time slated to see Henry Jeffries. The Boss has made good her promise. She's contacted her surgeon friend, who has recommended Jeffries, the very Jeffries that John has named as fast becoming one of the city's ranking surgeons. This seems a promising coincidence. Jeffries will be my man, I'm confident of it!

I'm with my retinue in the waiting lounge for only a few minutes before Jeffries, a sleek, good-looking man, sultanlike in his hospital whites, summons me into an examining room and has me once again in stirrups. As his gloved hands probe, I mention the few small ways in which my case doesn't conform to the classic ovarian pattern. My history of contraceptive use, for one. And another point, the pain caused by John's initial examinations. Only benign tumors cause pain, I've read. The malignant growths leave you numb as logs. Impatiently, Jeffries agrees—yes, yes, these are both good signs. When I ask, could my chances of having a benign tumor be as good as fifty-fifty, he doesn't give me any argument. It's as if I'm the stubborn customer and he's the distracted merchant—why not just give me the price I insist upon and get on with business.

Surely it's ridiculous, this ongoing quarrel I keep up with my fate. Why am I still quibbling, still trying to negotiate favorable odds? Haven't I been told by the man who is, plausibly, best equipped in his field to make an accurate diagnosis, that cancer is a certainty? I can only say on my own behalf that I know of no one—no lover of life at least—who wouldn't grow balky at this point, who wouldn't resist embarking upon the nightmare journey I'm about to undertake.

As I step out of the stirrups, Jeffries brusquely suggests that we settle upon a surgery date. I'm rattled. We haven't yet had a proper consultation. I know from my work editing medical material that in situations as grave as this, doctors are meant to listen, to answer questions; he's favored me with, at best, ten minutes of his time. The veterinarian you talk to about your dog's listless pelt gives you more attention than this. Am I to return to my loved ones and say, that's it, I'm on for Tuesday? I have family with me, I explain. They're understandably upset. They need a few minutes with him. He shrugs as if to say, what for? The gesture further unnerves me.

"Okay, bring them into the room across the hall," says Jeffries ungraciously. He's clearly irritated. I fetch my crew—why *are* they all here, I wonder, suddenly exhausted by the hubbub of the past week, the parade of doctors, my parents' constant, worried chatter, Jennifer's aggressive solicitude. We move into the designated room, furnished only with two folding chairs. There we are greeted not just by Jeffries, but also by his fellow intern, and nurse. I take one of the chairs, my mother, exhausted, collapses into the other. Six people remain standing in that room, quite enough of a crowd to keep one's nerves on edge. I feel as if my sense of privacy, whatever's left of it after having been examined so often and so intimately, is being raped.

"I understand you have questions," says Dr. Jeffries. "Let's hear them!" Why the imperious tone? Why the rush? It's clear that Henry Jeffries is absolutely chafing to be rid of us. Somebody, I can't remember who—the tension in this room is making my head spin—asks a question that skitters right by me. I can't concentrate. Maybe it's Jennifer inquiring about the possible duration of chemotherapy. Or is it my father, wondering for the umpteenth time, might not this tumor be benign. Whatever the question, whoever the questioner, the answer Jeffries gives is noncommittal and brief. Something like, "That remains to be seen," or "We'll know better after surgery." He's intent on moving us right along. "Next question!" he says, commandingly; then, once again, following some timid inquiry abruptly answered, "Next!"

"You're making me so nervous I can't think," I tell Dr. Jeffries.

"In that case I'm hardly the doctor for you." He seems pleased that I've taken him off the hook.

"Where's Dr. Lawson?"

"I don't believe Dr. Lawson wants anything more to do with you." The man is cold as ice.

Jeffries' harshness frightens and baffles me. What I fail to understand is that Henry Jeffries, number two man in gynecology at Community Hospital, has urgent professional priorities. His career, and this man is a comer, remember, is contingent on how deftly he plays the tricky games of departmental politics. Jeffries has come to think that he's made a mistake seeing me at all; he'll have offended Lawson, and Lawson is the chief.

Jeffries is not going to be my surgeon, that's clear enough, and as I realize this, I give way to panic. Is it possible that no one will operate on me, that this cancer, if cancer it is, will be allowed to run its lethal course unchecked? I flee Jeffries' office and take an elevator down to Lawson. I'm so disoriented that I've quite forgotten how uncomfortable I felt with the man. Right now, he seems my last remaining hope. He's *got* to operate, I tell Jennifer, he's just *got* to. Don't worry, she says, and flies off on some mysterious errand.

I plant myself in a free chair next to the desk in front of Lawson's office. "You can't sit there," says a large woman in technician's garb. "You've got to go back to the waiting room." I stay put. If I can just grab Lawson now, I know I can persuade him to operate on me. But if I miss him, he'll refuse to see me ever again, and will dodge all my calls. I'll be like the salaried flunky, summarily dismissed, who keeps pitifully pleading, please can't I have my job back? "Is that poor fool Creaturo on the line again? Tell her I'm in a meeting." The technician mutters something about calling security if I'm not out of that chair in five minutes, but bug-eyed with anxiety, I can't be budged.

My crowd has scattered; I don't know where they've gone, nor do I care. My mind has room for one thought only. I must regain access to Lawson. I'm so fixed on my purpose, on both the absolute necessity and near impossibility of it, that I almost believe I'm hallucinating when I see the surgeon strolling casually in my direction, a benign smile on his face. With a crooked forefinger, he beckons me into his office.

Jennifer has had her finest hour. While I sat like a stone in front of Lawson's office, she's been busy, phoning Helen, telling her about the odd situation that has developed at Community Hospital and imploring her to fix it. Helen has contacted Lawson who, though in the middle of some high-level meeting, has come to the phone immediately—the siren call of the Boss's celebrity—and allowed himself to be gentled by Helen's diplomatic arguments. She's told him that my initial bad reaction to him was really a response to the probable diagnosis of cancer. A classic case of hating the messenger. He's the best man in town, and she's sure I know it!

It doesn't hurt that Helen Brown is the one to argue my case. Nor is it unhelpful that an organization with which I'm affiliated has recently made Community Hospital a generous gift. What if

I had no Helen Brown behind me, no magnanimous organization, no leverage of any consequence? I'd be out on my ear, I'm sure of it.

So here I am, alone in Lawson's office, pouring out my hysterical apologies. I'm sorry, so very sorry; you see I just didn't know I was out of line consulting so many surgeons. Will he forgive me? Will he operate? Magnanimous, Lawson says I will not be denied his services. By this time, I am without will, docile, abject.

The rites of hazing have been a bit nasty, but my induction into Community Hospital is complete. I should count myself lucky—I've been granted entry into an institution of high prominence. And if, as I'll come to realize, Community Hospital has its factorylike aspect—if patients grab numbered tags before queuing up for chemotherapy, the same way you're serviced at a busy butcher's shop or at the bakery, well, that can't be helped. You see there are thousands upon thousands who are sick, and at least as many of them die as live. The doctors would exhaust their emotional reserves should they attempt even a show of sympathy.

I'm too stunned by the day's events to know if I'm pleased or wretched over the final outcome. I suppose I'm blessed at least with some small sense of relief. For good or ill—right now I can't possibly know which—the date for the surgery has been set.

. . .

For a hiatus of several days, between the unpleasant eruptions at Community Hospital and the afternoon I'm to check in for surgery, we retire the caravan. But not the party atmosphere. We have a steady parade of visitors. Jennifer comes often, and as she passionately relives every detail of our recent pilgrimage, her vivid presence threatens to overflow my small apartment. Diane visits too, and Carol—she and I have lived within a block of each other since our early twenties, when we both had too many boyfriends and not enough sense. We met at a pulp publishing house —our first jobs. She did *Modern Romance,* and I had *Screen Stars.*

Now my clever, amiable friend is a freelance writer. Over the years we've grown close as sisters.

Considering the stingy, square footage on Seventy-Sixth Street, this shapes up as quite some crowd. I'm alternately grateful for the company—it makes what could be an excruciating wait pass quickly—and resentful that I've so little time alone. I need to absorb what's happening to me.

I'm facing the prospect of a deadly disease. Incredible! That changes your life completely, yet in another sense, nothing changes at all. Whatever is good and strong in the structure upon which your daily existence rests will hold. But the points of stress, these are likelier than ever to give.

The friendships I've made are sustaining from the beginning, and, in most cases, will stand up impressively to the strains my illness will impose. One point for me. Professionally, too, I'm on firm ground. My colleagues are supportive, and Helen couldn't be a better friend. She calls frequently, and though usually a solitary person, asks if she may visit. I look over my two jammed, untidy rooms and say, um, I'm not sure you'd enjoy it here. We're kind of a mess. So we have our visit at her penthouse in the Beresford. Helen asks, how in God's name, are you getting *through* this thing, and I say, well, I stay mildly drunk most of the time. That helps. As I leave, she gives me a beautiful silk robe, black and fuchsia in an Oriental print. It will knock them out at Community Hospital.

But, oh, those points of stress! Every time Hugh runs out to the drugstore or grocery, I'm edgy, afraid he'll never come back. I've always been reluctant to rely one hundred percent on Hugh, and my situation hardly promotes a firmer sense of confidence.

Relations between my parents and Hugh pose an even more painful problem. After a brief honeymoon of civility, they are now barely polite to him. Hugh, in response, stays out of their way, to the extent that this can be accomplished in two crammed, luggage-strewn rooms. They've come to blame him for the crisis in my health. If he'd been stronger, a better provider, I'd never have gotten sick.

Blame. Blame and recriminations. The prospect of cancer issues an immediate summons to them both. People, and I don't exclude myself, find it next to impossible to acknowledge that they, or those they love, have been victimized by a monstrous cellular accident, as random as a lightning strike. There is simply no living in a universe as uncertain as this. Think what might happen next. But to blame offers comfort. Now you know what *caused* the terrible event. Some small sense of security is restored.

I'm no stranger to blame myself. Briefly, I've blamed my parents for my unthinkable circumstances. Suppose they'd supported my choice of mate instead of undermining and belittling it. Why then I'd have been happier, less emotionally torn, and everybody knows you don't get cancer unless your immune system is sent into mysterious collapse, exhausted by the demon stress. I'm in cancer-kindergarten at this point, and believe what "everybody knows" must surely be the truth. I don't yet realize that men and women of disciplined mind and serious intent have tried to establish a link between cancer and stress and come up emptyhanded. Nobody yet knows what causes a malignancy, but it certainly isn't stress.

As a guilty, Catholic-school girl, I can't cling for long to the notion that my parents are the ones who made me sick. No, if blame belongs anywhere, it must be put at my own door. This cancer is punishment, one I richy deserve because I have been a *bad person*. I "examine my conscience," as the nuns would say, remembering and regretting all my sins in the spirit and the flesh.

Fortunately, I haven't the opportunity to indulge in prolonged sessions of self-flagellation. It's far too hectic on Seventy-Sixth Street for that. In the ten days or so since it's been known I might be sick, there's been no pause in the rush of well-wishers who phone, asking how am I getting along, what can they do to help?

One call stands out in high relief. Locked in the bedroom for privacy, I'm talking to Geraldine, my health-editor friend, a woman of strong opinions and authoritative manner. Gerry assumes the role of Concerned Advisor, and though she's the first person to take this part with me, she'll be hardly the last. I'll have more than my fill of Concerned Advisors within the next few weeks, since everybody in my circle, and quite a few on its periphery, knows exactly what's wrong with cancer treatment in this country. They suspect the Medical Establishment, of course, and tell me exactly what I must do to avoid being done in by this well-credentialed gang of thugs.

Gerry's tone is considered, but not without a certain appropriate urgent edge. "At Community Hospital, they'll have you on chemotherapy before you come off the IV," she warns. "You must investigate your alternatives right now before it's too late." I'm to contact one Michael Guardini in Memphis, representative of the Klepper Institute, which offers an alternative course of treatment that's "entirely nontoxic and possibly more effective than conventional chemotherapy." I'm also to phone Bob Doherty, a medical writer situated in the Northwest, who runs a computer-assisted service for cancer patients, purportedly informing them of the best available treatments, traditional and unorthodox, both in this country and abroad.

Frantically, I scribble names and numbers into my notebook. As an editor of medical articles, I've come to share Gerry's skepticism. Over lunch she and I have often chatted about the arrogance and idiocy of doctors, how they line their pockets with tainted money garnered from unnecessary and probably dangerous diagnostic procedures, how they stupidly resist the incontrovertible data produced by practitioners of gentler more enlightenend healing arts—nutrition, acupuncture, chiropractic, and the like.

I'm not eager to be flayed by the murderous Medical Establishment. Having been so recently terrorized at Community Hospital—made to tremble by Jeffries, to grovel by Lawson—hasn't affirmed my faith in it one bit. A ready customer for the unorthodox, I file Bob Doherty's number for future use and phone Michael Guardini right away.

The voice on the other end of the line is cool, composed—no squeaks, no roars—and the man's diction is immaculate. I'm reassured. Guardini sounds nothing like a member of the lunatic fringe. Guardini applauds me for seeking out the Klepper Institute before my immune system has been completely ruined by poisonous standard therapies. Then he explains that while no formal studies have been done—Klepper is devoted to the arts of healing, not to research—he himself can testify to the many, many lives the institution has saved. Finally he drops his bombshell. Guardini tells me that there exists not one iota, no, not a jot of proof that chemotherapy has prolonged any cancer patient's life by as much as a single day!

The man's words leave me gasping. What, no proof? Chemotherapy doesn't work? You don't live any longer with than without it? Not so much as a day? I'm ready to sign up for the Klepper treatment immediately. What do I do? How much does it cost? How soon do I have to get there? Is he sure they have *room* for me?

Hold on a minute now, says the evercalm and reasonable Guardini in response to my urgent pleas. I must take my time thinking all this over. I should be aware that, if treated by Klepper, I'll be asked to demonstrate discipline and restraint. The program, which involves the elimination of all environmental toxins, including cigarettes, caffeine, alcohol, and meat, begins with a two-month stay in the institute's facility.

Guardini continues. My "inner environment" will be further purified by daily coffee enemas.

Coffee enemas? I may be terrified, I may be credulous, but still I can't believe that coffee introduced anally, is likely to cure me.

At this point, I know next to nothing about chemotherapy. I've been too preoccupied accepting the likelihood of my illness and tracking down a surgeon to have asked or read much about it. One friend has told me she thinks they put you in a lead-lined box and bombard you with chemical "ions." That doesn't sound quite right to me, but I'm not yet familiar with the means of administering cancer-killing drugs, which are, in fact, given by-mouth, by injection, and by slow intravenous drip. I'm aware that chemotherapy is considered quite dreadful—"the twin horrors are cancer and chemotherapy" is a phrase that's been imprinted on my muddled, half-informed mind—but apart from that I'm as ignorant of it as the next person who's enjoyed a long summer of excellent health.

And now the man from Klepper, who is as facile of mind and engaging of manner as a successful talk-show host, is telling me that this singular "horror" is administered to no effect. It simply doesn't work. What he's saying is patent nonsense. Millions of cancer survivors owe their lives to chemotherapy. But I don't know that yet. Fortunately, his mention of "the facility," and his prescription of coffee enemas have called forth the calm skeptic still residing somewhere in my terrified, anxiety-riddled mind. Suppose, instead of talking coffee enemas, Guardini had mentioned some complicated-sounding polysyllabic drug, said to be widely used in Sweden or France. In that case, I might have put my deposit in the mail directly. In that case, I would have almost certainly forfeited my life.

. . .

The morning I'm due to check into Community Hospital, just a little over three weeks since Weissman's sonogram, I swim fifty lengths. Since by now I look about seven months pregnant—my belly, bulging with ascites, has doubled in size in the past two weeks—I'm embarrassed to be seen in my swimming suit. I hide my spreading girth beneath a long towel wrapped around my waist, rush from the locker room to the side of the pool, and quickly plunge. Breath in, breath out, stroke, stroke, stroke—the repetition numbs my anxieties, and being able to slice so smoothly through the water makes me feel as if it's some disastrous illusion, my being sick. Look at this powerful, if misshapen, body! See how perfectly it works!

Hospital check-in procedures are completed, I'm in my room by four in the afternoon, waiting for Lawson or one of his subordinates to come by, but nobody sees me for several hours. My parents, Hugh, Jennifer, and Carol are in the patient's lounge, laughing, gabbing it up. High on adrenaline, probably. I dart back and forth between my room and the lounge, afraid to miss the doctor but anxious for company . . . and cigarettes. I'm nowhere near complying with Lawson's order that I cut back to five a day. All but give up smoking while preparing to find out whether or not you have cancer? Sure, that's easy enough.

A phone call from Geraldine catches me in my room. She has important instructions: "If it's cancer tell them you want a frozen section. And insist, as well, that a portion of the tumor be preserved in paraffin or Formalin. *Not* formaldehyde. Write that down, sweetie. And good luck."

Gerry's instructions are to prepare me for the possible later use of monoclonal antibodies, a promising experimental therapy. Live tumor is needed to be matched with the appropriate antibody, not cells pickled in formaldehyde, but as I lie in my hospital bed, waiting for Don Lawson, I've only the muddiest grasp of this. At last, the surgeon appears. He remains standing throughout what is to be a volcanic interview, surrounded by his fellow, intern, and nurse. This is a full-fledged visit of state.

Still terrified of the man, I gush sweetness and admiration. Oh, Dr. Lawson, how gracious of you to drop by. How wonderful of you to *see* me. The man's my surgeon, for God's sake, but I feel obliged to behave as if invited to the Oval Office for tea and crumbcake.

Then, like a conscientious schoolgirl, I read from my notebook, repeating what Gerry has said. Please, Dr. Lawson, could we add that to the consent form? Would you mind terribly? A trait is emerging in me, common, I'd guess, to both cancer patients and concentration camp inmates. Do whatever you must—simper, lie, howl, flatter, cajole—but survive, only survive.

The surgeon is suddenly, inexplicably fuming. "You want your pathology to be treated differently from everybody else's!" he booms. "Tell me, *madam,* if you please, who told you to ask for that?"

"*New Morning*'s health editor, Geraldine Terry," I reply. My voice sounds small and wretched.

"*Health* editor," snarls Lawson. If irony could kill! "I think I'd like to talk to that woman. Call her up!"

"She phoned as she was about to leave the office. Probably she's gone by now. I doubt I'll reach her." What in God's name have I gotten myself into? I hardly understand what I'm asking for. Why is Lawson breathing down on me like Jehovah preparing to hurl a lightning bolt? I'm scared to death.

"Go ahead, phone!" Feeling numb I dial Gerry's office number. "No answer," I say. "She's gone for the day."

Now Lawson is waxing ruminative. "Sometimes I just want to leave, to get out of this hospital, out of this city . . ."

"Maybe you'd like Hawaii," I interrupt inanely. "Hawaii's nice."

Lawson continues ignoring my preposterous effort to placate him. "I'd like to go back, to go back to a time and a place where the patient would look to you and say, *Doctor, make me well . . .*" Lawson's voice is gaining resonance, rising to near-oratorical pitch. "I'll tell you something, Madam, *you scare me!*" Conclusion of speech.

"Uh, you scare me too." I'm wearing the gorgeous black and fuschia robe, but I might as well be in tattered terrycloth. It certainly isn't doing me any good.

"I *mean* to," Lawson is booming again.

"Frankly, doctor, I don't know why you'd want to do that, why you'd want to scare me on the eve of so major a surgery." I manage this in a perfectly normal tone of voice. No fear-filled squawks or trembling whispers. I'm proud to have reclaimed a portion of my dignity.

"We *always* do a frozen section," says Lawson wearily, as if addressing a dull-witted ten year old. "And we routinely use paraffin."

"Then what I'm asking for isn't irregular?"

Lawson stares at his feet, hands clasped behind his back, nodding his head back and forth, back and forth. What possible use could there be in continuing to talk to me? His patience has been utterly exhausted. Afraid to start up yet another even more unruly tantrum, I sign the consent form with no emendations; he and his retinue depart.

I don't understand it. If they freeze tumors and use paraffin in any case, why has Lawson taken my request as an excuse to browbeat me? Still trembling from the aftershock of the surgeon's eruption, I rush to my group in the hospital lounge where I tell my story, lighting cigarette after cigarette. I'm talking loudly enough for other people to overhear, and realize by the end of my tale that I've the whole of the waiting lounge as my audience.

"It's even worse if you make the anesthesiologist mad at you," I say, addressing them as a group. "Then you're really in for it!"

A woman whose name I'll never know, though I remember she had a very sick husband and a very sweet face, laughs loudly, then walks over and gives me a hug.

"I'm so sorry this is happening to you," she says. "You're funny and you're brave."

The kindness of strangers. One has been properly warned not to rely upon it. Nevertheless, the calm I'd been trying to cultivate, all but shattered by Lawson's explosion, is partly restored by a stranger's hug.

· · ·

It isn't until nearly nine P.M. that huge Betty, an illiterate, astonishingly ugly nurse's aide begins to prep me for the surgery. And a nasty business this is. The bowel has to be completely clear before the surgeon can safely penetrate the abdominal cavity. I'm told to down glass after glass of citrate of magnesium, a killer cathartic. It makes me feel dizzy and nauseated. At fifteen-minute intervals, Betty administers a number of enemas. Her touch is rough. After each of my visits to the bathroom she checks the toilet bowl to see how far her work has progressed. "There be a drop of shit in you tomorrow morning, that Lawson, he have my job." Nice talk!

Mercifully, this violent assault on the bowel weakens you, so it's not too difficult to sleep. My group comes into the room for kisses and good nights; as they leave, my mother quickly makes the sign of the cross over my forehead. I skip the sedative put in a tiny paper cup beside my bed, and opt for two of my contraband Valiums instead. Patients are forbidden to keep any of their own "med's," but nobody ever checks.

Oddly, as I put my head on the pillow, I am not very much afraid. I've boarded the plane, it's aloft and flying, we'll see where it lands soon enough. Everybody is gone now—no more anxious mother, no more angry surgeon—and the quiet is a great relief. Softly, easily, I descend into sleep.

I've no memory of waking that next morning or of being wheeled into the operating room, the O.R. Maybe somebody stuck me with a hypodermic while I was still half asleep. The moment I've dreaded in imagination for the past two weeks is what I remember next, the moment when the doctor comes to you in the recovery room and says, yes, it's cancer. Over and over I've imagined how I'll feel—the sickening wave of anxiety because now you know the worst. You know you might die. And the piercing sense of loss. Gone, all gone, the baby works. Never for me that miracle most women take for granted—a child of my own body.

Of course, I could have imagined a happy outcome. You wake up and are told, hey, it's okay, no cancer. Expect to be yourself again in a couple of weeks. But I've hardly allowed myself even to think about that. Ever since I was a kid, I've been superstitious about envisioning the details of some much-hoped-for event. Imagine them, and they can never come true.

The moment, when it finally arrives, though hardly a happy one, isn't anything like what I'd imagined. I'm lying on a cot or gurney, and briefly, I come awake. Anticipating this moment, I'd feared only emotional not physical pain—I must have been living on Mars. It's unbelievable this pain, so intense I can still hardly believe you come through it and continue to live. I clutch weakly at my nose, which is clogged by tubing. I'm going to suffocate. Someone snatches my arm to make me stop.

Don Lawson is by my side, sitting, I think, on a chair or stool beside the gurney. Or maybe he's standing over me. I can't tell which. I ask him, "What did I lose?"

"Everything!" he says. His voice sounds robust, almost exuberant. The voice of a man who has behind him a good day's work well done. Then he corrects himself. "No, not quite everything. You kept your cervix."

"What are my chances of surviving?" If you can think the words, you can usually manage to say them, no matter how grave your physical distress.

"Superb!" says the surgeon.

I don't firmly register the impact of anything Lawson has said. I feel no terror, no numbing wave of anxiety, no desolation, not even any relief that, yes, the surgeon expects me to live. Only pain and more pain. I slip back out of consciousness.

And so it passes, this much dreaded moment, with little suffering of the psychological sort. I've no reason to doubt Don Lawson when he tells me my chances of surviving are superb. Certainly I'm in no condition to quibble, to say, hey, doctor, what makes you so sure? How exactly do you know that?

In fact, on this, the judgment call, my surgeon is way off-base. He's routed a good deal of the cancer, but it has been running wild inside me. There's plenty left. My chances of surviving for even a few years, far less into my sixties or seventies, are terrifyingly scant.

But lying on that gurney, weaving in and out of consciousness, I'm not thinking about survival. For now, there is only the pain and the monumental effort of enduring it. Later I'll come to that wretched state of awareness—fear, the sense of loss—that I'd thought to experience right after surgery. How naive to have imagined I'd be frightened or depressed when the agony is simply this: not even to silence your screams, because you haven't the strength to scream, but to hang in and keep on breathing, an effort more strenuous than any other I've ever been called upon to make.

PANIC

November—December 1986

*F*aces loom into my own. They are huge and sad. The faces of sorrowful giants. Tears trickle from their enormous, pitying eyes. Jennifer, Carol, my mother. How have they gotten so big? Why are they crying? The sludge of unconsciousness claims me.

I wake, gasp, cast my eyes around the room. Carol hunkers in a corner. How strange she looks, squatting in the shadows, knees angled sharply outward. How strange that she is wearing green harem trousers.

More sludge. Then I'm pulled awake. My mother, grown small again, speaks softly to me. "Do you want me to stay?" she asks. "Yes," I whisper, "yes." I grasp her hand, spin back into darkness.

What is this in my room now? A man, strangely costumed. A policeman. He carries a billy club. The man takes my mother away. I only watch, feel no impulse to protest.

Daylight scorches my eyes—morning. A man, lanky, elegant, lies beside my bed, stretched out on a gurney. He's as languorous as a cat. Hello, says the cat man, you're looking well. Thank you, I croak. He tells me his name then is up and away, slithering off the gurney.

. . .

Disoriented by pain and drugs, I'm catching only bits of business now and they are unearthly, out of sequence. But the man with the billy club and the cat man are both real; neither is a morphine-conjured apparition. The policeman is a security guard. My mother, denied permission for an overnight stay by the nurse, has bypassed channels and hidden under my bed. She was discovered, though—some whistle-blower called security.

The cat man is Helen's friend, Ben Payne, the thoracic surgeon. During the night, as I lay in drug-drenched sleep, I was brought to a different room—some reason they had for changing me. I was transported there on a gurney. Ben Payne, asked by Helen to say hello if he found the time, visited me after exhausting

51

hours in the O.R. He couldn't resist a quick lie down when he saw the opportunity.

It is weeks before I fully make these connections. Right now, as I tunnel in and out of consciousness, the world is a painful and peculiar place, full of quirky mystery.

. . .

My mother orders private nurses. That wasn't in our plan, but then nobody anticipated I'd be this weakened or this anguished after surgery. Fortunately, my excellent insurance policy covers the cost of the nurses, as well as almost all of my other huge medical expenses. The first of my nurses comes, Lucy. She is small and homely, wears big, clumsy eyeglasses. I fall in love with her immediately. She gives me little slivers of ice to wet my mouth. I can take nothing orally, not even water, until the tube comes out of my nose, and this won't happen until my bowel, sluggish from being mauled during surgery, begins to move. Lucy tells me I must walk the hospital corridors, pushing the stand that holds my IV, to make the bowel come awake.

This is my job now, to walk, in spite of the pain. I try. I double over. I cannot stand erect. To do so stretches my long line of stitches, extending from breastbone to groin. I don't care if I die of thirst; I can't walk anymore. I collapse into bed.

Lucy gives me a gadget called a spirometer. Like a baby-toy, it is. You blow into a tube, and try to make the little domino in a tiny stand attached to it bounce up and down. I blow, feebly. The domino barely moves, though the effort causes a new pain. Something dark and wet wraps itself around my chest, pressing, gripping. Lucy says, blow, blow, keep on blowing anyway. You have to work the lungs. The idea is absurd. I push the spirometer away.

. . .

I am still unconscious more than half the time but the fog is lifting. I see the people in my room distinctly. Carol drifts in and out, not wanting to crowd me, but Jennifer seems to be here nearly all the time, more often even than my mother. She watches and listens as with every breath I gasp with pain. "Does it hurt all the time, or does the pain come and go?" asks Jennifer. "It's a pain that doesn't get any better when you analyze it," I snap. How angry she makes me.

I am suddenly quite warm. Lucy takes my temperature. One hundred two degrees. The next moment Lawson and company are in my room. Lucy is acting flustered, ashamed. She doesn't seem to be telling them about my temperature. One hundred and two, I call after the surgical team as they are about to leave. My temperature is one hundred and two degrees.

Furious, Lawson wheels on Lucy. "You'll never work here again," he shouts. Lucy starts crying. She leaves in disgrace. What have I done? I love Lucy. She gives me ice to cool my mouth, without her I will be parched as the Sahara. "Spit out the ice," commands Lawson. I swallow it instead and glare defiance. "Don't send Lucy away," I cry. "Please don't send Lucy away. Lucy has been very kind to me." Lawson yells out some orders. Antibiotics are swished into the sugar-water filling the bag that supplies my IV.

Lucy was on my side, but Lawson makes me afraid. He is one of them. They call the cops on my mother, send Lucy away. They are the enemy.

. . .

I push through the night, bumping through ruts of pain. Morning. I have a visitor, a woman, sweet-faced, young. "Have you any problems?" she asks. "Tell me if anything is bothering you." The young woman is a hospital shrink. I'm fine, I say promptly —no problems. Oh yes, there is one thing she might like to know. My surgeon is trying to kill me. Funny, the look of alarm on her face. My blood is rich with morphine.

. . .

Another visitor. A man, tall, pale, and skinny. Herbert Bernard. Dr. Herbert Bernard. He seems to be telling me this is just the first of a succession of cancers I will have; I should expect many more. I'm wild with terror when I tell this to my mother, who tries quite futilely to calm me.

Dr. Bernard serves as fellow to the medical oncologist, the man who oversees chemotherapy. And I, of course, have misunderstood Bernard badly. He has come to issue the official warning given to all patients before they're asked to consent to chemotherapy. It is known that people treated for one cancer are many times more likely than the average person to develop another malignancy, and it is thought that this heightened susceptibility may be the result of chemotherapy. Procedures at the hospital call for the patient to be so warned within a pain-and-drug flooded day or two of surgery.

More official statements are issued. Lawson is in my room, bristling threatening energy. He has also come to Mirandize me. Like the policeman collaring the hood, he rattles off his cautions dully and by rote. I will be put on either a five- or ten-month protocol of chemotherapy; assignment to one or the other is made randomly. This is a research hospital; I will be drawing my treatment by lot. But which is the *best,* I say, I want the protocol that will *cure* me. They don't know, the data isn't in. There must be trials and more trials. And so it is that I'm inducted into the world of research, with its stiff, unbending gaits, its doctors so taken by the correctness of their sacred procedures, so disinclined to mourn their many, many mistakes.

Lawson doesn't like this interruption. He continues impatiently: "Seventy-five percent of all ovarian patients treated with chemotherapy are clinically free of disease after completion of the protocol, though of these, fifty percent show microscopic disease upon a second surgery." Quite a mouthful, this is, and I don't get a tenth of it. What about the twenty-five percent who aren't clinically free, do they die? What about the fifty percent of the seventy-five percent, do they die too? I can't grasp this strange arithmetic—the arithmetic of death.

But there is more. Lawson gives me a couple of sheets of

Xeroxed paper. They concern something called the Tyrone program which, as I writhe and gasp, I am apparently meant to assess. I may have a different course of treatment entirely. Different, higher doses of drugs, given over a three-month period, followed by a second operation, then something called "intraperitoneal therapy" for three more months, and a third surgery. Three surgeries! Jesus God! They say that's the only way they can know the cancer's gone—to open you and look. Intolerable! And what is intraperitoneal therapy? Jennifer writes everything down. I could no more manipulate a pencil than grow a womb again.

"Is this Tyrone thing better for me?" I ask. I am supposing it must be or they wouldn't bring it up. "We don't know, we hope so," says Lawson, adding that they have excellent reason to believe it won't be *less* effective than the standard therapy. "You mean you do this to people because you *hope* it will work!" I am unbelieving, quaking with outrage. To torture people without knowing they will benefit seems unbelievably cruel to me. I am also a quick study. I have got it exactly right. Except my outrage is partly—only partly—misplaced. I will learn in the months to come that this torture, founded on hope, does sometimes—only sometimes—lead to cure.

· · ·

My night nurse, Phyllis, is beautiful; she is pleasingly rounded, has café skin and almond eyes. Phyllis also models plump-girl fashions and sings sometimes in nightclubs. Whenever I wake during the night, I see her cozy in a corner, knitting. I feel cared for, safe. Phyllis, unlike the new day nurse who adheres to strictly scheduled order—she's afraid of Lawson, I think—gives me morphine whenever I ask for it. As two nights pass into three and four, it becomes harder to find a spot for the injection. Big, knotty bumps cover my backside. "No, not there," I tell Phyllis as she positions the needle. "Find another place, that hurts!"

I've always been a night person, and now it is three and four o'clock in the morning when I feel moved to sweep athletically around the hospital corridor. "You want to walk now," says Phyllis, with an encouraging smile, her big, bold teeth shining— "let's go then!" I don't stop with three or four tours of the floor, I want a marathon. I can do another one. I'll try for nine, for ten!

Phyllis has gifted hands. I'm achingly tense from twisting in the bed, trying to escape the pain; my muscles have gone all stiff and rigid. Ah, I cry, as she works me over, her hands slippery with warm oil, ah, that's better.

Then one morning, on the toilet, my bowels twitch releasing a small, purply-black splotch of feces. That day, Rader, Lawson's resident, comes to my room and without warning—he doesn't say a word—snatches the tube from my nose. I stare at him in amazement.

· · ·

One night, I don't know which night, Susan comes. Susan, my friend from college. I remember the first day I saw her at Josselyn, the rich-girl dorm at Vassar. Why they put me there, I'll never know, a scholarship kid of obscure origins. I even complained about it to the warden. Susan, small, compact, hurrying so briskly, so surely, to wherever she was going. Crisp in her white blouse and pleated skirt, she was straight from the world of private schools and horses. I didn't even hope to know her.

Now she is at the hospital, her newborn and my godchild Alexander strapped to her chest, but she is turned away. My mother says I'm too weak for visitors. Susan leaves a letter. "I just want to tell you, a thousand times over, that I love you—my beautiful friend for almost twenty-five years. . . . There are millions of things I want to talk to you about, and then I just cry for you. In the same breath I want to tell you to hang on tight—for you and for all of us who love you—and do whatever you desire. Ask me anything. I want to help in whatever way I can. . . . I'll wait for you in all this—just know how much we love you."

I read and know I'll keep the letter forever. I can tell though, that Susan thinks I'm going to die. I'll fool her.

. . .

I wait to cry until I see Courtney. Courtney is Carol's daughter and I've known her since she was a baby. Now she is twenty, a sensational-looking girl, passionate, vital. We've always palled around together, walking all over the city when she was ten, eleven. Nobody but Courtney, who was all over motion, dancing up and down doorsteps as we went, ever wanted to walk as far as I did. Later, in her teens, we swam in Narragansett Bay, always going out too far—insistently they'd wave us back—when I visited her mother's summer house in Rhode Island. We did gymnastics together, too; Courtney was so talented, and I ambitious for her. Form, Courtney, form! Don't pause on the cartwheels. Now she's a magnet to me, claims she learned from me how to be a "hussy." Courtney is as close as I come to having a daughter.

Now we've switched roles. She's my coach, and with her I'm moved to race the hospital corridors. We leave the room together, bump heads as we get tangled up in the IV stand, laugh—ouch! that hurts!—then together burst out crying. Oh, Courtney, Courtney! We neither of us hold back, we're hiccupping, sobbing. Courtney and I collapse together in the lounge, her head in my lap, my hands working her thick tangle of auburn hair. We're clutching at each other, tears streaming. Some of the other people in the lounge cry too. They think she is mine, are moved by her devotion. Oh, if she were, if only she were, my child, my beautiful, well-grown daughter!

. . .

My room fills up with flowers. Nobody on the floor has as many as I do. Lawson will know I'm somebody, I think, when he sees so many flowers. I ask my mother, please collect all the notes and mark on them the kind of plant or bloom so I can do the thank-you's correctly. I want my mother, too, to be impressed that so many people think of me. It isn't what she wanted, the life I lead, but she admits my friends do seem supportive.

. . .

Where is Hugh, my father? I hardly ever see them. There are only women in my room, except for doctors. Later my mother says, Hugh couldn't wait to get out of that room, he didn't care enough to be with you. But my father, I object. I didn't see Daddy either.

They stayed away partly out of concern for my modesty, Hugh and Daddy. I am always being bathed, my bottom bared for morphine. And partly because the women crowding my small room left no space for them.

My mother—fierce in her love, tormented by fear—she will not admit Hugh cares for me.

. . .

On Thanksgiving day, they say I can eat. Oh good, turkey! But when the meal arrives, it smells foul. Tag ends of turkey heaped in a mound like a cowpie, covered with steaming khaki-colored gravy. I gag on one bite, can't even swallow the Jell-o that sits neatly on the tray beside it. Eat? They must be crazy.

But I am getting better. I know because I resent my new nurse, a high-strung girl named Anne, who won't leave me be, is always saying, time to walk now, in a tone that's falsely chirrupy, or approaching my bed, her eyes alight with purpose, then pressing me to use the spirometer. Other patients mustn't like her either or she wouldn't be working the holiday. The popular nurses are all off on Thanksgiving. Please leave me alone, I finally tell her, out of patience. Stop hovering!

Lawson's resident, Rader, is back. Without even a hello, how-are-you, he starts snipping away at my staple-stitches. I wince anticipatorily, expecting this to hurt, but it doesn't. Why doesn't he tell me, don't worry, this won't be painful? Before, when he snatched the tube away, I wasn't alert enough to register even a silent complaint. But now I think, what a lousy bedside manner.

Next, a visit from Lawson. A dedicated man, I'll give him that, he works right through Thanksgiving. I can go home day after tomorrow, he says. Go home? So soon? I hadn't even thought of going home. I'd supposed I'd probably be here forever.

The Friday after Thanksgiving Helen comes in the morning. I'm wearing the robe she gave me, and have smartened up a little, run a brush through my hair, put on some lipstick. Helen tells me I look beautiful. Others have said the same, marveling, how is it possible, sick as she is, that she can be so pretty? A week on sugar-water gives the skin a glow, makes the eyes sparkle. Helen brings a huge stuffed bear, a Gund animal—they cost a fortune. Bosco, I tell her, I'll call him Bosco, thinking, no doubt, of warm milk with chocolate, and other innocent comforts of childhood. I try to "chat," but taking the breath you need for words pulls painfully at the incision. Helen remarks that I seem serene, mistaking my slowly-articulated speech—each syllable costs me—for composure. The Boss is thoughtful, though, her visit brief. "You've been charming for long enough," she says. "I should be going."

Next day, there's the flurry of leaving. Which flowers to take, which are three quarters-gone? Pack up, call a cab, keep the nurse for an extra day—it's a new, kind nurse, Liza; I fired the annoying Anne—the patient must be comfortable. I stagger down the broad, imposing stairway that leads to the front entrance of the hospital, with nurse, lover, parents, friends. I'm bent over, hands protectively on my middle, still stuffed with painkillers, still feeble and hurting. I feel like a prisoner released after long detention, afraid of the "outside" and unbelieving. Are they really letting me go? How, after being so closely guarded, will I handle freedom?

It is over; it is just beginning.

. . .

After being so totally enfeebled, each step in my recuperation delights and thrills me. Being able to sleep on my side is the first small victory. Then a cup of coffee in the morning taken by my bed. What a pleasure! How is it that I never properly appreciated this before? Food goes down, although in very small amounts, and with the help of laxatives, is processed normally. After a day or two I can move from couch to bed unassisted.

I start to take small walks. First five blocks, then ten. I am afraid to walk alone, however—I need Hugh with me. I cling to his arm as we cross the street, marveling at the other people crossing, how fast they are, and confident. It seems unlikely I'll ever manage street crossings again quite this ably. Still, I do walk. Progress.

I set myself a task to write all my thank-you notes. What an undertaking! I have many people to address and insufficient stationery. I need expensive, understated stock for executives at Hearst, casual cards for friends. I wouldn't feel right without a job to do —I have always, always worked. I call in at the card shop on the corner, and get down to business.

My parents have decided to stay on with me awhile. They've nothing pressing to do back in St. Louis, and of course, they're wild with worry. And so we huddle together, like any family anywhere, bickering over trifles, quarrelsome and untidy. The anxiety in my apartment is high, very high. It fouls the air.

What to do to dispel it? A VCR, that may do the trick. My father loves old movies. Hugh and I stumble out onto Broadway to our local Crazy Eddie's where we buy a VCR, then stop at the video club to purchase a membership and check out some films. Five hundred dollars gone in five minutes. The nearness of death has made me a spendthrift.

I need new clothes, too, clothes for my convalescence. On to the Gap. What do you know? I am down two sizes; now take an eight. Twenty-three pounds gone in the six days I spent in the hospital. Ten of them were put on in the two weeks prior to the surgery, from the bloat, the ascites. But the rest was real weight. The clothes at the Gap designed for skinny teenagers, now suit me nicely—I buy a handful of bright turtlenecks, with jogging pants to match. Three hundred dollars. What's money!

In any new circumstance one must immediately establish customs, regular habits in order to feel secure and rooted. Hugh and I start to make little outings of our walks, each time stopping at Julia's, a pretty place on Seventy-Ninth Street, for a drink. I have one beer, or a cup of mulled cider. I don't really want the alcohol, just the feeling of comfort, the sitting-there on the bar stool, chatting up the person next to me. Julia's is festive with the approach of the holidays—they've put out tinsel and wreaths and blinking Christmas lights. I feel normal there, like any other person, not a cancer-person, as I carefully manipulate my sore bottom, a pin cushion for morphine needles, onto the stool and order up my drink.

Carol, sensing my need for some gaiety, offers to decorate a tree for me. She has a gift for these things, tree-trimming the old way, with hand-made ornaments, lit candles, but I have to say no. There's hardly room in the apartment for the four of us. A big blue spruce, and Carol, a splurger, would settle for nothing less, shedding its spiky needles onto the floor would be more burdensome than celebratory. So instead, Carol bakes us Norwegian krum ka-ka cookies. They're so delicious the family devours them all in a quick half hour.

Waking hours aren't so bad, but in my dreams I grieve. An old lover of mine appears in one, a passionate man, a man of genius. I approach him. He says, there was a garden inside you, full of flowering vines. Now it's rank with weeds. He turns me away. Another dream features a young writer, my protégée Laura. She tells me she thinks it would be better if she forwarded her work through another editor now. Someone healthy. I think in my dream, what perfidy, after all I've done for her.

I grieve too for my devastated body. In the shower where I stand uncertainly, I close my eyes as I scrub. I don't want to see the puckering flesh around my long scar, don't want to look at my newly emaciated body, my breasts so small and shriveled, shrinking away from the rush of water as if from a battering. I block out the sight of this strange new body, this body that has betrayed me.

61

. . .

It's December third, a week after my release from Community Hospital, and I've an appointment with Dr. Nash, the medical oncologist who'll oversee chemotherapy. I walk erectly now, no more caved-in, postsurgical slouch, and although I don't like my body naked, my new skinniness looks good in clothes. I'm eager to present myself at Community Hospital, thinking I've done well. Surely the doctors will be proud of me.

Jennifer and I are conspiratorial while we wait for Nash; we sneak a cigarette on the fire stairs, then decide to drop by and see Lawson. Under "Other" on my discharge papers, he's scribbled "adjustment disorder—recommend psychiatric consult." I suspect my odd, morphine-inspired remarks to the hospital shrink were leaked.

Hmmph! Adjustment disorder, what does he mean by that, I say, affecting mock outrage. We'll have to ask.

We walk the few steps to Lawson's office, Jennifer trailing behind me. I'm slender as a girl in flecked black-on-beige wool jersey, hemline dropped to midcalf. I feel pretty and I feel bold. He'll have to like me. But Lawson barely looks up when I approach. Certainly, it's not possible he's failed to recognize me. "Hi, Dr. Lawson," I offer timidly, hoping for a smile, for a how-well-you-look. "Mmmrrgh," mutters the surgeon and turns away.

"He's really a very *small* person," says Jennifer bitterly. I'm hurt. Okay, we had our differences, but we fought a war together, didn't we? And now, after we've clambered out of the trenches, I'm expecting some old-soldier joking, some foxhole camaraderie.

My name is called; Nash is ready for me. I'm into stirrups yet again, grateful that I'm covered by a sheet. You can count my ribs, and my arms and legs are fragile as a child's. Nash reaches far inside the newly-hollow core of me—I've stiffened, braced—then says I'm healing well.

Jennifer and my father join us for the consultation. Aware by now that when everybody comes along it makes a circus, I've said, only two of you at a time, please. I don't think the doctors like a crowd. My mother and Hugh elected to stay home.

Nash explains which drugs will be used against my tumor—Cytoxan, Adriamycin, and platinum, called CAP for short—and tells me the doses, which are measured in milligrams and grams. I will receive these queer-sounding substances for six months, then have a second operation, the check they told me about when I was still so weak from surgery, to see if the tumor's gone. The names of the drugs are so queer-sounding they shoot right out of my mind, and the doses mean nothing at all to me. I do grow more attentive, though, when Nash starts talking about "toxicities." The Adriamycin can be counted upon to damage my heart; the platinum hurts the hearing, nerves, and kidneys.

"How much damage will there be?"

"Very little. You won't notice it. Though it can be measured clinically." Some people's hands are twisted into claws after platinum, I learn later. He tells me nausea is a common side effect of all the drugs, and also refers to possible "fatigue." I will also learn later this "fatigue" is caused by the drugs' action on the bone marrow, the body's blood-producing factory. And I'll also find out that this suppression of the marrow may be severe enough to require a lengthy hospitalization and massive transfusions.

These transfusions don't always come in time. The patient's immune system, stripped by chemotherapy of the white cells that provide protection against disease, functions haltingly, and the most common parasites, the most everyday bacteria, turn deadly. Sometimes they keep two steps ahead of the saving blood, seeping into the heart and brain, hurting, even crippling their host.

Well, I'm not sure I would have been able to absorb all this in any case. And had I absorbed it, I might have sped away; bolted flat-out; run too fast for them to catch me. On the other hand, had I understood, perhaps I wouldn't have found myself hovering near death some months later, my lifeline a length of clear tubing attached to a succession of tidily mounted bags of blood. Too little information and you're insufficiently warned against the dangers that may await you; too much and you're pushed into panic—a dilemma no doctor or patient ever entirely avoids.

Dr. Nash continues with his cold and cryptic warnings.

"What about hair loss?" I ask him. Like everybody, that's what scares me most. "How extensive will it be?"

"Total," says Dr. Nash.

"And how fast will I lose it?"

"Within three weeks after the onset of therapy."

He says nothing to soften the impact of these dread words. I can expect to be bald in a month. Molten fear hardens into a rock of agony; it lands down low in my middle, someplace near where my uterus used to be.

"Can I use the cold-cap?"

A recent issue of *New York* magazine has run an article about coping with chemotherapy; the writer has explained that something called a cold-cap, an icy covering for the head, worn while you're receiving chemotherapy, can minimize hair loss.

"We've tried it. It doesn't work. It's just an extra encumbrance and makes the nurses' lives more difficult." Nash doesn't know for sure that the cold-cap doesn't work, I tell myself—I'll wear it anyway.

I inquire about the Tyrone program, the new experimental treatment Lawson told me about when I was still in my morphine fog, a day or two following surgery.

Nash's eyes are slits as he seems to take me in, head to toe, as if assessing a job candidate. "That's for women who have their heads screwed on straight, and want to take an aggressive course against their disease," he remarks acidly.

Up to this point, Nash's manner has been icily neutral, but now he's outright hostile. Hasn't my body gone through enough? Must my feelings also take a battering?

I persist. If the Tyrone program is going to be better for me, I want it, I say. Nash explains that nobody can say whether or not it will be better, and that "the side effects are much worse than we'd anticipated." The women on it don't budge from their beds for months. This shuts me up. I stop pestering Nash about the Tyrone program. I don't want to be this sick. Who would?

I still don't know if I missed an opportunity here. I do know that the chemotherapy I'm later to receive will be far more rigorous than anything Community Hospital can dish out, and that my body, my amazing body, having once betrayed me, comes through like a champion, handling all manner of outlandish poisons.

Is it that Nash doesn't want to have to bother with someone who's been tagged a "difficult patient"? The issue here is the smooth functioning of Community Hospital. It's been determined, who knows why—because of what I told the hospital shrink, because my distraught mother hid under the bed—that I'm likely to be a cranky cog in the well-oiled Hospital machine.

I ask my last, my most important question. "You've seen my slides," I say. "What do you make of my chances of being alive five years from now?" I know from reading in my small but growing collection of cancer books that five is the magic number of years; only then do they pronounce you cured. All the books refer to "five-year survival rates."

"Well, you don't have a little bit of cancer but you don't have a lot," says Nash. "I'd put your chances at from forty-five to fifty percent."

My father and Jennifer sigh with relief. I really don't know why they're so thrilled with forty-five to fifty percent. As I construe it, what the doctor has just said is that I'm slightly more likely to die than live.

The jauntiness I brought to the hospital that day has run right out of me. As we leave, I'm flattened, spiritless. The elation of the recuperative period has passed. This chemotherapy; it is real and it is dreadful. And even with it, I may not survive; that too is the reality. Jennifer and my father are very "up," however. Jennifer is thrilled by my chances. She's sure I'm "special enough" to find myself in the lucky fifty percent. My father pronounces Nash "intelligent and articulate."

In the taxi going home—the driver's off today, we travel by

yellow cab—their high spirits irritate me. You two aren't going to go through chemotherapy, I say. You're not going to have "clinically measurable" damage to your heart or your nerves. You two are both going to keep your hair. And then I fall silent. A sodden lump of wretchedness.

I don't like Nash very much. Nor has my experience with him made me any more comfortable with Community Hospital. They're indifferent to my suffering here. If I don't make it, nobody will blink away a tear. I have already made my decision, though it's still only half-conscious at this point, and it's nothing I'm yet ready to share.

I'm not going to be treated at Community Hospital. I need somebody who *wants* to pull me through this thing. To hell with reputation, to hell with size and resources and eminence. I suspect I'll die if I stay there.

. . .

A realization dawns, though dimly. Information is important here. I want to know who lives through this thing, who dies, and why. The gaining of knowledge, often a pleasure for me—the excellent student, the scholarship girl made good—has become an urgent necessity.

I make several phone calls. The first is to Roy Graham, a friend of Susan's. Roy is a researcher at the Shelburne Cancer Clinic. I call him at Susan's suggestion. He's smart about these things, she says, he's working on some hot, new, research project, phone him, you'll see. The word from Roy isn't good however. "Look I hate to tell you this," he says, "but your chances of being alive five years from now are under fifteen percent!" Roy is very *au courant*. Previously, it had been thought that from thirty-five to forty percent of patients with ovarian cancer lived. The new data rolling in is less promising. It is now thought that "ovarians," as they're known in the trade, are out there dying like fruit flies on a sweltering summer day.

"Our people are bald as bats and barfing like crazy," continues

Roy Graham, "but at least they've got a shot. You better get down here right away. Who did your surgery?" Roy is thrilled when I tell him Lawson. "Great! Great! MacGregor—he's in charge of the protocol—MacGregor knows Lawson well. He'll take you. You're *our* sort of patient."

How nice that I'm eligible for this club. I will be permitted to go bald as a bat and to barf like crazy. I tell Susan later, you know your friend Roy Graham, I think he's short on tact.

The second phone call is to John Frederickson, just to say hello, to check. I don't hold it against John that he failed to diagnose the cancer; as a friend he's first-rate. John tells me there's a paper in the new issue of the *Journal of Obstetrics and Gynecology* about ovarian cancer. Maybe I want to read it. Yes, yes, I want it right away, I'll send a messenger.

I don't find the paper hard to understand. As an editor, I'm what they call a "generalist"—I know a little bit about a lot of things. I'm also on easy terms with language; writers each have their individual style, sometimes lyric and fluid, sometimes cryptic and terse. The medical "style" is just another way of arranging words; doctors, too, write for "effect." They go for balance, a tone of nicely-reasoned judgment. Doctors' prose is cerebral and very distanced. But I can blue-pencil it in my mind, cut through to the meat of it.

The paper is about the restaging of ovarian cancer. Patients are "staged" after surgery according to the amount of cancer the surgeon has been unable to cut out. Survival is closely linked to the bulk of tumor remnants. The more cancer you have, the more steeply your chances of cure decline. They've recently broken the staging process into finer, more discrete categories and in so doing, have more closely calibrated survival chances. One of the new categories is stage IIIc, describing patients who, after surgery, are left with three centimeters or more of disease. That's me, IIIc; it says so right on my discharge papers. "Largest remaining tumor nodule, three cm. in diameter." I calculate my chances. You don't need a computer to do the necessary arithmetic; long division is enough. With three centimeters of cancer, quite a large growth, I find myself near the very bottom of the survival scale. My chances of being alive in five years are roughly seven percent. My teeth chatter with the chill of it.

My parents and Hugh all try to reassure me. I must have gotten it wrong. They said *fifty* percent at the hospital. I'm not wrong, I tell them; it's here in black and white. Seven percent. Seven, not fifty. I'm in deep trouble here, I know it.

I make a third call, to Dr. Nash. I sneak up on him, don't say anything about having read a paper—I sense he won't like that. No, all I say is this, "Tell me, Dr. Nash, why exactly did you put my chances at forty-five to fifty percent?"

Dr. Nash sounds a little tired, a little off his speed. "That's more or less what we tell everybody," is what the doctor says. He sounds as if he's stifling a yawn.

I'm not surprised that Nash hasn't leveled with me. Keep them quiet, that's the ticket, never say they're all but dead. They'll kick, they'll scream, if you do. Lie instead, or rather, in the spirit of compassion, muffle the truth a bit. Tell yourself it's in the patient's best interest, that you're bolstering them psychologically. Don't let *them* decide, hey, if my chances are so poor, I've got to really go for it, I've got to find some treatment somewhere that will work, I've got to sail off that cliff.

No, keep them quiet. Tell them little. They'll keep still and take their medicine nicely. They'll keep as still as a corpse.

· · ·

Christmas shopping. At the best of times—you're healthy, loved, the boss has just given you a raise—it's no pleasure to shop Manhattan during the holidays. People do murder just to get a cab, the stores are jam-packed. Outside it's clammy, December-damp, and inside overheated—you strip off coat and sweaters, lug them up escalators. Other shoppers press in on you, elbows sharpened. An ache starts up in your lower back as, laden with more and more parcels, you progress exhaustedly from floor to floor.

This Christmas the strain of approaching the stores is hugely magnified. I'm weak and terrified and hurting. I still fortify myself with Percocet every time I go out the door. And what an odd list of purchases I must make to see me through the holidays. Turbans, lightweight, to cover my bald head, a cold-cap because if I use it, maybe, maybe—I can't help hoping—I'll be one of the lucky few who won't lose her hair, and back to facing facts again, a wig. It says in the *New York* article you're smart to procure this item before the chemotherapy begins, so the wig stylist can see and try to match the natural color and texture of your still-undiminished crop of hair.

First, we go to Saks for the turban; my theory is that Saks has everything. My theory is wrong. Hugh is busy trying to find a garage—parking is impossible, it's bumper cars out there on the street—while my father and I scoot around from department to department and finally buy a stiff, dressy, black silk helmet—cost: $150—because it's the closest thing Saks has to the turban I'm almost certainly going to need. I never wear the helmet, of course; it is to molder away, forgotten in some bureau drawer.

Next stop, Cole Dominicks on Fifty-Second Street, off Fifth; that *New York* writer never said where to get the cold-cap, and I've found out about Cole Dominicks only after making two dozen phone calls. There are no parking garages nearby, no turning into Fifty-Second Street either; traffic there is at a dead halt. I climb out of our Toyota at the corner of Fifth, telling Hugh I'll meet him back at this point as soon as I can. A Santa is on the corner, ringing and ringing his merry little Christmas bell, the sound mixes into the cacophony of crankily honking horns. I tell myself, remember this moment, don't ever forget it, because this, girl, is maybe the achingest moment in your life. Christmas of '86 —a Santa on the corner ho-ho-ho-ing as you carry out your strange mission.

Finally, we meet Nicholas and his assistant Andrew at Nicholas Piazza, a salon for the fitting and styling of wigs, on Fifty-Seventh between Madison and Park. Right away I know I've found some friends. Nicholas doesn't supply Dolly Parton-style whipped-cream toppings to the rich or frivolous; he deals with the sick and aged every day. Many of his customers have cancer, others are old, with barren temples, or suffer from alopecia, hairlessness caused by chemicals or disease. Nicholas understands how scared I am; he's gentle and methodical. The webbed-lace base is lightweight and it breathes; that's best for comfort. The Italians mix synthetics with real hair—a nice effect and maintenance is easy. Like a mother with a loved child, he brushes tenderly through my long hair, getting the feel of it, the heft.

I go for the top-of-the-line item. A wig, custom-made to fit my scalp out of bona fide human hair. It costs two thousand dollars, but I've been assured my insurance will cover a "hair prosthesis." I hope this check is good, I say, I'm really kind of confused, I can't remember where my money is anymore. Nicholas is calm, seems unconcerned—so, you'll write me another if this one bounces. Take it easy. It's not going to be as bad as you think it is, losing your hair. I know, I've been doing this for a lot of years.

Lessons of the cancer patient—so many of them and so hard to learn. But I'm a ready pupil. I note it's surprising, the way people are. A doctor, icy and rigid as a field marshall awaiting his salute; a wigmaker soothing as a lover, feeling your distress almost as his own. Yes, it's surprising, very surprising, the way people are.

. . .

A package arrives. I have contacted Bob Doherty, the medical writer, and proprietor of a service that helps cancer patients choose among available therapies. "He knows more than anyone else *I* know about cancer," Geraldine Terry, my health-editor friend, has said. The package is thick with information about other programs or approaches I can take if I choose not to be treated at Community Hospital. And I've already so chosen, though I haven't told anybody yet; even from myself, I'm keeping it a half-secret, this decision to leave Community Hospital, to break free from enemy ranks, even if that rash move puts me smack into no-man's-land.

Seven percent, seven, and they said fifty. Liars, thugs, I have to get away.

The package Doherty has sent me includes a single-spaced, six-page letter, chock-a-block with names and concepts and treatment programs that are dizzying in their number, their wildly exotic unfamiliarity. Perhaps I should go to the Whiteside Research Institute to get a "spectrum of biological agents extracted from urine called antineoplastons." Or maybe not. I may also choose to be treated with "selenite, a special form of selenium and copper . . . balancing the organism's acidity and alkalinity and its anabolism/catabolism phases." Wait a second, on to page three— I should book a ticket to Paris where I may receive a "purified version of natural antibodies that form against cancer cells' surface antigens." What confusion: This is No-man's land indeed!

Along with the six-page, single-spaced, typed letter, there are fifteen pages of computer printouts describing "whole abdominal irradiation by a moving-strip technique" and "simultaneous presentation of carcinoma involving the ovary and the uterine corpus." Wisdom seems to dictate that I skip the printout altogether, and try to make as much sense as I can out of Doherty's letter.

I read again, more closely. I read the letter five or six times more. Hopeless, I still can't determine what a plausible next step might be. I have to talk to Doherty.

Doherty is pleasant, responsive, and patient when I finally reach him on the phone after half a dozen missed tries. He also speaks with what appears to be dazzling expertise. The medical writer breaks down his overwhelming torrent of advice into more manageable parts. His best advice: go to Munich, Germany, for treatment at the Lang Clinic, under the direction of the distinguished physician, Doctor Erich Rapp. "Rapp is the very best oncologist I know," Doherty says, with persuasive certainty. "In chemotherapy he has no peer." He uses a combination of drugs, two I've never heard about, but the other is platinum, the same platinum that's used at Community Hospital. The drugs are used along with whole-abdominal radiation, a combination, Doherty assures me, that results in "an astonishing synergy." He says he's discussed my case with Rapp, who awaits my call, and the Munich doctor has said I have "a real chance." "Believe me," Doherty insists, "he does not make such prognoses lightly."

I copy country code and number for the Lang Clinic into my notebook and prepare to set up communications with Germany. Doherty has told me that treatment abroad is covered by Blue Cross, and that a relative can stay with me at Lang at only a tiny extra cost. If I decide to go, the trip will be affordable. To reach Rapp, I'll need to call at the end of his working day, 7:30 A.M. New York time. And for the next week, I will indeed speak to Erich Rapp nearly every day. I will be groggy from sleep and pain and weakness, he will speak to me with a thick, fudgy, German accent, and what we will be talking about are per-meter-square doses of drugs called "iffosfomide" and "4-epirubicin." My hands will shake with anxiety as I beg him to repeat again and again how to spell the drugs. I, of course, have absolutely no understanding of what we're talking about—even if he'd an Oxbridge accent I wouldn't understand. Still, I'm determined to get it down, and to get it down right, and then I will somehow, somewhere, find someone smart and qualified to tell me whether this Munich doctor is a quack—I've only Doherty's word that he isn't—or whether he is indeed the world's most gifted oncologist.

Still it isn't enough that I contact Germany, Doherty says. First, I must look into treatment with monoclonal antibodies. Monoclonal antibodies, yes, that's the ticket, Gerry has already told me about them. And I have just read an article in the *New York Times* Sunday magazine about a former researcher, Doug Clancy, who has set up a facility, Oncomedics, Inc., where for $35,000 a year, you can receive the experimental antibodies. The medical establishment has upbraided Clancy because he is subsidized by patients' fees rather than research grants. Cancer business isn't supposed to be conducted this way. Monoclonals are in the news; monoclonals are hot; this Bob Doherty *must* know what he's talking about.

I should try for monoclonals first, as Doherty tells me, because they are nontoxic—no "clinically measureable damage" to anything, what wonderful news—and if that doesn't work out I fly out to Munich to be cured by Rapp after just three months of his amazing therapy. I never need see the inside of the loathed Community Hospital again. There are other, better, if more obscure, roads to travel and I, now energized by the spirit of adventure, am about to set foot on one of them.

My enchantment with Doherty is short-lived. When, at the medical-writer's suggestion, I call the Brandis Institute, "the center for monoclonal research worldwide," I get a lab; there are no doctors there, no patients. What earthly good are a bunch of test-tube men going to do me? I call Doherty back, as disillusioned with him as a girl in love at first sight who has a lousy second date. Hey, I say, that Brandis place is only a laboratory. "Of course it is, you start with them, then move along to the doctors conducting the experiment." Does Doherty know that I have about six days to get started? That's when Nash said I had to begin chemotherapy. Delays are dangerous. There's cancer inside me. You zap it quick or it grows. There's some really urgent deadline pressure here.

Doherty understands my problem. A good shortcut might be to contact Dr. Richard Wirth at Wilson Medical Center; Doherty believes he has some involvement with monoclonals and may be able to direct me to a treatment center. This offhand advice, all but randomly solicited—suppose I'd decided to pursue selenite instead, it would have taken months of phone calls to follow all of Doherty's leads—will put me into contact with one of the country's most eminent research scientists, a man who will turn out to be both caring and responsive. As I wind my way through this crazed labyrinth, composed in equal measure of quack-talk and good medicine, Dick Wirth will serve as my guide. And though I will not always follow his recommendations, they will certainly advance my education. And sharpen my awareness that within the maze into which the cancer patient is so often flung—in our flawed system even top doctors cannot point to the best and clearest corridor to cure—one must be alert indeed to sidestep a deadly cul-de-sac.

· · ·

Such a time, such a jumble of anxiety and hope, of hectic days. I try Dick Wirth. He's out of town for a few days at a conference. I leave my number, not really expecting a call back. Rushing, rushing, I call MacGregor, in charge of the Shelburne Cancer Clinic protocol Roy Graham has told me about. He's out as well. Well, isn't there somebody who can help me, I naively insist. I want to know about their new ovarian cancer protocol, and I'm in rather a hurry. Disarmed, I think by my ingenuousness, the person on the phone cuts through the skein of red tape that distinguishes the Clinic, and puts me through to a Doctor Jansen, who sounds nice, young, the coordinating physician on the protocol.

Dr. Jansen is astonished to be hearing from me. He asks two times, to be sure he's got it right, am I a *patient?* Yes, I say, of course, a patient—I've got ovarian cancer and I'm not sure what to do about it. Dr. Jansen says he's never heard from a patient before. Doctors call in *behalf* of their patients, he explains. Oh, my doctors, they wouldn't do that, I say. You don't know my doctors. Jansen's long pause baffles me a bit. I don't yet know enough to realize how surprising my candor—and my brashness—must seem to him. Most patients do exactly as their doctors tell them, not daring to investigate on their own. Depending on the skill or lack of it of their physician, this can either be a secure or wildly dangerous path to take.

About this protocol, I say. What are your success rates? Jansen is an unusual fellow. He doesn't fudge, or say I must talk to my physician, or explain that this information can't be given out on the phone—standard operating procedure at the Shelburne Clinic.

Instead, he just reads off the numbers and, as I glance back at my notebooks, I see the success rates are precisely the same as with standard therapy.

That isn't so good, is it, I say. I believe your numbers are about the same as with the, what-do-you-call-it, the CAP. Yes, says Dr. Jansen, we've very disappointed with the results, then adds that the neurotoxicity has been far worse than anticipated. Some patients have trouble with fine coordination, buttoning shirts, that sort of thing. Dr. Jansen doesn't yet know the extent of the nerve damage to be caused by the protocol. In a month or two, the Clinic will cancel this treatment program. By then, several patients will have been so severely damaged by it that they will have exited this research center, funded by the federal government, in wheelchairs.

Well, I guess I won't come down then. Doesn't seem much point in it, I say. Jansen agrees. And adds, look if you're going to do this, to play an advocacy role—I'm not sure what he means by "advocacy role," I'm just asking questions—let me give you a tip. Go for the most aggressive treatment that you can, go for the high-dose chemotherapy. That's the best way to get well.

I thank Dr. Jansen and tell him I'll keep his advice in mind. I do. And this information, casually relayed by a helpful doctor, proves important. Oh, the randomness of this, my education, the bits of information gathered here and there, that might have been as easily forgotten as remembered! But Jansen is right. Radical problems need radical solutions, and aggressive treatment, more aggressive by far than what the average oncologist, fearing complications—and litigation—is willing to prescribe, is what is needed to defeat a difficult malignancy.

There are tricks, though, to this business of aggressive treatment, tricks that are hard for doctors, far less patients, to get the hang of. It's not just the more, and the more toxic, the better. No, not at all. Treatment must be aggressive, yes, but it also must be most prudently, adroitly administered. For it can kill as well as cure.

You might liken the treatment of cancer to a dangerous voyage of discovery. Or a circus high-wire act. The doctor/explorer/tight-rope walker must indeed be bold, but he must also be constrained by the meticulous cautions that enable any daring venture to succeed.

Of the dangers of aggressive treatment, and of the cautions that must accompany it, Jansen says nothing. I'll learn these lessons myself. And in the hardest way.

. . .

Doherty has also given me the name and number of a woman, Ellen Jenkins, who was dying, *dying* of her disease—a recurrent breast cancer—she couldn't walk, was confined to her bed, her breaking bones, shredding, turning to chalk, until he, Doherty, took her in hand, and put her on that plane to Germany. He just corraled her, used force practically. He wasn't going to let her die. She needed Erich Rapp. And now, what a miracle. She's walking again, she's cured, brought forth from her bed of agony like Lazarus summoned from the dead!

Ellen Jenkins is so plain and homey when we talk. She sounds very happy. She has "just the most darling little wig," and she's put up her tree—"only a little one, but it's pretty"—all three of her grown children are coming home to visit. In the last few days, she's often managed without her cane. She is doing nearly all the housework herself, can mop, use the vacuum. Oh yes, she is a great admirer, a very great admirer of Erich Rapp. He saved her life.

The pity of it, the terrible pity of it! Is this what cancer does? Turns the bones inside your living body into dust? So diminishes your life that you trill with delight because you can manipulate a vacuum cleaner? I'm appalled by Ellen Jenkins's suffering, bowled over by her amazing plain-housewife bravery. I could never be so brave. Please, God, let me never have to be so brave!

But Rapp has got Ellen Jenkins's vote. I wouldn't mind that, having Ellen Jenkins's vote. This Ellen Jenkins, who is so happy with her wig, her Christmas, she seems quite formidable to me.

. . .

I put in a call to Carl Whiting, because when I was shopping for surgeons, he was the kindest man I met, to tell him I'm thinking of going to Munich and to ask what he thinks of Erich Rapp. Whiting has been all day in the O.R. the evening he calls me back. I'm not his patient, he's exhausted, and yet he phones. I wouldn't dream of contacting the distant Dr. Nash.

Dr. Whiting sounds as weary as God after a really trying day in the universe. Eagerly, attempting to muffle the excitement in my voice—I think I may be onto something here—I tell him about Doherty, about Rapp. He hasn't heard of either one of them and the not-again, the not-another-patient-with-a-cockeyed-plan note in his voice is plainly audible. Never mind, he's bound to be defensive. Doherty has told me how all-knowing American doctors never admit that European treatment is better.

Listen, listen, you've got to listen, I tell Whiting. I bring my whole card into play, I tell him about the miracle cure, about the amazing Ellen Jenkins.

"It always starts this way," somebody, somewhere is cured, and it's a miracle! Don't you think we can do that here? Bring about remissions? Even when the disease is so far advanced? Yes, —the doctor takes a deep, let's-be-patient breath—yes, even when disease is far advanced. Poor Whiting. He's been in and out of two diseased abdomens today, and now there's me!

"I'll bet you don't even know what drugs he uses," says the surgeon. Oh yes I do. I dash for my notebooks. I tell him about the iffosfomide, the 4-epirubicin, the platinum, and how they're used in conjunction with radiation therapy. Haltingly, I recite the square meter doses for each six-day treatment cycle. I'm the girl who never once came to school without having done her home-work!

Whiting's tone changes a little. He explains that 4-epirubicin is similar in its activity to Adriamycin, but thought not to be so damaging to the heart. The two drugs are what they call "ana-logues," almost but not exactly the same. And the iffosfomide, it works in much the same way as Cytoxan. What do you know? This German doctor's treatment isn't so very off-the-wall. Whiting continues, explaining that "we know in theory that radiation can activate the chemotherapy." That's Doherty's "amazing synergy." "For all I know," concludes Whiting, "this might be the best treatment in the world."

"For all I know"—the words of an honest man. I'm moving along in my education. *Nobody really knows, nobody is sure of what the best treatments for cancer are. Nobody knows for certain if or how I'm likely to be cured.*

. . .

As all this goes on, it's miserable and tense on Seventy-Sixth Street. Two weeks have passed since my surgery and I'm still tremendously enfeebled. We are, the four of us, crowded into my bachelor girl's apartment, piled on top of one another, tormenting then pleasing each other by turns. Our moods and needs keep clashing and somebody's feelings are always getting bruised. For three and a half weeks, until I finally commit to a chemotherapy plan, we live this way. It feels like months, like years.

My baffled, tension-wracked parents don't know quite what to make of all the calls, the notebooks, and I can tell my frugal mother is, out of long habit, appalled that I keep phoning Germany. Think of the expense! She's terrified as well by the thought I might go to Munich—so mysterious, so far away, and the doctor may be crazy! Still, she knows me to be adventurous; as a writer for *Cosmopolitan* I've traveled the world, seen the bazaars of Marrakesh, fairytale castles of Prague, sea cliffs of the wild Galapagos, and, to her surprise, I've always returned from these exotic places quite unscathed. I'm also the best-schooled member of the family. My parents are accustomed to my affinity for exotic information. Now I am talking "analogues" and "epirubicin" the way I talked when home from school about James Joyce and Sean O'Faolain. My mother hadn't heard of them either. She's terrified, but in her way, she trusts my judgment.

The person she doesn't trust is Hugh; the tents of our two enemy camps are in place now, securely pitched. I still have dreams: a family finally reconciled by tragedy, as in a made-for-TV movie, all of us together in Munich, me in mink and a tall silk turban, glamorous as Marlene Dietrich, all of us talking up a storm in some cozy little café. You don't stop fantasizing—a happy time, a happy ending—even when you have cancer. Where would you be without fantasies?

The reality is far, very far, from these reveries. The reality is my parents and Hugh speaking only when absolutely necessary. Hugh tells them there's a Catholic church on Eighty-Second Street. They have Mass at eleven. My mother asks, grudgingly, does he want a piece of chicken. Thanks, Hugh. Good morning, Hugh. But outside of that, my parents ignore him. And though Hugh tries to take these snubs serenely, sometimes he burns with scorched pride, bristles with resentment.

Hugh doesn't, however, as I once feared he might, bolt and run. On the contrary, he stays very close, his responses finely tuned to my moods, my needs. We are coming closer, Hugh and I, reaching out for each other amidst the clamorous confusion that has besieged our life. Perhaps there is more than I knew to the bond that links us. No, we weren't happy with the roles we played, I, the reluctant provider; he, frustrated in his need to command, to succeed, but my danger has begun to distill the heavy vapor of these misgivings. And the concentrate that emerges seems to have the clarity, the density of love. My situation might have caused Hugh to take a step away. Instead, he moves nearer, instinctually, protectively, and I take shelter in his unconstrained concern.

My need for Hugh, and for my parents, whose love also buttresses me, tears me in two. To love him seems an insult to them, and vice versa. A tortured equation. I find myself carefully parceling out my conversation—so much for my mother and father, so much for Hugh. Switching my attention from one to another with as much nervousness and as little real joy as an anxious hostess. I must make everyone feel wanted, needed, and the effort is exhausting. My most peaceful times are spent outside, walking with Hugh—my mother and father barely leave the house—or else come late at night, when my early-bird parents have gone to sleep and Hugh and I are alone together in the bedroom, reading. Though I'm still too weak by far for a real embrace, just feeling the warmth of his leg against mine is a balm.

. . .

My friends keep coming, and I'm grateful. Their presence mutes the overpowering din of the antagonism between my parents and Hugh. Jennifer, Carol, and now Jimmie. Carol and Jimmie started up a romance while I was at Community Hospital. They met tragic. Jimmie brought roses, and Carol had sobbed all her mascara away, and now they appear a little ashamed that their jubilant connection was occasioned by my misery and offer up food and talk by way of consolation.

Jimmie brings kelp and sea salt and rice cakes from the health food shop on Broadway. Cancer cannot grow, he assures me with absolute certainty, so long as you sharply restrict the intake of fat in your diet. He brings along a book by Michio Kushi, chief guru of macrobiotics, to prove it. The book purports to dispel "the myth of carcinogens" and to supplant it with "the unifying theory of yin and yang." I'd never have gotten ovarian cancer in the first place if I hadn't been so fond of pork chops; my pork-chop habit caused me to menstruate at the time of the full, rather than the new moon, and that's where all the trouble started.

I don't for one minute credit any of this. As a magazine editor, I've seen fad panaceas and pop-psyche discoveries come and go, I've shrugged away everything from Dr. Atkins's high-protein diet to the hullabaloo raised over the "G" spot (do you have one, can you *find* it, and if you do how much more pleasure can you *actually* expect?). When downwind of horse manure, I can usually smell it.

Still, fat intake has been linked to the promotion of various cancers—it says so right in the *American Cancer Society's Cancer*

Book, which I've begun reading, and which I am more inclined to trust than I do Michio Kushi, so why not cut out the pork chops for a while. Couldn't hurt. Oh yes it could. After several days of raw carrots and fish broiled with squirts of lemon juice, I'm losing weight. Continue with this and I'll be a skeleton. My father runs out for steaks, I slather my bread with butter, eat chocolate-chocolate chip Häagen-Dazs from the carton. A pound or two climbs back on. Good! There are some hard times coming ahead; my body needs to mainline protein, and I have *no* reserves of body fat to be depleted. The hell with water-packed tuna and unsweetened mango dates. Besides, the health-store stuff tastes terrible.

And so it goes on Seventy-Sixth Street. Much company at night, much talk of yin and yang and whether or not the German doctor is a madman, and during the day my persistent, if haphazard, investigations. What could they be but haphazard? I haven't got a fraction of the time or resources to obtain a proper education. "I went through the school of hard knocks," said a million self-made men, the accustomed and expected answer when asked about their schooling. And here am I, physically and emotionally battered, struggling to gain, from every jab at my backside, every blow to my soul, a little precious information.

Meanwhile my parents—how small they seem now, in their late sixties, how fragile huddled on my sofa together, how unlikely to deliver me, their overcherished daughter, into salvation —continue to circle around Hugh like wary, frightened children. He tries, oh, how he tries to win them over. To my father: here, Joe, your shirts, I took them to the laundry. Let me drive you to the church, Ann, it's cold outside and a little nasty. But they're having none of it. It breaks my heart. How much, how very, very much, I want for us to be a family.

My parents are stony, unyielding. They know what to blame for this disease. Jimmie says it's pork chops. Just try a little yin, a little yang, you'll be all better. My parents, they take a different view. Hugh's been in and out of half a dozen businesses in as many years; my steady salary is what has carried us through. That wasn't right. Their girl, their beautiful, talented girl, the one who might have married the ambassador. Made to carry so much of the load. Small wonder she got cancer.

Through all this Carol hangs in, a constant visitor at my apartment. She's frantically chatty and charming, not so much trying to distract me as attempting to quiet my parents' nervousness, to make a bridge between them and Hugh. She's tilting at windmills though. Carol can't alter my parents' conviction that Hugh was in some way responsible for my illness. In their fear and desperation my parents need a scapegoat. Dismally, for all of us, they've chosen Hugh.

. . .

It's the third week since surgery, and time is closing in. I have but a few days to make a decision. Though nearing the crossroads, my mind is jammed by fear and confusion, and my will, overheated by my panicky desire to survive, sputters and fails. I have no idea which way to turn. Then one night, at about nine o'clock, the phone rings, and the steady, cultivated voice on the other end of the line identifies itself as belonging to Dick Wirth. Oh yes, Dick Wirth, the doctor from Wilson Medical. I'd almost forgotten him. Wirth apologizes for having taken so long to get back to me, first he had the conference, then a crush of work awaiting his return, but what can he do for me? His secretary has told him I have ovarian cancer.

I really have no idea to whom I'm talking. I don't know that Wirth, Director of the Wilson Medical Center, has, among his other accomplishments, developed a blood test that screens for the presence of ovarian cancer. It is a major diagnostic advance and it has brought glory and honor to Dick Wirth, whose name is known to every oncologist in the land.

All I know now—but it's enough to impress and thrill me—is that this Wirth has not only called back but actually apologized that it took so long for him to reach me. Fancy, a doctor who apologizes. I'm still reeling from Lawson and Nash.

I had intended to ask Wirth about monoclonal antibodies. But I have by now read the *New York Times* article on monoclonals more closely. And I've realized that, although the antibodies show great promise in the laboratory, nobody's been cured by them yet. Slowly, I'm grasping the ethical guidelines that govern cancer research. You wouldn't treat somebody with *any* chance of cure with established therapies—and I do have a chance, a small one, a seven percent chance—with an unproven technique. The patients at Oncomedics Inc., paying $35,000 a year for monoclonals—a disgrace, according to the research establishment, buying your cure as you might a Porsche—have exhausted all other possible avenues.

So I say to Wirth, well, I originally called up to find out about monoclonal antibodies, because I heard you were working with them, but they wouldn't be right for me, would they? I mean, I don't think I could even *get* them. Wouldn't it be unethical to treat me with monoclonals when I have some chance, even just a small chance, with chemotherapy?

Yes, says Wirth, patiently listening as all this tumbles out in a rush, a torrent. The monoclonals aren't by themselves considered appropriate therapy, even of last resort.

But now that I've got you, I chatter on, would you like to hear about my plan? You see I'm thinking of going to Munich, Germany, for treatment with Erich Rapp. Have you heard of him? No, Wirth hasn't heard of him, *nobody* has heard of him except Bob Doherty, and I am beginning to realize this is a less than excellent sign. Well, anyway, he has this treatment program, and says he has a fifty-five percent, four-year survival rate for stage III and IV ovarian cancer patients. That's good, isn't it? Better than we're doing here, as I understand it?

Yes, says Dick Wirth, if true, that is very, very good, about forty percent better than what American doctors can claim. Oh, good, I thought so. Look, hang on a minute, I'll get my notebooks, tell you about the treatment exactly. Can you wait a sec? Of course, says Wirth, he seems to have all the time in the world.

I read from my notebooks, the drugs, the doses, the treatment schedule, the radiation therapy. Wirth says, I don't want to diminish your enthusiasm in any way, but there are a few things you might want to know about. The radiation can be effective, yes, but there are problems with it. It scars the abdomen. And with a scarred abdomen you wouldn't be eligible for intraperitoneal therapy. Oh, yes, intraperitoneal therapy. They talked about that at Community Hospital. They put the drugs inside your belly somehow, through some sort of tube I think—I've never been much of a one for gadgets. The mechanics of this treatment stymie me.

Radiation can make trouble for the surgeon too, says Wirth, should I need another operation. The abdomen may be so scarred that the surgery becomes very tricky. The soft-spoken Wirth is understating his point. A good surgeon won't go anywhere *near* a patient who has had whole abdominal radiation. It fries your insides; they don't hold up under the knife. You can die on the operating table. Wirth's warning about radiation, often given to ovarian patients but with disastrous results, is crucial to my survival. Radiation is the one insult to the abdomen and the bone marrow that really cannot be tolerated. With the ravaged innards and chronically lowered blood counts it causes, I'd never have managed the heroic therapies I'll later come to need. Thank you, Dick Wirth!

What he would suggest—the man's manner is so mild, so patiently instructive—is that I see a man named Alan Thornton, head of gynecological oncology at Central Hospital, before making a commitment to any form of therapy. This suggestion is very sound, very on-the-mark. I have, in my naiveté, bounded right up to the top; Thornton, along with Wirth himself, is known in oncology circles the world over. Thornton, one of the earliest pioneers of contemporary chemotherapy, is now one of the deans, the elder statesmen of cancer treatment in this country. I don't know this as I talk to Dick Wirth, who, I've wrongly concluded, can't be that highly placed in the research establishment himself. If he were, why take such time and trouble over me?

Okay. I'll make an appointment to see Thornton, I say. I want to do whatever this nice and rational man advises. Good, says Dick Wirth, if I need any other advice, please don't hesitate to call. He's a bit busy, however, it may take him a little while to get back to me. He hopes I'll understand.

So it is that I make contact with one of the country's most distinguished cancer researchers. And find myself a little less enthusiastic about going to Munich, in spite of my fantasy visions of me as the Marlene Dietrich of cancer patients, my family gathered adoringly around me.

· ·· ·

My old life, my life of deadlines and lunches and office gossip, has disappeared, is all but forgotten, somehow waved away by some evil fairy's wand. How strange, this transformation, practically overnight, from busy editor trying by sheer force of energy to steamroll through the conflicts of her life, to cancer-sleuth, madly phoning, scribbling into notebooks. Not that the deadline pressure has lifted, far from it. In fact, I've never worked so fast and furiously. Subject under investigation: ways to sidestep death.

Bobbie Ashley, *Cosmo*'s executive editor, calls, and after she asks how I'm doing and listens to my report, we settle in for a little talk about doings at the office. One of my ablest young writers—the girl deftly juggles the most diverse material, everything from "The Crisis in Daycare," to "The Heart-Piercing Pangs of Sexual Jealousy"—has run into trouble with several stories. She just needs better direction, both of us cluck. And Helen is getting compulsive again—fine-combing recipe-copy for God's sake. Picky, picky! Keeping the boss's eye on the Big Picture, that's self-appointed sentry duty for Bobbie and me.

This kind of talk is more calming than Valium; it's still out there and it's waiting for me, normal life, with its pressures and its pleasures, its pettiness and vanities. A wave of nostalgia for my paper-strewn gray-walled office, where I'd curse over copy describing some skimpy bugle-beaded minidress, done sixteen times over—"Hey hot-stuff, want to *cook?*"—overtakes me. I long for the jokiness, the tumult, even the droning humdrum of the everyday.

. . .

An outing. I have not yet left the house at night; my days are busy, exhausting really, and there have been friends enough to come to me. But I feel I must see Susan. Susan, she managed the miracle-child, indeed she managed *three* miracles—three babies after forty, they just rolled right out of her, the last born on the bathroom floor. She was on the toilet, anticipating a bowel movement, when she began to crown.

Susan's late success points up my own failure quite pointedly. We led such parallel lives. Vassar girls together, honorable and sweet, though I was the more outgoing, the more expansive in temperament. Susan did her senior thesis on Virginia Woolf, while I chose D. H. Lawrence. That tells you something in itself.

Then after school the City, where Suzie and I swung together into lusty overdrive, not wanting marriage—that didn't seem like the beginning of life to us but the end. No, we wanted love affairs so wild and turbulent, they'd sweep us right away. Blood heat!

We got what we wanted, and, yes, the punishment fit the crime. Exhausted, wrung-out by our adventures, we retrenched in our thirties, attempted the settled life. But only one of us, only Susan, really succeeded. Only Susan had babies.

I continue to love my friend in spite of her triumph. And I spread the love around, embracing also her young husband, Alec, many years Susan's junior, and her three sons, Ari, Nicholas, and the new baby Zandy. I'm his godmother and proud of it. He's a solid, husky infant, with quite the determined air.

But Zandy isn't the pick of Susan's litter, at least not for me. I like Nicholas the best; Ari and Zandy resemble their industrious, effective father, but Nicholas is like Susan—mysterious and beautiful. He is a creature of obscure, unfathomable moods, a dreamy blond, eyes as blue as a northern sea.

I pick the occasion of Nicholas's second birthday to visit Susan. I know there is danger in this outing, but I am resolved to face it, to see Susan's babies swarming over her, to register and move beyond the pain. I am determined to continue to love them all, not to be embittered by the damage done me by my disease, not to start hating babies because I can never have one of my own.

Hugh and I go late to the birthday party, thinking we'll thereby avoid nearly all the guests, see only Susan, Alec, and the boys. But Susan's enormous loft apartment—it's big as a roller rink—still holds a handful of handsome young mothers, their toddlers squirreling around, making noise and trouble, when we arrive. Susan is busy wrapping up wedges of birthday cake and chasing children, leaving me to make small-talk with strangers, a task of great difficulty. I'm only three and a half weeks out of the hospital, just over a month from the day of terrible discovery, and I'm to say to some woman I never met before, how nice, you're married to the painter who did the lovely abstract on Susan's wall. It's fantastic! What colors! You plan part-time work next fall? When your child's at preschool? Terrific! Which one's yours?

I can't believe I'm saying these things. I have *cancer,* I want to shout. I may die! Who cares about your ratty, snaggle-toothed little kid, your pretentious, no-talent husband! Will I ever be able to make chit-chat with strangers again? Doesn't seem likely. It just isn't possible to talk to anyone who doesn't know and love me, and who isn't nearly as scared as I am that I may die.

The party's nearly over. The children who remain are tired, cranky. A little girl trips over a tiny battery-driven car as it races around in crazed, jumpy circles. She falls, shrieks, erupts into tears. You're a big girl, you're okay, I say, trying to soothe her. But the child stumbles wretchedly away, she wants Mommy. She stares at me sullenly, thumb in mouth, as she clings to, all but climbs up, her mother's leg. What do I know about the special murmurings of mothers, the wonderful comfort their bodies bring?

Alec talks to me about a couple of brassy new publications on the newsstands—*Spy* and *Seven Days*. Do I think they have a market? A sharp editorial focus? Alec is a banker; talking business is his way of bridging gaps. He's trying to make me comfortable, to take my mind off my troubles.

My eyes keep roving back to Nicholas, Susan's double, Susan again, my friend's best biological link to the future. He rips apart his presents in a spirit of sober greed. Just for him, just for him. The aggressive older boy and the cherished baby, this isn't their day. Nicholas's little limbs are solid, compact; he moves with grace. Like his mother he'll be an excellent athlete.

I look at Nicholas and I know—the knowledge brings even more pain than I'd anticipated—that there will never be another Barbara. Another intense, dark-eyed child speeding through the world, curious and energetic—read, Mommy, read—never ready for sleep. I would have loved a child like that. I would have loved a child like *me*.

At last Susan has a moment free. She doesn't talk about *Spy* or *Seven Days,* doesn't try to distract me. "This is going to be very painful for you," says Susan. Her gaze, which is steady and very sad, resembles Nicholas's. It is full of secrets.

Time to go. Susan, Alec, and the babies scramble into the elevator with Hugh and me, and we move down through this building full of warehouse-sized "spaces" to the well-locked doors that open up to the winos and crack dealers of Thirty-Eighth Street. I've told Susan and Alec about my plans; the chemotherapy, the trip to Munich. "I think you're very brave to have chemotherapy at all," says Alec.

In the car they come, all the tears I've been saving up throughout these frantic weeks, these weeks of pain and fear and looking for the the Cure. They spill right out, no, they don't spill, they *roll* in a violent, violent surge. Somebody—it must be me—is pounding at Hugh, at his face, his shoulders. It's your fault, your fault, I sob and scream. I would have *had* a baby, if it hadn't been for you. Never enough money; never enough security. You gave me this cancer. It was you, you! Loser, lifewrecker—I hate you, oh, how I hate you.

Hugh doesn't even duck; he takes his battering. He was busy reading books and manuals meant to help relatives of the cancer patient during the long days and nights in the hospital when my mother and Jennifer were crowding my room. Expect the newly-diagnosed cancer patient to lash out in rage. Expect to be blamed for the disease. The relatives of the afflicted must be prepared for emotional turbulence. Remember, cancer is a family disease.

I sob all the way home, dash half-blind from tears up the stairs to my apartment, where Jennifer is waiting with my parents. "What's wrong?" they ask. "Susan's babies! Susan's babies!" I wail and wail.

There is a full, economy-sized jar of Maxim instant coffee on the butcher-block-topped bar that serves as a "wall" for my miniature pullman kitchen. I grab it, and mindlessly I let it sail—over my mother's head and past the TV, toward the pretty windowed alcove that encloses an ornate three-legged table covered with Italian lace.

"What are you doing?" my father shouts, his olive skin gone gray. "You're trying to kill your mother!" Jennifer, who is solid and strong, has locked her arms around my chest, trying to restrain me. Powerful as a sinewy, barefoot savage, I have no trouble breaking free.

"Kill my mother, kill my mother, what a laugh. I'm not trying to kill anybody. Don't you know *I'm* the one in danger of dying here."

All at once the rage drains out of me and I feel slack, as empty as if the demon anger had been exorcised, routed by some grade-B movie priest. Have I really been party to this melodrama? This ugly, squalid scene?

Munich, Community Hospital, the Shelburne Clinic—who cares where I have chemotherapy. I don't want to live anyway.

What's the point, what's the point? Why don't they just let me die?

I'm quieter now, but still accusing. "I would have *had* a baby," I say to my parents, "if it hadn't been for you two. Hugh wasn't good enough for you, nobody was good enough for you. So I never married, never sealed the deal. You'll kill your mother, you'll kill your mother. I've been hearing that since I was ten. Oh, the irony of it, the wonderful irony of it, it's so amazing. You're still saying it. You said it *tonight!*"

My parents, evidently, have temporarily forgotten whatever they read in the hospital. They're not thinking now about the feelings of a cancer patient, how they evolve from shock and fear into rage and bleak despair. They see only that I'm on the attack and, when attacked, it is their custom to hit back forcefully.

My mother strikes the first blows and she packs a formidable punch. I have always depended too much on her approval, permitted her to pull my strings, a guilty marionette. We wrangle. I sob. Sometimes I hear myself making a strange sound, a strangled, baffled laugh. There is love here, too much love perhaps, but there is little enough understanding. I mismanaged my life, my mother claims. I counter—she's never understood my generation. Back and forth we go with my father and Hugh, the peacemakers, trying to stay out of it, trying to stay calm.

Hey, something interesting is happening here. Always before I have backed away from my mother's anger, unable to endure it really. I took my stand for independence secretly, did what I wanted but kept it hidden—middle-of-the-night stuff, covert actions. Up to this point my grab at life has been a near-miss, bungled because made by stealth. I needed daylight. But now I'm giving as good as I get, tangling with my mother, no holds barred. I am fighting, I am sobbing. I fight and sob myself right out. But I am no longer deferring, no longer hiding. I'm several decades behind schedule and it's taken a runaway cancer to nudge me out of the nest, but I am finally, finally coming of age.

Exhausted, we two warring parties retire from the field of

battle. Jennifer picks up to go. My God, she's been here the whole time. I hardly noticed that. As she leaves, I realize that at least one other person in this drama is acting out of character. Emotional, opinionated Jennifer, who is herself accustomed to operating at a very high pitch, has stayed quiet throughout the whole of this.

· · ·

There isn't much time to nurse hurt feelings in this wounded family. Countdown to treatment day nears zero, and still I have no plan. I'm on the phone again, this time to John Frederickson and Harry, asking about Allen Thornton. They both confirm Wirth's view: the Central Hospital man enjoys a reputation for great eminence. He's top-notch. Great, I think, I'll have Thornton treat me. But when I call his office, his nurse tells me he's in Paris for the month and isn't taking new patients in any case. All I can hope for is a consultation. Perhaps that would be enough to set me on the proper track, or maybe I can talk him into treating me. But a month! I can't possibly wait a month before having treatment. Every day that passes without chemotherapy provides the cancer with a juicy opportunity. Three centimeters of tumor will grow to four, to five, and quickly.

Phone Nash, I tell my mother, stall for a week. Say I caught cold, am running a temperature. Chalk-colored from worry, drained by the emotional violence that has so recently battered us both, my mother complies. She is very, very afraid of this delay.

Just after my mother puts down the phone, it rings again. My good friend Barbara Lee is eager to talk to me. Like Carol, Barbara will be among the friends destined to stay closest to me throughout my ordeal. We've known each other for nearly twenty years—twenty years of sharing and sniping, of sunny and of crabby days. Jennifer is very *here,* very on-the-spot, indeed she's practically living in our laps. But Jennifer's a sprinter, fast and showy, and beating this cancer will be a long endurance race. Our relationship won't go the distance.

Barbara has life-saving bulletins to disclose. There's a doctor in Peru, she believes, who has constructed some special kind of box. You step into it and vavoom, the cancer's gone, just like that. That has always been her plan—if she got cancer, she'd just pop down to Peru and climb into the doctor's magic box.

"Oh Barbara," I say, "I can't believe you're *telling* me this." My brilliant but somewhat other-worldly friend also believes in haunted houses and in casting the I Ching. She maintains that her durable relationship with her husband can be attributed to astrological compatibility. He's Pisces, she's Aries; together they make the ends of the zodiac meet.

But I read about the Peruvian doctor in *Esquire,* Barbara objects. He wouldn't have been written up there if he were some kind of fruitcake. Oh no? I say. You believe everything you read in *magazines*. Okay, okay, says Barbara. My friend worked with me at *Cosmopolitan* for ten years before moving to the country to marry, have her daughter Kate, and take up the freelance writer's life. She knows how desperate any publication can be for the selling cover line, the grabby, if somewhat hokey scoop that will get the reader to shell out a dollar fifty at the newsstand.

Barbara's second bulletin is more intriguing. There's a drug called carboplatin, she remembers reading about it, can't be quite sure where. But she's positive the article said it worked for ovarian cancer. The headline went something like, "Takes the Agony out of Chemotherapy," Barbara tells me. I'm interested. She offers to run to the library to find out more for me, and phones back that evening to tell me that carboplatin was patented by Bristol-Myers in 1985, and is in use all over Europe and Canada. It is as active against ovarian cancer as cisplatin, but unlike the latter does no damage to the hearing, nerves, or kidneys.

It will be a full year before I realize that the FDA's stubborn refusal to approve use of carboplatin except in a research setting is, in the eyes of enlightened oncologists, a national disgrace. An "analogue" of cisplatin, it's as effective as the latter drug in killing cancer cells, but has no permanent side effects. No torpid kidney. No crippled hands and stumbling feet. How the leviathan FDA inches forward, even with a drug such as this one, which can spare so many so much suffering. (Carboplatin will finally be FDA approved in late 1989.) I call the Corbin Institute in Boston and the Shelburne again, but nobody has a research program in place that makes use of the drug. It's too exhausting to go further with this. Besides, at present I don't even know for sure if carboplatin works. There's just Barbara's Xeroxed newspaper clip that says so, and even then they could be wrong in Canada and Italy and France.

So it is that bits and pieces of information reach the cancer patient, much of it quackery, a clinic in Canada, magic box in Peru, but some of it pure gold. How to know the difference between the nugget of information that can keep you whole and safe and the dangerous skulduggery. And how to make this determination in a few, fast, death-chased weeks!

So it is, too, that I begin to learn where my true emotional lifelines will be. Imagine that, busy Barbara, taking time away from her precious four-year-old Kate, her deadlines, her charming but falling-down old stone house in the Catskills, where just last week the rain gutters were choked with bumblebees, to wade through the poky local library—they don't even have microfilm there—to find out about carboplatin for me.

Oh, and to find out more, as well, about the magic box. An article ran in April '74, she tells me. Couldn't hurt just to check it out, insists stubborn Barbara Lee.

· · ·

Luck. The random factor. It may ruin or save you. It bestows the gifts of beauty and intelligence, then blights them both. Raises you up high, then brings you low. In the midst of battle, or of cancer, luck may be the one to turn your head when the burst of killing missiles flies. Or maybe you're the one who's felled. Luck. In the West we lie and say you make your own. In the East they own to half the truth and call it Destiny.

As luck would have it, Janice Trama, *Cosmo*'s sometimes-beloved, sometimes-berated office manager, whom we pet or curse, depending on what terrific or demented thing she's done that day, has a favorite aunt suffering from an advanced lung cancer. Community Hospital dumped her after surgery, or so Janice says. They said there was no hope for her, the cancer had gone too far, she couldn't be saved by chemotherapy.

So Janice's aunt, as plucky as she was sick, went to the library to do some digging, to find her cure. And now she's being treated at Memorial Hospital in Cityside, an undistinguished urban center, a small-town half grown into a shapeless metropolis, a few hours drive from New York. Janice thinks a miracle is heading earthward, toward Cityside. She sends me a clip from a magazine that describes the brilliance and dedication of Dr. Jacob Marek, Cityside's maverick oncologist, savior of her aunt.

The article might have been titled "The Most Unforgettable Cancer Doctor I Ever Met." Born into a well-to-do European family, Marek narrowly escaped the Nazi death camps, was saved by his gallant country's underground and, dispossessed of all but his native brilliance, made his way to the United States to scale the ladder of scientific achievement. Marek joined ranks with the bold, brave few, the doctors who pioneered modern chemotherapy. He helped achieve the first of the childhood leukemia cures, then held even deadlier cancers—of the brain, lung, bone—at bay, with high-wire, high-dose treatments of His Drug. His achievement brought him the highest honors, tribute from his peers, public acclaim.

In a magazine, the oncologist is quoted as saying he has no time for traditional research methods—won't treat a sick or dying patient with a placebo—and doesn't much care for the way the medical bureaucracy follows experimental procedures, and even if his colleagues think him a maverick, saving lives is more important to him than piling up a bunch of statistics.

I like the sound of this, I must admit, I really do. Having already sensed that at Community Hospital, I will be little more than a "good" or "bad" number, fearing that my life, myself, quite possibly my very death, will be reduced there to a fractional figure, a digit after a decimal point, I am very taken by Marek's profession. I keep imagining my unmourned death discreetly deposited in the data bank. I look into a future that may very well not contain me and see a researcher, narrating a slide presentation that shows monster cells, undissuaded by chemotherapy, and saying to his colleagues, "Look here, look here, the CAP is only minimally effective when tumor has spread throughout the peritoneum. We had a success rate of only five point six percent." A dead statistic is what I very much fear I'll be. I think I'll give this Jacob Marek a call.

I should do a little checking first, though. Carl Whiting probably is good for one more phone call—only one. Yes, he's a wonderful man, but he's also a busy surgeon; it's not his life's work to hold my hand. I get him right away and quickly say, what about Jacob Marek, do you know his work? "I'd rather see you go to him than Munich," says Whiting. "At least he heads up a major federally-backed research program." Thank you, Dr. Whiting, you've been so kind, I say, I promise not to bother you again. I can tell by his exasperated-sounding sign off, his "Well, good luck then . . . and good-bye," that he hopes I'll make this promise good.

When I phone Memorial Hospital, I'm told Marek is in his laboratory, but that he'll get back to me soon. He always returns his calls. And so he does, phoning me a few hours later. But when I say, may I come in for a consultation, his words are hard to understand—the accent impossible on the telephone—and his manner impatient and decidedly eccentric. He seems to be saying something like, "Consul*ta*tion, consul*ta*tion, what is this consul*ta*tion? You want to come here to be treated? Fine. I treat you! But consul*ta*tion . . . I don't understand."

Rather than explaining that a consultation is a preliminary meeting between patient and doctor to discuss treatment possibilities—surely an award-winning oncologist ought to know that —I simply say, "Can I see you, please?" "O-kay, I think so."

Marek's voice now sounds childlike in its good nature, appealingly naive. A man of quick-changing moods. "But what is a good day. Let me see, let me see. All day Thursday I'm at the lab and the big hospital. No good, no good. Ah Friday, Friday. You can come to my office Friday. Sometime in the afternoon. If I'm not there, you wait."

I am not encouraged by the Unforgettable Cancer Doctor's stunningly offhand manner; if I made my appointments with writers for "sometime Friday afternoon," we'd never fill the magazine. Still, there is Janice's aunt to consider, Marek's distinguished history, his expressed dislike for research techniques that also appall me, and the bottom-line fact that at this point, except for the dreaded Community Hospital and the uncertainties of Munich, I seem to have nowhere else to go.

On Friday, Hugh drives my father, mother, and me to Cityside. It is now three and a half weeks after discharge, but still the ride is difficult. I must sit upright for several hours, and the weakened muscles of my lower back now called upon to support my weight ache with the strain. The Percocet I've swallowed begins to wear off as we drive, and the pain from the incision creeps stickily back. By the time we have lost and found ourselves again in the unfamiliar slums of Cityside, which are littered with rubbish, its street corners occupied by derelicts, lounging in attitudes of desolation, I am exhausted. At last, Memorial, a sprawl of parking lots and cinder blocks that looks shabbily at home in this dreary urban landscape. Like a broken swing on a tumbledown porch.

Once inside its doors, however, Memorial isn't quite so awful. Unlike streamlined Community Hospital, with its immaculate interiors and quick-march procedures, there's a comfortable clutter here. People move to a shambling human pace. A nurse hands a tissue to a frail old man, wheezing on his gurney; a mother just out of the sonogram room scolds her straying toddler. The walls are a motley of crammed bulletin boards, kids' crayon drawings, and cut-out Christmas angels, halos askew, dripping glitter dust.

It seems an average hospital, with a typical patient population and a staff of ordinary decency.

Marek's floor is different, of course; it's set aside for cancer patients, most of them end-of-the-road cases. The doctor is best known as an oncologist of last resort, and on his ward, the special exit through which they wheel bodies of the newly dead is used with shocking frequency.

The physician is who-knows-where when we arrive—Marion, the lovely young woman who assists him, thinks he's probably in his lab at Memorial's larger sister institution. She recommends we wait for him in the hospital's cafeteria and grab some lunch—she'll come fetch us when he arrives. Eagerly, we follow her suggestion. None of us has eaten yet. I fill my tray with grease-glazed short ribs and black-eyed peas. A mistake. Sour acid floods my digestive tract, still tender from the surgery.

We're halfway through our dismal meal when Marion comes scurrying toward us. He's back, Marek's back, and we must rush to meet him. A very imperial summons, but one which I, now so sadly, strangely lost in what writer Susan Sontag has called the "kingdom of the sick," rush hurriedly to meet. The oncologist is pacing the floor of his office when we meet him, a man of furious energies. Almost totally bald, his grey-blue eyes flash aggressive intelligence under bristling white eyebrows. With his six-foot, trim frame he has the look of a warrior or daredevil.

I tell him of my plan to go to Munich for treatment with Erich Rapp. He dismisses this idea with a savagely impatient wave of his hand. "Rapp! Rapp! For years he treated CURABLE CANCERS, CURABLE CANCERS, HODGKIN'S DISEASE, with mistletoe extract. MISTLETOE EXTRACT!" At last, someone who has heard of Erich Rapp. My disillusion with Doherty is finally complete.

Treatment will be bearable at Memorial, Marek explains, because it is so homey on his ward. A family member is allowed to bunk with the patient throughout chemotherapy, and if I find the hospital food unappetizing—a cramp grips my insides as I recall the black-eyed peas—we may make use of two kitchens on the floor. "You'll like it here," Marek says. "Everybody cooking, laughing. We have some fun, you know, while we do all this."

"Fun." Did the doctor really say "fun"? I don't quite, in all my pain, my fear, my terrible distress, believe that I am hearing this.

"I can cure you," Marek announces boldly. "I'm not talking about remission. I'm talking about cure. c-u-r-e, cure!" A cancer in remission is still present, but has been held in check; cure means the deranged, malignant cells have gone away. The CAP, he says, won't do the job by itself, but he will boost it with high-dose treatments of His Drug, so potent they must be followed immediately by a chemical rescue—without it, you'd poison the patient to death! There is one problem though. Both the platinum and His Drug are toxic to the kidneys, and so can't be given at the same time. Treatments must be staggered.

Marek then outlines a schedule of chemotherapy that sends me reeling. I'm to spend several nights in the hospital for the CAP, then to take a short rest at home, followed by a much longer stay at Memorial for dangerous death-defying treatments of His Drug. I'll be two weeks out of every four in the hospital for the next six months. Then a surgery, and if no cancer remains, yet another year—a year!—of maintenance chemotherapy.

Fun! The man wants me on chemotherapy for *eighteen months*. "Bald as a bat and barfing like crazy" for a year and a half. I couldn't possibly endure it. In fact, this is to be exactly the duration of my treatment, though not all of it will be taken with Marek. "Eighteen months," I say, "Why, at Community Hospital they said only five." "You know nothing, *they* know nothing," responds Marek angrily. "The name of the game with cancer is the Last Cell. You have to kill the Last Cell." He is, I will later find out, quite right, precisely right, about this.

Suddenly, the oncologist changes tone, tempo, subject. He looks me over, lets his head drop disconsolately. "You're too young for all of this, you know," he says, and then, more brightly, "but you look in good condition!"

Marek, evidently, hasn't been properly schooled in the handling of cancer patients. Oncologists, as a rule, disclose very little information and are very steady, very monochromatic in mood. They play a close hand, keep a poker face. Why overload a jumpy and presumably hopelessly ignorant patient with too much information? Knowledge can be inconvenient, it triggers panic. The patient may become ungovernable. Like politicians, doctors usually favor you with a much simplified version of the truth. Some slogans, a few formulas, that's all.

But Marek shatters the mold. He's mercurial, intellectually jumpy, sheds raw emotions and complex ideas quite shamelessly. "Your drug," I say. "It's experimental, isn't it. Nobody knows whether or not it works. Am I correct?" "No!" shouts Marek. "It is *not* experimental, *not* experimental. We have proven it." He moves to one of the bookshelves lining his office and pulls out a thick loose-leaf folder jammed with Xeroxes of medical papers, all about the excellent results obtained treating ovarian cancer patients with His Drug. I note the dates of the papers—many were published long ago—and the authorship. "But *you* wrote all of these," I object. I want some corroboration. Some evidence that at least one other doctor in the world thinks ovarian cancer can be cured—C-U-R-E-D, cured—with His Drug. "Of course I wrote them," Marek says. "It's My Treatment."

Now this fierce doctor is shifting subjects yet again, treating us to a complicated lecture on the interleukins, naturally existing or sometimes genetically engineered proteins, thought to fight cancer by abetting the body's immune response.

"*I* was working with interleukins as early as '72," brags the cancer doctor, a man not much restricted by modesty. "And you know what?" Here's the little-boy eagerness again. "You know there are three hundred and eighty unidentified lymphokines, and fifteen known ones!" "Lymphokines?" I ask confusedly. I'm out of my depth. "Lymphokines, interleukins, they're the same," says Marek impatiently. Any fool ought to know that!

I rather wish Marek would save the science lecture for another occasion. My stomach is cramping, my incision stinging, and I am faint with exhaustion.

"I had wanted to see Alan Thornton," I tell this wild man oncologist. Marek's large, intelligent-looking ears seem almost literally to flex at the mention of Thornton's name. "Thornton, you want Thornton, I get him for you," Marek says. "Al Thornton, he is my good friend. I've known him for twenty years."

Marek then tells me about a dear friend of his, who also had ovarian cancer. "She was worse than you, bulging out to *here,* with ascites," he says, his hands miming the girth of a woman seven months pregnant. "I sent her to Thornton and he cured her, I *hope* anyway." Now the expressive hands are pressed together as if in prayer. So, I think, here is yet another vote of confidence for the man Wirth suggested that I see.

"You say Thornton will treat me? His nurse said he wasn't taking patients anymore." "Oh, yes, if I ask him, he will treat you. I can arrange it. Although I truly think you would do better with My Drug. I think I could cure with it, even without using the CAP, and—" this last remark is made quite slyly—"you wouldn't even lose your pretty hair. It keeps on growing with My Drug."

"Let me think it over," I plead. I am half-dead with fatigue, worn out entirely by my afternoon's encounter with Marek. I say good-bye-for-now to the Unforgettable Cancer Doctor, and after gobbling two Valium and a Percocet, curl into the backseat of our Toyota and sleep all the way back to New York.

· · ·

At home I review my notebooks, looking over the jottings I made in Marek's office. All my other notes are neat, coherent, and legible. But today I've made only scrawls, beginnings of sentences with no endings, jottings that might be useful to *Time* magazine's science desk but don't much bear on my case. I screw up my eyes, ball my mind into a fist, and after dipping into the papers Marek has handed me, manage to understand. Marek's drug is itself part of the established arsenal of cancer treatments. What is experimental are the tremendously high doses he gives, and the special "rescue" administered directly afterward.

I find myself not much wanting to take Marek's special treatment, not only because it means spending the major portion of what may be my much-abbreviated life in the hospital, but also because I sense that for Marek, this high-dose protocol has become an *idée fixe,* his last hope for recapturing the now-tarnished prestige of his early glory days.

Still Marek intrigues—and frightens—me. I'm intrigued because he's given me so much time and information, because his understanding of cancer appears profound, and because he is so human, angrily blasting Erich Rapp, sad that someone as young as I am must go through this ordeal. On his ward my mother won't have to hide under my bed to be with me. She can scramble my morning eggs in one of Marek's kitchen's, bring me cups of tea.

But I am frightened as well. I think Marek is probably a little crazy. Speaking always of His Drug, His Treatment, His Rescue —why he even handed me His Curriculum Vitae as I left, and though it is packed with honors and awards and has stapled to it a sixteen-page bibliography of Marek's published papers, I am not so naive that I don't recognize this both as a baldly aggressive attempt to recruit me as a patient—Marek is thrilled that I am a magazine editor, sniffs the sweet aroma of possible publicity— and the act of an ungovernable ego.

The drug Marek uses is mentioned in my fledgling library of cancer books, but not as a treatment for ovarian cancer, and I find no discussion of his high-dose technique. I would have to browse a medical library for days to check Marek's information on this obscure modality, and I don't have days to spend this way, nor the energy to find somebody to smuggle me into a restricted students-only facility. The most fruitful aspect of my lengthy, exhausting interview with Marek, I decide, is his promise to put me into Thornton's hands. I have no reason to doubt that the two men are friends; they're of an age, were young, pioneering scientists together. Marek will, I think, make good his promise to have Thornton treat me. Why would he not?

. . .

Next day I formulate my plan, and quickly, I *must* make a decision to act on it. I phone Marek to ask if he'll treat me right away, I'm in such danger every day I wait, but with the standard treatment only, not with his frightening megadrug. I'm too scared for that. Then, after a single treatment, will he please dispatch me to his old friend Thornton; after I see him, I can decide what to do next. I could, of course, return to Community Hospital for standard treatment, but I can't bear the thought of going back to so impersonal—even hostile—a place. Nor would my desire to see Thornton be well served by my signing on at Community, where the arrogant self-regarding staff considers itself totally top-of-the-line. They wouldn't look kindly on my desire to see a physician at another, supposedly inferior, institution. As far as I can see, my best access to Thornton is through Marek.

"You want to be part of Thornton's research?" Marek asks. The doctor's voice is darkly playful. "Fine. Fine. I give you a first treatment, and then we see."

I'm smart all right, I know I'm onto something here, have met a man of brilliance. But I am also deadly stupid. Even if Marek could persuade Thornton to take me—not a likelihood, Thornton's policy about not signing on new patients is firm—he isn't apt to try. Why yield such a tempting morsel as myself, with my youth, my strength—I'm such a really excellent research subject, such a robust guinea pig—to the man he outshone in his youth who has now risen far above him. Why indeed!

Well, I have never been famous for my sense of strategy. But in my own defense, let me say that my danger is formidable, the horns of my dilemma rough and knobby. I have to be treated immediately. The cancer may well be spreading already, like mossy fungus on the wall of a cave. With standard therapy I've only a remote shot at a cure. I will need something extra, something special; I've no idea what this might be, but I'm hoping that Thornton, whose services will be procured for me by Marek, will provide it.

I am also up against what Marek has described as the system of "fixed formulas or what doctors like to describe as protocols." If I choose a particular "protocol" now, a six-to-ten-month course of therapy, be it standard or experimental, I will find it difficult to change, to hop a different bus, one with a more pleasing destination than the grave.

You see, a research institution like Community Hospital, or even Thornton's Central Hospital, likes "virgin" patients best, those who haven't been treated yet. These hospitals are not just dispensing medical care, they are also gathering data garnered from their research protocols. You've no statistical value to them if you've taken only half or three-quarters of the medicine they prescribe. You need to be with them, start to finish, to be counted as one of their survivors, or even to be included in the nameless rollcall of the dead.

I don't suppose this system would seem particularly offensive to the well population, to healthy people involved in their sex lives, their golf games. But when you enter the strange "kingdom of the sick," and realize, my God, I am a number first to these physicians and only incidentally a person with hopes, memories, plans, and dreams, the bile rises from deep within you and it floods your gullet. You feel dehumanized and you quiver with outrage. You don't want to play the game this way. But it's their game, not yours, and the rules of research have been firmly in place for better than half a century. Who can change them now? Who can even try? Certainly not a woman veering dangerously toward death. Certainly not me.

Marek has encouraged me to believe that with his help I may bend the rules a little; I can begin treatment with him, and because of his special relationship with Thornton, still be considered for research at Central Hospital. He has baited his little line quite prettily and I, a gullible fish, have taken the lure. In fact, just this one treatment, the one I can't safely postpone, am courting death by delaying, will make me ineligible for anybody's research anywhere, and will make even those who practice only standard therapies shy of me. So I'm not such a top-notch student after all. I've missed quite a key factor in this equation. And in so doing have made what will turn out to be a near-lethal mistake.

I wonder, after putting down the phone with Marek, why he has been chuckling so merrily. I only half sense that his is a laugh of victory!

. . .

Reactions to my plan are mixed. My father, a good Sunday painter and would-be film director—he could have made *Dr. Zhivago* he always insists, life just didn't give him the opportunity—enjoys and trusts men of temperament. Marek's caged-beast pacing and lightning mood shifts, though they've sounded an alarm in me, have persuaded Daddy that the doctor is a genius. My father's love for me is profound; he was the one who, before the operation, denied I could be ill the most vigorously. And now he will not, *will not,* accept the possibility that I might die of my disease. Nobody but Marek has said I can cure her, C-U-R-E, cure. My father needs to believe.

Hugh is more cautious. He senses there could be danger here, but after so many years with me, he knows I'm stubborn, can't easily be talked in or out of a decision. Realizing I need to be given my head in this, Hugh says I'm with you all the way. My mother, a tightly drawn knot of love, anger, and anxiety—her rosary beads haven't been out of her hands for five minutes since she's been here—is so wildly relieved that I've determined to go *someplace, anyplace,* for treatment that she offers no objections. She sees this as yet untreated cancer as a stalking killer, with me, her beloved daughter, as its prey. The evil must be stopped immediately.

Jennifer is the only one who tries to dissuade me. She cannot believe that I am leaving Community Hospital, an eminent institution thrust up by a great metropolis, for an obscure facility in grubby Cityside. "Nobody but you and your father think that doctor's any good," she fumes. "You're out of your mind to go there!"

Curious Jennifer has also been busy reading, a book by a therapist, dubiously credentialed, who has rushed in where Nobel prize winners fear to tread and announced that the causes of cancer are psychogenic, in the mind. Wrongheaded attitudes give you the disease; right-thinking cures you. Jennifer has brought me this book like a priest rushing the Bible to a condemned man and has urgently admonished me to read.

I don't finish the book. After reading certain key passages— "Cancer may be viewed as the ultimate primitive representation of an extreme separation of the self-contained positive and negative forces motivating our lives"—I fling it across the room. Nothing but pseudo-knowledge here! Jennifer disagrees. I am a classic, *classic* "type C," she insists, a cancer-prone personality. "Your goddamned negative attitude is what gave you the disease in the first place," she insists. "And you'll never be cured until you get rid of it!"

She levels this accusation the very evening that I return from Cityside, when I'm doubled over with pain and exhaustion, and the lunacy of this attack goes right by me. I'm struck mostly by the astonishing unfairness of it. Not only am I fated to suffer from this disease, I am to be blamed for it as well. I know from my own less flashy reading that sad and happy people both get cancer, that introverts are no more protected from it than extroverts, and that neither doing good in the world nor doing ill will keep you cancer-free. Cellular disaster strikes most democratically. There is no particular cluster of traits that puts you at risk, no person who is type C.

I'm edging away from Jennifer. I'm under assault enough as it is; I don't need to be battered further by her accusations. It will prove simple enough to make my escape. For Jennifer isn't just angry, she's also getting a little bit bored with me. And edgy. One day of fear and wretchedness followed by another and another—that's arduous, that isn't what she contracted for. My friend is looking for a guilt-free exit, and she's got one here. It's all my fault that I got cancer, my own foolish doing that I didn't properly vent my anger or direct my love. That I turned into that uptight bundle of rage and frustration pinpointed by the looney-birds of psychology as type C.

. . .

We leave for Memorial. Again, there's a flurry of packing, of stuffing our bags and tracking down affordable berths in Cityside —the whole family is going along, but only one person can stay in my room on Marek's ward—and I have travel nerves, as if setting off on some particularly complicated kind of holiday. We hasten along, packing a dozen different bottles of vitamins—I'm covering my bases here—along with a tiny ashtray, which I plan to hide in my bedside drawer. I haven't quit smoking yet. I'm too strung-out, too terrified. We pile in the car, and silently—we're all too anxious to talk—hasten onto Cityside.

As we drive into Cityside's slummy outskirts a second time, I'm more sensitive to the squalor here. *This* is where I'm going for cancer treatment. Maybe Jennifer was right! How could I leave beautiful, efficient Manhattan for this fifth-rate place! Jesus, the doctor is probably fifth-rate as well. Who gives a fig for his precious awards, what the hell is he doing *here!*

We have been told to come in by way of the emergency entrance. The dull-eyed security guard waves us toward admissions; a patient or two shambles along, a hugely pregnant black woman, a one-legged man clad in filthy jeans and a baseball cap. This is not an all-cancer hospital. These are clinic patients. But I can't help but think, people were certainly better dressed at Community Hospital. Admissions has only a modest desktop computer. At Community Hospital, a beautifully ordered printout, complete with credit rating, issues from their beautifully modern machines. Oh God, this is all a terrible, terrible mistake. Those doctors at Community Hospital weren't so bad. I want urgently to go back to its gorgeous equipment, its crisp technicians, its patients who read the *Voice* or the *New Yorker;* here the only reading materials I notice are cheap adventure novels or bodice rippers. Why, I even see one fellow thumbing through a comic book! I'm being treated along with people who *don't know any better,* and I, a sophisticated editor, had at my disposal the best of the best, the now, in my mind, terrific Community Hospital with its top-rated staff, its sleek CAT scanners, imperturbably silent corridors. I must be mad, totally mad!

For a brief, unsettled moment I find myself alone by the elevators. Hugh and my parents are all elsewhere, making their rooming arrangements, toting bags upstairs to Marek's ward. A woman stands alongside me. Though dressed in street garb, she reminds me strongly of the nuns who taught me during childhood. She has that nun-skin, so clear and shining, and the whites of her eyes are unnaturally pure and clear. I am flooded by memories of all the nuns I ever knew, and I remember particularly the ones we called by those funny double names. Sister Frances Joseph, she had me in third grade; Sister Teresa Claire in eighth. They were so kind, these clear-skinned, clear-eyed nuns. This nurse seems just like them. Her face is suffused with the mild, steady light of kindness. It shines on all the world.

I grab her hand, which doesn't startle her at all. She acts as if people who are wild with terror grab at her every day. Unruffled, the nurse beams her steady light of kindness onto me. This disease has made me so strange. I cry at the oddest time. "I have cancer," I tell her. "And I'm going to let Marek treat me. Am I crazy? Is *he* crazy? Do you know anything about him?"

The nurse is very calm. "He's a fine doctor," she tells me, "you're in very good hands." I pick the oddest times to cry. Because suddenly I'm sobbing, my arms thrown about her shoulders. She stands quite firm, doesn't shrink away.

"Oh God," I say, "I am so *scared!*"

EXPERIMENT

December 1986—April 1987

Marek's ward is hard to get the hang of. Procedures here are very odd, the doctor is a wild man, and the patient population desperately sick. Most of the people here have been around the block. Their cancers didn't respond to conventional treatment, and they've found out about Marek after long hours spent in medical libraries or following a computer search. I am the only newly-diagnosed patient. Fresh meat.

Soon after settling in I am told by the nurse that I must pee into a "hat." I imagine a top hat, a fedora—how on earth will I accomplish this? But the "hat" is really a plastic basin that slips under the toilet seat. They are monitoring the quantities of urine I produce, a measure of the health of my kidneys. I will need good kidneys, if I'm to excrete the toxins to which I'll soon be introduced.

I am summoned for tests: lung X-ray, CAT scan, even a bone scan, courtesy of the department of nuclear medicine. Perhaps they can bomb this cancer away. I am not eager to know the results of any of these procedures. The news nowadays is so rarely good. Following the tests, I am hustled into Marek's office for a conference. He's assisted by another doctor, Newman, who spends his spare days chasing butterflies. Dr. N. is a thin, jumpy fellow. It isn't difficult to imagine him swatting at the air with a net. Well, I wanted an environment less sterile than that offered by Community Hospital—what is it they say about answered prayers?

At the conference—the whole family comes along—Marek mounts slides from my scan on the wall and begins to point at large black splotches, as well as at areas that look polka-dotted. All cancer, it would seem. The largest darkened area is seven centimeters in diameter. "But I only had three centimeters after surgery," I say, jumping up in protest. "So, it grew," Marek booms. Desolate, I sink back into my seat.

Seven centimeters of cancer—this is insupportable, a catastrophe! I know from my reading that even three centimeters is too great a load to be successfully challenged by chemotherapy. With this much cancer, I haven't a chance. My hopes plummet. Later, I pound out my despair on my hospital bed, chanting. "It's too big. It's too big!" I sound like a tormented child.

My parents and Hugh are alarmed and baffled by this outburst. "But you're just starting treatment," Hugh protests. "The chemo will take care of it," my father adds. Such baseless optimism! I'm wildly impatient that they haven't been counting centimeters as obsessively as I have. Don't they know that it's the *bulk* of the tumor to be reduced that tells whether or not you'll live or die. How can this family be so ignorant!

In fact, the radiologist has made a mistake, but I won't know this with any certainty for many months. And in the meantime, I will live with the dispiriting belief that inside me there is a surely untreatable hunk of cancer bigger than my fist. It will help keep me with Marek, this error, for I know that standard treatment alone can't possibly work against such bulky disease. Without it, I might have gone to some less eccentric physician. And yet, as mistaken diagnoses go, this one's trivial enough. Except in the most sophisticated cancer centers, and sometimes even there, more serious errors occur with shocking regularity. I will meet patients whose disease went entirely undetected by doctors for better than a year, plenty long enough to make the difference between life and death.

"So . . . let's see what you want for chemotherapy," says Marek, his eyes alight with mischief. He hands me an open book, an oncologist's manual. "You pick!"

"Me? But I've no idea what I'm reading," I object, and Marek, who's playing to—cartooning, really—my desire to be a partner in my treatment, takes the book away. He has made his point. Only one person in this room is knowledgeable enough to direct the chemotherapy, and that person is he. How foolish I would be, then, to decline His Drug.

For now, though, he doesn't press. He plays me, lets the line go slack, recommends only the standard treatment, the CAP. There is more than one recipe for the CAP, however, and he chooses the combination that is strongest, most aggressive.

. . .

That night I am prepared for chemotherapy. A special nurse comes by to "stick" me. She searches my hand for a prominent vein and sighs in vexation. My dainty veins frustrate the IV nurse, who is obliged to prick me several times before she succeeds in implanting the needle. My mother watches her like a hawk.

Come morning, it's time to begin. I don my synthetic cold cap but it isn't very cold. No, not at all icy. The nurse says they have an old-style one in the kitchen that might work better. She fits me with a big cloth bonnet, filled with actual ice cubes. My mother nervously adjusts it, out of long, devoted maternal habit. Just as she straightened my skirt seam when I was in high school, brushed the wool-balls off my sweaters. The nurse also suggests a tourniquet for my scalp, to provide added protection, and improvises one from some hospital tubing. As she wraps it tightly around my scalp the blood flow to my head abruptly stops. I feel chilled and dizzy. This is even more unpleasant than being pricked.

Another nurse arrives to administer the Adriamycin, the "Adrio" as it's known in patient's slang, the "red death." This is among the harshest of anticancer drugs. The nurse explains that she will "push" the Adriamycin, into my veins, emptying the vial filled with cherry-red liquid all at once. This is a prudent way to proceed. The Adrio is very abrasive. If it seeps out of the vein into surrounding tissue, it can corrode the flesh, like acid. Adriamycin burns are treated with skin grafts but even they don't always heal. You can lose a hand to one.

I don't know this as the nurse "pushes" the Adriamycin, and in my ignorance I feel safe. Safe but foggy. They have mixed a strong sedative, Ativan, into the other drugs that are now drip-dripping into me out of bags suspended from an IV stand. A heavy metal box, attached to the stand at about my eye level as I lie in bed, regulates the flow. It goes click-click, click-click, lulling me into unconsciousness.

What a strange bedtime this is! It's nine o'clock in the morning, my head is burdened by its weight of ice, and the whole of my family has gathered round. They seem to pulse with anxiety. Click-click, click-click. A sudden rush of adrenalin rouses me. This tourniquet, it's intolerable. I must be rid of it. I grab wildly at my head, tossing the bonnet to the floor and ripping off the tourniquet. I call out to my mother, my God, this is just the *beginning*.

It occurs to me I could break free entirely. I bolt upright in bed, thinking to pull away from the tubes, the poison. Strength, I have no strength. Befogged again, I slip weakly into the darkness. Dead weight.

. . .

Throughout the day and well into the night I wake at intervals to vomit up bile and queer, grayish, chemical-tasting stuff. There's no food in my stomach. What I'm losing are secretions produced by my own digestive tract. My mother, who must be the one to spend the night in my room, sets a plastic basin beneath my chin whenever I gag awake.

Next morning I'm amazed to find myself alive, well, and famished. A tray has been left in my room and I slip out of bed—my mother's still asleep—and steer the awkward IV stand to which I'm still tethered toward breakfast. A big, bulging sausage sits on the plate and I gulp it down, barely pausing to chew.

After two days of "hydration"—a mineral-rich saline solution flushes through my veins, washing the toxins away—I'm discharged. It is now Christmas week. The family will spend the holiday on Seventy-Sixth Street, and then, when I'm strong enough to travel, we'll drive to the country. I'm really looking forward to this. I'll see my animals again—two dogs and a cat—Hugh had to put them in a kennel when he first returned to New York on that long-ago weekend when I signed into the Medical Institute for tests. And at last, we'll have a little space. The apartment is jammed with suitcases and tension, the air too thick to breathe. Another thing, I'm proud of my country house, anxious for my parents to see it. They'll think, she hasn't done that badly for herself. It's a nice house.

But first, we have our city Christmas to get through, and as holidays go, this one's dreadful enough. I request that my mother cook the full feast and she outdoes herself. But then I can't eat a bite—I'm anorexic at this point, a mysterious side effect of the therapy—and the friends who've kept us occupied are scattered here and there, busy with Christmas. A somber silence—I've banned the radio, carols really would be too much—rules on Seventy-Sixth Street.

Then, the day after Christmas, Marek has requested our appearance in Cityside—he wants me to have another scan. The man is downright eager to see how well his chemotherapy has worked. Off we go, early, early in the morning and my sour, empty stomach aches. I'll have a nice glass of barium, mixed into a sickeningly sweet syrup, for breakfast.

In the parking lot at Memorial I look at my father and say, "It's not worth it, really, it's not. I'll die in the end anyway, after they've had their fill of all this." Well, I'm never at my best in the morning. And this morning, anticipating the barium and yet another "stick"—they inject contrast dye into the veins before the scan—I don't feel human at all, but rather like some poor wounded creature, some suffering, wordless part of nature that endures without complaint.

. . .

CAT scan rooms are kept quite cool—at about sixty degrees, ideal for the machinery, if not the patient. Shivering, I take my place on the scanner, a flimsy cotton sheet draped over me, and listen to two X-ray technicians as they chat about the holidays—gifts given and received, parties still to go to. The whole world has been having Christmas and I'm having a CAT scan. Sorry for myself, I let the tears slide down my cheeks. "Is anything wrong?" one of the technicians asks. "No, there's nothing wrong," I say. "I just don't care for this procedure very much."

After the scan, we wait around a bit, my parents and Hugh buoying me up—surely the news will be good—then meet with Marek, who's only partly pleased with the test results. The polka-dotted areas are now entirely clear, but the large black splotches haven't shrunk. He has expected better from His CAP.

I am expecting Marek to bring up Thornton, to say he's phoned his old friend, set up an appointment for me. But instead he is muttering about His Drug. There would have been more shrinkage, he is sure, had they used it. I am too stupid to understand—His Drug has great potency!

But our plan was just this one treatment, I say, just to use the CAP. Has he had a chance to phone Thornton yet? "Oh, Thornton, Thornton, of course . . ." There is an interestingly-timed pause, "but he is still out of the country, I believe. You had better come back here for your next treatment. It's not so bad, eh, the way we do things? I'll see you in three weeks." And then Marek is suddenly, bafflingly out of the room.

I'm too fatigued, and confused, to know what to do. Surely Thornton is back from France by now. Marek seemed to be stalling. But why, why? As the doctor darts quickly away, it's as if he's been surprised in the midst of making some secret, and possibly devious, arrangements.

I am here. And I am vulnerable. This is Marek's advantage. And he will press it, as would any skilled seducer, quite ruthlessly.

A day or two later, we pack our bags and leave for the country. I haven't yet lost my hair though my tresses do seem strangely lusterless, and so I am not too worried that Nicholas hasn't yet delivered his painstakingly crafted wig. Secretly, I believe I will keep my hair—surely I won't go bald all at once—but I do pack several scarves just in case.

As we approach the house I expect my parents to rave about the view—from our mountainside perch we can see five states—but they only remark that at least this house seems solidly built, unlike the "shack" I so unwisely rented when Hugh and I first began our weekend commute. I'll settle for that. Praise is praise.

I myself take enormous pleasure in the cozy clutter of the house's interior; I love my rocking chairs, my hand-painted hurricane lamps. But neither Hugh nor I score any points for decor. My mother likes her solid, suburban furniture. She doesn't see anything particularly wonderful about rooms full of rickety antiques.

Even our animals—and everybody loves our black labs, Winnie and Bert, and the marmalade cat, Thunderfoot—don't win them over. The animals are rambunctious after their long confinement in the kennel and they race hysterically around and around the house. My parents find them noisy and a little menacing.

I'm disappointed that my life in the country has failed to impress my parents. Disappointed and aggrieved. For I experience their indifference to this household as yet another rejection of my relationship with Hugh. It is here, not in the tiny city apartment, that as a couple we've put down roots most firmly. This house is what we've made together, the edifice that has contained our only half-shared life. Do my parents feel that to praise this house would be to ratify our union? Is that why they fail to remark upon its charms?

Even so, I am feeling physically much better. I've begun to eat again—the anorexia has vanished, as suddenly and mysteriously as it began—and Hugh and I plan an expedition to South Lake, our special spot, a little jewel of a lake high up in the Catskills, where we have skated and skinny-dipped. We visit it in every season and are ourselves there as we can be in no other place.

The day is bright, and we've recently had a snowfall. Hardly anybody but us visits South Lake in the winter; the snow there is always pristine. We take the dogs, who are frisking ecstatically in the yard, literally twirling in the air, they're so excited by the cold. We find the lake frozen solid when we arrive and decide to trek across it. Every now and then the ice groans spookily beneath us, as if about to break apart. On the shore, the pines bend gracefully beneath their weight of snow, and in the perfect, winter-wrought silence, I forget Marek and bone scans and the metallic taste of cisplatin in my mouth. I am happier than I have any right to be.

Energized by this outing, I take charge of the food for New Year's Eve—we're having a late supper of ham and potato salad, the same supper my mother prepared through all the New Year's Eves of my childhood. The mood in my country house is unusually relaxed as we settle down to an after-supper game of poker. When my mother has the deal she capriciously declares a long sequence of wild cards—one hand, it's red threes, deuces, black sevens, and one-eyed jacks. This is the mother I have always loved so much, pretty, high-spirited, flirtatious. Whatever our differences, she is irreplaceably dear to me. We laugh uproariously as three out of four of us bring in a royal flush, then have to do some fancy figuring to decide who has the winning hand. For a moment there, we are actually acting like a family.

The next day this briefly-found peace shatters like glass. I am sitting in the porch room, grateful to be curled up on a sofa and not struggling to adjust a hospital bed or vomiting chemicals. I have decided to reread Graham Greene, an old favorite, and as I flip through the pages of *Our Man In Havana* I run my fingers through my hair. What's this? The long, silky strands don't hold, they cling to my fingers, slip into my lap. I run out of the sunny porch room, as startled as if I'd just caught fire, screaming. "My hair! My hair!" Nobody else is as amazed or alarmed as I am. I think, resentfully, they *expected* me to lose my hair, they *knew* it would happen. During the next two days nearly all my hair comes out, as I indulge in a marathon of weeping. I don't stop crying. Even when I think I've quite exhausted myself, I find more tears.

In the *American Cancer Society's Cancer Book* it is explained that many patients experience hair loss as the most stressful part of cancer treatment. The authors note that this is odd, given the life-threatening nature of the disease. But then the authors have never lost their hair. They don't know that it makes you feel as if you are disintegrating, that you feel ugly and maimed. Why, I believe many people would choose death over disfigurement. Indeed, some have done so, refusing chemotherapy, not because they fear the nausea or the death of cells in the bone marrow—the first is a passing condition, the second, to the patient at least, an abstraction. The doctors fret over the exhausted cells but you don't feel them go. No, what people fear, quite reasonably it seems to me, is the loss of their silky hair.

. . .

We've come back to the city. I need to do something quickly about covering my all-but-bald head, and besides we've only a few days before my next visit to Marek's hospital. First stop, Nicholas Piazza, the salon for wigs. The few strands left on my head are all quite dead, like the leaves of a tree after frost, soon to be carried off by even the slightest breeze. I cannot wait for Nicholas to finish fussing with my custom-made wig—it's just a wig, after all, not an artwork—and I insist he supply me immediately with a synthetic hairpiece. I pull something short and curly from the rows of mannequin heads on his display shelves, and say, here, I want this. This will do just fine.

As Nicholas fits me with the wig, I am forced to look in the mirror. I remind myself of some space creature from Star Trek—very peculiar-looking, to be sure, but not unattractive. "You have a near-perfect head-shape," Nicholas remarks mildly, and I can see what he means. My head is small and delicately molded, in its way not unlovely. I realize if I had sufficient confidence, I could carry off this "look"; all that would be needed is eye makeup (without hair my eyes seem huge), and big, showy earrings. This is but a passing thought. I must learn how to put on my wig. On the first try, I've slipped it on backwards, for a not very engaging Neanderthal effect. But after a little coaching, I'm in and out of it like a pro.

. . .

It has been seven weeks since my surgery and the ban on strenuous physical exercise is now lifted. I have to find out if I can still

119

swim. I think that probably I can't, that I'll sink to the bottom of the pool like a stone, but the only way to know for sure is to try. I ask Hugh to drive me to my swimming club, and though he's hesitant—it's cold and blustering snow outside—he agrees. Hugh knows how much my swimming means to me, understands, too, that it emblemizes my return to a life that's fit and active. I'm thumbing my nose at this disease.

I carry a special tote bag for my new wig and plan my strategy. I'll change from wig to swimming cap in the club's locked bathroom stalls, come to think of it, I'd best change into my swimming suit there as well, since I seem also to be losing my pubic hair. That might draw some unwanted attention in the open changing area. Then I'll lock up my valuables and attempt to swim.

What do you know, I can still do it. Breathe in, breathe out, stroke, stroke, stroke. I am slower than before surgery and a good deal chillier—no more comfortable layer of fat insulating me from the cold—but I still have endurance and buoyancy. As I slip out of the pool, I can't help but notice I'm attracting admiring stares. I haven't been this thin since high school.

How very odd! I am to be prettier in this illness than I was in health. But then my whole world is exploding, is upside-down. The unimaginably strange is becoming familiar to me. The new world that I inhabit in this lean new body is very different now. All its features have been irrevocably changed.

· · ·

I cannot wear the wig all the time—it's uncomfortable to have a mop of synthetic fur on your head. I will need turbans, too. I've resolved that while bald may indeed be beautiful, it probably isn't for me. And remembering my frustrating shopping expedition at Christmas, I think I'll probably need to have the turbans custom-made. I've phoned Ingeborg, a designer friend, and described my predicament. Of course she'll make me a batch of turbans, she's delighted she can be of help.

I decide to go directly from my swimming club to Ingeborg's loft, but by now the snow is piled high and there are no cabs. No matter, I'll walk across town. Stomping through the snow, I revel in my restored physical competence. Following a fifty-length swim with a trek across town in a blizzard—what a feat!

My friend Ingeborg is also proud of me, when I arrive all flushed and wind-stung. She's a very physical woman and can appreciate my resilience. Ingeborg is also quite fastidious, though, and she doesn't deal well with the sheer mess of my hair loss. Like a dog in the springtime, I am constantly shedding. And since to fit properly, the turbans must be fashioned while actually on top of my head, my friend is kept quite busy trying to keep the insides of these head coverings clean. She never stops tsking, her sense of order and beauty offended by such havoc, such slovenliness.

I've brought along a bottle of white wine, and as I proceed to consume nearly all of it, grow quite drunk with sentiment. I'm in a mood to reminisce, and Ingeborg, a Viennese who possesses the romanticism native to her city, gladly goes along. We have two decades of friendship behind us, a rich lode to mine. Ingeborg and I remember being young together and full of hopes—the hopes thinned out a little when we were no longer quite so young. And as we run through the men in our lives—he was basically a social climber, don't you think? Oh him, definitely an artist—we reserve the kindest judgments for the ones who really loved us.

Ingeborg and I talk and talk, and all the while, my industrious friend has been sewing me dainty cotton turbans in colorful, cheeky prints. They are as gay as this strange, snowbound afternoon, as light as the air.

. . .

My holiday from treatment is over. We're back again at Marek's hospital, peering at yet another set of CAT scan slides. "I don't know, I don't know what this radiologist is seeing," Marek says, his pointer aimed at the big black splotch, which is still interpreted by the radiologist as a seven-centimeter growth. "He may be reading the slides incorrectly. I *hope* he is. We don't want to have to poison you to death."

Marek invites first me, then my father up for a closer look at the slides, as if we were colleagues in a lecture hall who could easily be made to understand. But this is all theater, all a sham. We are none of us "partners" in this treatment, for all of the doctor's stagy tricks. It is Marek's towering ego, not lack of talent —he has proved himself to be marvelously gifted—that washed him out of the scientific mainstream. He wouldn't defer to the judgment of lesser men, wouldn't play the game. And now that he operates in professional exile, this same ego has turned cagey, manipulative. He invites us up to his blackboard so we'll feel part of a consensus, but in fact the decision Marek has reached is all his own.

The doctor then explains that this time around I'm to receive three grams of His Drug to "boost" the CAP. Dr. Newman wrings his hands in dismay: in his view, this is a most inconsequential dose. But from my vantage point, it is three grams too much. "I only wanted the CAP," I protest. "You said you'd give me the standard treatment, then refer me to Alan Thornton."

"Thornton isn't taking patients anymore!" Marek barks.

"But you said . . ."

"Don't tell *me* what I said. Look, you will be getting three grams of My Drug. If you don't want it, go someplace else for treatment."

"It's too late to find another hospital. I have to have a treatment right away!"

"Oh, so you understand that much at least," Marek says, with a small, tight smile.

It is becoming clear—the man has trapped me. Either I take His Drug, or risk being late with a treatment that must be administered at precisely timed intervals. And where exactly would I go should I decline Marek's plan? Thornton remains as inaccessible to me as before. And it won't be easy for me to get back on track with Community Hospital after having snubbed them in favor of Cityside.

"All you have at stake is your career," I beg. "I'm worried about my life."

"I'll *save* your life," the doctor booms.

It is only now that I understand completely. Marek's behavior isn't bound by the usual restraints. He is in love and at war. At war with cancer, and a real hawk at that, willing to use the hydrogen bomb of treatments to defeat it. And in love—bitterly, resentfully, narcissistically in love—with his own talent, his beautiful mind, which is no longer honored by the fickle world as once it was. Marek is not fitted by temperament to play Thornton's *éminence grise*. He is an explorer! But the world now thrills to the work of younger men: the gifted Joseph Gallo, ambitious Steven Rosenberg. It has all but forgotten a proud old tiger who once roamed the jungles of science roaring out his terrible discoveries.

I say I'll think it over, this treatment plan, which Marek has told me will go from three grams of His Drug to six, and then to twelve, and finally to twenty-four. As Newman whines, but only three grams, it's not nearly enough, we take our leave. "Well, I've been tricked," I tell the family as we settle into a booth at a nearby Howard Johnson's. I've decided to feast on fried clams. Afraid I'll soon be anorexic again, I'm warehousing calories.

"*I'll* say you have!" says my mother, steaming. Behind her anger, there is terror. The most prudent of us all, she's terrified of what Marek may do to me.

"I don't know, His Drug might work," offers my father, more hopefully.

It might. Or it might not. Marek has got what he wanted, a subject for his research, and a robust one at that. Before I consent to treatment, I phone Dr. Jansen, the doctor from the Shelburne Clinic who told me to go for aggressive treatment, for high-dose chemotherapy. I need to check this treatment plan with somebody and Jansen has been open and cooperative with me—I'll get a good reading from him. The doctor comes on the line right away. I mutter my sorry-to-bother-you's, then quickly ask if he thinks the CAP can be effectively boosted with high doses of Marek's drug.

"It's not an unreasonable idea," says Jansen, somewhat non-committally.

I'm back in the hospital but still wavering when Marek proposes a tour of his laboratory. The doctor drives us there himself, and I realize he is trying both to soothe and to seduce me. The special attention is meant to quiet my misgivings, the laboratory tour designed to dazzle me. As we drive Marek reminds me, without undue modesty, that he is a much-honored, prize-winning scientist. His lab work involves forays into immunotherapy, from which I can also benefit.

In the end I do decide to stay at Memorial. And should you wonder why I came to the decision in the face of Marek's dubious strategies, I can only say that I thought—and still do think—the man a genius. I've also learned that the CAP, by itself, is minimally effective against three centimeters of cancer, far less the seven centimeters I still believe I have, and I have Jansen's word that it is "not unreasonable" to proceed. Also, for the present, Marek is keeping doses of His Drug unthreateningly small.

Finally, I must admit that while the courtship has been bumpy, I've fallen a little bit in love with Marek. He is daring and imaginative, and if he doesn't scruple too nicely, well, what would you expect from a mad genius? I want to put my hopes in him, just as you want to think love is possible when you meet a man who is both dashing and a little sinister. We have begun this adventure together. Now let us see where it leads.

. . .

Having made a commitment to Marek's ward, I now take stock of my environment. During the day or so of pretreatment hydration—they're obsessed here with my kidneys—I look around, absorbing the sights, sounds, and smells of the place. A place where people are not just patients to be cured, but human subjects whose survival, though few enough of them will survive, will serve to validate Marek's research, restore the luster to his rusted, creaky reputation.

Mostly, the ward smells of food. The two kitchens on the floor are in constant use, with patients' relatives making huge vats of spaghetti sauce, thick, aromatic soups. A tincture of garlic permeates the corridors. The sounds are less inviting, though. Marek's hospital houses a disproportionate number of brain cancer patients—His Treatment is particularly effective against this malignancy—and not all of them are of lucid mind. Some of those who've slipped their moorings make queer, inhuman noises as they sleep. Nor is what greets the eye particularly reassuring. A skeletal girl, just twenty-three, leaves the floor on a litter. Her parents—they've tapped data banks throughout the country to find Marek—are taking her on holiday. Two brain cancer patients schmooze in the hallway, their stubbled heads scarred from surgery. They're tethered to IV stands that drip outlandish helpings of Marek's Drug.

The doctor wishes me to meet a few of his most prized patients. There is Margot, who is frighteningly thin and whose frail body is wracked by a terrible, deep cough. Margot's long cancer is far advanced; she should be dead by now. That she breathes at all is testament to Marek's wizardry. Next I meet Emily, a buxom young woman with a thick thatch of coal-black hair. "See what pretty hair she has," says Marek slyly. Admiringly. "And she's just had fifty grams of My Drug." I understand that he wants me to know I can take vast quantities of his special chemotherapy, and still not lose my hair. This is a bald appeal to my vanity. It's not as effective as it might be, though. I notice that poor Emily seems too enervated even to speak.

In this eerie environment, I hold on fast to Hugh. And he is firmly, quietly in place. In the years we've been together, amidst a life smothered, as everyone's is, in dailiness, I've all but forgotten what first drew me to Hugh. But now I remember. He has always been a man who loved to be needed. And who, when he feels my need, responds with his best, his kindest traits.

Sometimes, I know, I've made him feel valueless, unnecessary, the body in the next room, the man at my arm at an expense-account dinner, a screening. After all, I earned a living, had my own friends, a busy social life. A face that says, I'm fine on my own, thank you, is what I've learned to show the world in my tenuous, materially unsupported circumstances. And I've sometimes showed this face to Hugh. He shrank from it.

But now, at the darkest moment of my life, in this strangest of strange places, I am vulnerable and frightened. And Hugh is glad to be with me, to be so much needed. He keeps busy, making friends with the other patients, helping figure out what Marek's next move may be, bringing me flowers or some attractive trifle that caught his eye on the street—a jeweled belt, a silvery headband to hold my wig in place. And with these small, thoughtful gestures, he distracts me from my terror, helps me believe that however lost I may feel right now, I will one day find myself again.

. . .

My second treatment in early January is uneventful as these things go. Perhaps the nausea is a little less severe; certainly the anorexia doesn't last as long. My adaptable body seems already to be adjusting to the poisons Marek has prescribed. I relax a little. And my parents, no longer rigid with terror, begin to unbend as well.

Daddy starts a friendship with a young girl two rooms away, Amy. She's just seventeen, has a runaway lymphoma. He takes his sketchpad in to visit her and does a quick portrait of this pretty child. It pleases her no end, he says. He shakes his head, marveling at the girl's sweetness, her bravery, how she always asks how *I'm* doing, how she's praying all the time for me. An amazing girl, Daddy says, really just amazing.

But though I mumble my isn't-that-wonderful's, I stay away from Amy. I don't want to know this beautiful, dying, seventeen-year-old child. I can't afford to. Not with my own fears mounting, swelling, threatening always to crest. The pull of sympathy will be strong, and painful. It will be dangerous for me, I sense, to make too many friends on Marek's ward, and Amy, because she is so young, so good, constitutes a particular danger.

I am right to be so self-protective. Amy will be dead within eight weeks.

. . .

About a week after discharge, we have a February snowfall. It carpets the streets. But as for me, I'm finally shaking awake after my long winter's sleep. Good God, have my parents been here since November? It's nearly February, how exhausted they must be! Struck by a furious rush of energy, I clean out my closets, exhume the contents of my bureau drawers, sweep and swab the floors. Delighted that at last I seem able to fend for myself, my parents book a ticket for St. Louis. On their last night in New York City, I'd like us all to celebrate. I want my parents to have something else to remember besides the sanity-cracking strains of this disease. We plan dinner out and I ask Carol to come along. She'll deflect the tension that is always present between my parents and Hugh, a role Jennifer used to play.

Jennifer is easing out of my life and I'm not struggling to bring her back. I haven't the emotional energy to deal with her continuing insistence that I'm a "type C." The last time we spoke, she argued that only psychotherapy could cure me of the emotional bad habits that brought about my disease. I gave myself high marks for forbearance for not hanging up the phone, and some few days later, was delighted to hear from Carol via Jimmie that Jennifer had plunged headlong into the animal rights movement. It's my surmise that this new enthusiasm is occupying the emotional energies she'd previously reserved for me.

So now it is Carol who plays mediator between Hugh and my parents, and on our night out, we have pasta at a local Italian place, a party of six, counting Carol's friend Steve who, out of deference to the coolness that's sprung up between Jennifer and me, she's brought along in place of Jimmie. The outing goes as smoothly as I could have wished. My mother talks a blue streak, Daddy presides over the table with patriarchal dignity, and Carol addresses enough remarks to Hugh to make up for my parents' pointed silences.

After our meal, Carol proposes we go back to her apartment for after-dinner drinks. As we look out the frosty doors that open onto her garden and watch the snow pile up outside, we seem a normal enough group, groggy but happy after the heavy food, a little too much wine. Carol's stereo blasts country's hottest hits, and mellow after my second brandy, I hum along to the sweet, sad tunes. Right now I am feeling queerly happy with this strange, troubled life of mine. It seems still to promise some mystery and gaiety.

The next day my mother and father board their plane at La Guardia, with, I hope, at least one pleasant memory of this troubled time, and I begin in earnest to reclaim my life.

. . .

About a week after my parents leave, the phone rings early in the morning. Half-asleep, I listen as a silky-voiced Marek outlines a surprising plan. "I've decided I want you to see Alan Thornton," the doctor tells me. "I've made you an appointment." This is an entirely unexpected turn-around, but of course I go. I'm thrilled that at last I'm going to see the eminent Central Hospital oncologist.

Thornton, a smiling, avuncular man, puts me at my ease. He seems distraught that such a "young girl," as he refers to me, should have so grave a disease. When I read from my notebooks, which are filled with jottings about my treatment to date, including details of Marek's chemotherapy, Thornton's smile is friendly. "Ah, so you're an amateur oncologist already," he says, not unpleasantly.

As he reviews Marek's plans for me, the doctor knits his

brows and ruminates. "I've never thought Marek got enough credit," he says. "There's a quality about him that reminds me of a Frenchman with a nose for wines. He *sniffs* out the cancer somehow." Dr. Thornton seems quite pleased with his metaphor. "Don't misunderstand me," he quickly adds. "You are in danger of dying of this disease." I hear, but don't really absorb, this remark. I am finding it difficult to comprehend the idea of my own death.

The reason so many die, Thornton explains, is that neither surgery nor chemotherapy is aggressive enough, but I've nothing to worry about there—Thornton reviews the notes Lawson made after my operation, then casts his eye over Marek's proposed chemotherapy, steeples his fingers, and pronounces all satisfactory.

"It's very *weird* out there in Cityside," I comment leadingly, hoping Thornton will offer to rescue me. I don't say outright, look, I only signed on with Marek because he promised to refer me to you. I don't *want* His Drug.

Slippery Marek, he knows his way around. He has referred me to Thornton, yes, but not as a potential Central patient. Please see *my* patient is what, evidently, Marek has said—she's a little nervous, in need of settling down. He doesn't want me saying later, why, you conscripted me into treatment, promised a referral to Thornton that you never delivered.

I sense, I'm sure correctly, that if Thornton were to treat me now, he'd be "poaching," stealing another physician's patient. Thornton's remarks about the Cityside physician have been entirely approving; he has offered no criticism of Marek's unorthodox treatment plan. If he has reservations about the therapy I'm receiving, I am not to hear them. Nor am I to be invited on board at Central Hospital. The two men are former colleagues, old friends. Thornton respects Marek's claim on me.

I feel bemused and let down as I prepare to take my leave. "Wait a minute," the doctor abruptly says. "I want to show you something." He fishes into a wire basket on his desk and produces a black and white glossy photograph of a woman with a sixties-ish bob and heavily-mascaraed eyes. She's clad in a swimswuit and just at the bra-line emerges a narrow tube. It seems to be coming right out of her chest. "This is a Brouviac catheter," Dr. Thornton explains, "and you may need one before very long." "Oooh," I say with a shudder. He tells me that most people's veins can't stand up to the six months of intensive chemotherapy I'm slated to receive, and warns me of the burn that could result should the needle ever slip out of an exhausted vein, allowing the Adriamycin to "infiltrate" the flesh. I think with longing about the beautiful pool at my club. I've managed the baldness compe-tently enough, but nobody's going to let me swim with a tube coming out of my chest. Do I really have to have this catheter, this ugly intruder in the flesh, which Thornton has so casually, so bafflingly brought into my life? Is there no end to the indignities imposed by this disease? "Oooh," I shudder yet again, at this news, which should, of course, have been delivered by Marek. He's the man who's treating me. This is a singular lapse in so "brilliant" a physician.

Dr. Thornton seems pained by my distress. "I know, I know," he says, "cancer really changes your life."

· · ·

Bobbie Ashley phones from the office to say the staff plans to make me a gift. There's nearly a thousand dollars in the office kitty and Helen has suggested a cashmere robe—would I like that? A thousand dollars is a great deal of money, and Bobbie has decided to ask me how I'd like it to be spent.

"I could use the cash as a travel fund," I say promptly. I can't tell how eager I am to take a vacation from this disease. Bobbie and I plan an inexpensive holiday—I will write a brief travel arti-cle, and by so doing obtain a press discount on hotel rooms and airplane tickets. The cash gift from the office will help cover the rest of our costs. A few phone calls later, a trip to Jamaica has been arranged. Hugh and I will spend several days at the Trident in Port Antonio. Bobbie tells me it's a fancy-ish, upscale resort.

Will some hideous side effect of the therapy prevent me from going? Marek has mentioned that mouth ulcers may result from taking His Drug. I phone Cityside to find out, and while the doctor thinks I'll probably be well enough to travel, he seems annoyed by my call. I am quite a frivolous girl to be planning vacations when my mind should be on the serious business of getting well. "No more holidays after this," Marek scolds. "We have work to do."

Hugh and I pack our bags, run down to Rockefeller Center for our tickets, and are soon drinking rum cokes aboard a 747 flying south to Kingston. In our haste, we've neglected to arrange a connecting flight to Port Antonio and so must hire a cab to drive us the hundred or so miles of bumpy, rutted coastal road that links the two towns. As we lurch along in the tinny car, our driver plays bad reggae very loudly, and a hot wind whips through the open windows, stirring up the mildewed junk stashed in the backseat. I soon give up trying to sleep.

The Trident is right out of Somerset Maugham. They've given us a small suite—sitting room, bedroom, and porch—in a bungalow near the beach. Two rare Albino peacocks cruise the grounds at teatime, looking for treats, and on a point that overlooks the open sea, there sits an exquisite gazebo. What a change from the bizarre clutter of Marek's hospital!

We're vacationing during what is called the "January hole," a slack time after the crush of New Year's and just before the onset of the February season, and in the dining room where we take our lavish five-course meals, we see only a handful of other guests. I notice a patrician-looking woman in her sixties and guess her to be a lady of leisure. But what about the rakish-looking middle-aged man who converses with his nubile young companion in German? I have no theory for him. Hugh and I have the bungalow next door to this pair, and late one afternoon, catch an intriguing glimpse of them, not making love, as one might have expected, but doing stretches and jumping jacks. An odd couple indeed!

We buddy up with a doting married pair in their late thirties, Rick and Mary Lynn, who are escaping the Toronto winter. With their help we try to figure out the rest of the guests. The resort with its tea service at four and its miniature man-made beach has a certain self-contained shiplike aspect. One can't help but wonder about the other passengers aboard.

The patrician older woman turns out to be the vice president of a department store. She's come here to convalesce from a tricky back surgery. And the German, a minor film celebrity, is also a semi-invalid; he suffers from a degenerative disease of the nerves. The young woman with him is his driver and personal secretary, and the jumping jacks, evidently, part of some program of physical therapy. Mary Lynn confesses that she herself has a heart problem, the result of a congenital defect. Though she looks the picture of health, nobody can say how long she'll live. And I— well, of course, you know that I have cancer.

I marvel over the coincidence of this strange assemblage. Here we all are, so seemingly privileged with our money and our pretty clothes, watching white peacocks prance at teatime, stuffing ourselves with rich food, as we watch a squadron of waiters whisk away the complicated cutlery. And yet, along with our beach wraps and gaudy summer silks, each of us has also brought a suitcase full of pain.

· · ·

People tell tall tales on Marek's ward—tales of disappearing melon-sized tumors, of people brought to the brink of death, then daringly rescued. The father of one patient claims he's talked to the president of the Shelburne Clinic, who supposedly told him that if he himself had cancer, Marek would be his man, though he wouldn't throw any research money the doctor's way. Marek won't do research properly, won't follow fixed protocols. He is like some jazz artist of chemotherapy, improvising as he goes.

The jazz artist has instructed me to come early to his hospital; they're going to take a pint or two of my blood, to "bleed" me, as they say. They plan to separate the white cells from the blood's other components, and mix these with white cells obtained from healthy donors. I'm then to be transfused with my own blood, enriched from other people's tumor-fighting T-cells. Or that, at least, is how the theory goes. Nobody knows if, or to what extent, this process, a form of immunotherapy, works. The well-grounded suspicion is that it's minimally effective. Some people even hold it can be dangerous, abetting tumor growth, strengthening the malignant cells, even as it reinforces the patient's immune response.

A technician, Janet, wheels a big unwieldy machine into my room; she feeds my blood into it and as the white cells are somehow separated out, Janet and I chat companionably. I am quite pleased to be getting immunotherapy; it doesn't make you sick to your stomach, and it's thrillingly avant-garde.

I angle for a pass to leave the hospital grounds after this procedure is finished. Marek gives his reluctant permission—he'd rather I were always under his watchful eye—and Hugh and I decamp, feeling like truant children set for a day of play. With my parents gone, we are now quietly, undefiantly together, no longer the off-again, on-again couple we used to be. Cancer has obliterated our modern, one might even say fashionable, ambivalence. It's a luxury cut from the emotional budget when faced with such long-running catastrophe. Echoing my parents' aspirations for me, I, too, wanted Hugh to "do better," to be "a success." But now I wonder, what is "better," what is "success"? I've no longer a head for such ephemera. And Hugh, for perhaps the first time in the whole of our decade together, knows without question that when I park my head against his chest, I'm coming home to rest. My need has sparked in him a powerful emotional loyalty. I do not dream of being apart from Hugh, nor he from me. We are solid, a unit.

And so we go out. I've learned that you don't need to venture as far as Jamaica to take a vacation from disease. Hugh and I make a festival out of every smallest outing. And the pleasure we find together makes me feel there is a life for me beyond the depressing confines of Marek's ward. We find relief—from the tedium, the fear—wherever and however we can. I think without these breaks the monotony alone of illness might have defeated me.

Together we seek out the picturesque old quarter of Cityside. There Hugh hires a hansom cab, and I'm absurdly pleased to be seeing all the sights. I'm quite chipper, as Hugh and I hold hands in the surprising bright February sunshine. What a fool I'd have been to have lain passive on my hospital bed while the doctor played his interesting, scientific-seeming games with my blood!

We return that night to find there's been a mixup in the lab. Somebody's lost my white cells. Janet and I are a little short of conversation when she wheels in her huge machine a second time. We've talked ourselves out. This time they manage to hang on to my blood. The pretty young nurse who comes later to transfuse me with it warns that I may experience a light chill when I receive the enriched serum.

A light chill? Suddenly I am shivering all over, my teeth chattering a mile a minute. "Do-Do-Do—you, you, you, you—thi, thi, thi, thi . . . nk, nk, nk, nk . . . this, s, s, s . . . is, z, z, z . . . psy, psy, psy, psy . . . co, co, co, co . . . som, som, som, som . . . atic, k, k, k?" I ask Hugh. "So far, nothing else has been," he answers wryly. Hugh is never frightened, or distanced, by the peculiar changes my body is going through. As long as it is my body, nothing about it is alien to him. What strange intimacy this is. Illness makes you more vulnerable than sex. Nobody in my life has ever seen me in so undefended a state.

Hugh's comment breaks me up. I am laughing even as I continue to shiver like a reed in the wind. I am out of control. Why, this immunotherapy, it's absolutely hilarious!

A nurse comes in to give me a shot, and in a minute I'm still as a statue.

. . .

On the day devoted to collecting my urine into a hat I also insist on going out, promising Marek that I won't pee any place else but the hospital. He regards me suspiciously. How can I promise that? Look, I'm a big girl, I'll just hold it, I declare. Okay, okay, have a good time, Marek says.

Hugh and I have bloody Mary's and crab cakes at a lovely old ship that's been converted into a restaurant. It sits astride a broad river. Next, we find a pleasant little mall in the old quarter where I splurge on sweaters and pants, cramming as many rewards as I can into my day of freedom. Trying on clothes is a bit of a challenge though, since I can't slip the sweaters over my head without losing my wig. I lift the wig off, letting it dangle from a hook in the changing room, and slip down so nobody will have a glimpse of my bald head, a smoothly executed move that leaves me feeling like the Chemotherapy Kid. Slim-hipped as I am, I've never looked this good in pants. The saleslady is impressed with my trim figure. You could model for this store, she says, you really could!

I feel cocky. Other people may be laid low by chemotherapy, but not me. When I return to the hospital, I lay out my purchases on the hospital bed so the nurses can see and admire them. Marek happens by. "When the going gets tough, the tough go shopping!" I say, pointing to my parcels. The doctor giggles obligingly. I recognize that this jaunty mood of mine is quite strange, is probably not "normal." But what would normal be in these unlikely circumstances? I've absorbed too much, too fast, and now I'm speeding on straight adrenalin. As it shoots through my body, I feel charged up, spectacularly alive.

During this, my third monthly treatment with chemotherapy, Marek and I have a set-to in the halls. Suddenly, out of nowhere, it seems, he has changed the treatment plan. Well, I've been warned that he is instinctual, quirkily intuitive, in Thornton's metaphor, a sort of cancer connoisseur. What do I expect?

Marek wants to quadruple the scheduled dose of His Drug, upping it from six to twenty-four grams. Frightened—I've seen other patients laid very low after such high doses—I try to negotiate.

"You said six grams," I object.

"I've changed my mind. I didn't like the looks of your latest scan!" The big, seven-centimeter splotch of cancer doesn't seem to have shrunk. By now I've checked in with Lawson for my postsurgical exam—I took care to be very composed with the surgeon, very ingratiating—and he hasn't been able to detect a growth that large. Still, I can't be sure that Cityside's radiologist isn't providing the more accurate reading.

"You promised that Thornton would treat me," I remind him. Marek is playing fast and loose with my life, and my instinct is to flee.

"Thornton, Thornton, that's all I hear from you! You know that Thornton—you think so much of him—in his whole career, he hasn't discovered one thing. Not even one. I have discovered *three* things." Marek's boasts aren't empty. His creativity as a young man was indeed remarkable. The discoveries to which he's now referring brought him tantalizingly close to a Nobel prize.

Marek is on a roll. "And now *I, I* will discover that ovarian cancer can be cured if you use My Drug along with the CAP and with immunotherapy. And then after I do this, Thornton will repeat my work on a dozen different cohorts of patients, and it will be so-called *proved*." Heavy irony drenches this last word. Marek evidently holds in some disdain the scientific method, of demonstrating and redemonstrating the efficacy of a particular treatment before accepting it as the standard.

Steam seems to be coming out of the tall man's ears. He is the creative genius of chemotherapy, Thornton a mere plodder. He is furious that I've failed to grasp this distinction, outraged that I'd prefer Thornton, the rival of his youth, to him. It doesn't occur to Marek that my agenda is different from his. Unlike him I've no discoveries to make. I want only to live.

I hear my own voice and realize I am snorting with laughter. Though shocked and rattled, I'm also amused by this flamboyant display of ego. I'm not going to be laughing long, however, if Marek gets his way. I've seen other patients laid way low following Marek's megatreatments. After twenty-four grams of His Drug they'll be wiping the floor with me.

"Look, give me the six grams and I'll take as much of the immunotherapy as you want," I offer, in the spirit of compromise. I am literally running after Marek, who, still fueled by his anger, is racing for the stairs as I make this proposition. "What is this, a bazaar?" Marek asks, and I find myself snorting more laughter. Why the man is a wit!

I offer to take twelve grams; it's a final offer.

"Do you want me to lose interest in you as a patient?" Marek threatens. Careful, doctor, there are witnesses to this exchange. And on the consent form it's stated that I am entitled to treatment without prejudice, even if I decline experimental therapy.

"Twelve grams, no more." I'm digging in my heels.

"Have it your way!" Disgusted with my stubbornness, Marek disappears into the stairwell, leaving me quite unsure as to who has been the winner in this curious exchange.

. . .

Quite the seasoned patient now, I know to hold out for the special IV nurse—she's very handy with her needle—when it's time for the hydration to begin. Nobody else can find a way into my small veins, which are growing worn and scarred from too many pricks, like a drug addict's, I suppose. Even the skillful IV nurse has had some difficulty. Twice, a needle that she thought well-lodged has slipped out of the vein, causing the saline solution to spill into the flesh of my hand.

I remember Thornton's warning about Adriamycin burns. There is danger here. The needle must stay tightly wedged in the vein. When the nurses begin setting up for the chemo, I'm given Ativan, but, like a soldier on watch, I fight the drowsiness. I need to stay alert, to warn the Adriamycin nurse that the needle isn't secure.

"Watch out for an infiltration," I mutter groggily when she arrives. "The needle, it keeps on coming out."

The fresh-faced blonde nurse concentrates intently on my veins until the vial of red liquid is empty. I can't hold out too long against the Ativan, however, and by the time the Adriamycin nurse goes, I'm weaving in and out of a drugged sleep.

I wake. My hand feels wet. It's drenched in cisplatin. "Infiltration! There's been an infiltration," I cry out, and, fortunately, there's a nurse in the room to hear me. Quickly, very quickly, she withdraws the needles from my hand. Luckily, cisplatin is not quite as treacherous as Adriamycin because it isn't corrosive. The IV nurse is summoned to find another, stronger vein to receive the rest of the chemotherapy.

The prominent veins on the inside of my elbows have been exhausted—they've completely collapsed—as have those on my forearm and wrist. The nurse must penetrate another vein in my hand. Being pricked there is particularly painful.

After the chemo, I go from room to room, questioning my fellow patients—long-time veterans of chemotherapy, they all have exhausted veins—to find out how they've avoided chemical burns. Jack, who has brain cancer, is visited by the hospital's general surgeon each time he checks into Cityside. The surgeon cuts into a central artery leading to his head. Elizabeth, who, like me, has an ovarian malignancy, has a subcutaneous catheter just beneath her collarbone. It's about the size of a Ping-Pong ball and looks very odd resting on the frail bones of her emaciated chest. Yet another patient has a tube protruding from between her breasts, like the one I saw in Thornton's photograph. I ponder these options, none of them pleasant, as I nurse my sore hand, which is beginning to swell. A cortisonelike medication to help heal the burn is mounted on the IV stand, and I'm told I must remain in the hospital until the swelling is under control.

I have been at Memorial for over a week and am growing claustrophobic. I want very badly to take a long walk in the sunshine, to swim. I want to be back at my gym on Fifty-Seventh Street where I take tumbling classes and work out on the rings and trapeze. Instead, I'm confined to an ugly room at Memorial. I hate the hospital's dingy green walls, the crude crucifix that is mounted on the wall opposite my bed. I hate the cooking smells, which have begun to sicken me. I hate the loathsome plastic basin into which I vomit during chemotherapy.

I have never been any good at being sick. I am absolutely

simmering with restless energy. Marek wears a long face as he enters my room. He looks inconsolable. "Oh, your poor hand, your poor hand," moans the doctor, cradling his face in his own two hands. I am glad he's come; I need his advice on what to do to avoid another burn. Clearly, my veins are useless.

As I begin to ask him about the various kinds of catheters, Marek's attention slithers away from me. He's on his feet before I've formulated my first question and seems to be walking out of the room. "Talk to me about it in *March*." Marek orders quite imperiously.

"Come back here," I shout at Marek's departing back. "You come back in here and talk to me. You *have* to talk to me. You're my *doctor*." The word doctor issues from my mouth like a roar. I realize I have an audience. A number of patients have collected right outside my door.

Startled, Marek turns on his heels and walks back into the room. I pat my turban, which in all this excitement has slipped rakishly over one ear, back into place. "Don't you see, I don't know what to *do*," I say. But instead of talking to me about the catheters I now quite certainly need, the doctor makes a great show of forgiving me for my unseemly outburst. Gallantly, Marek kisses my injured hand and pats my cheeks, which are plumping out a bit. "She's becoming a real little beauty, isn't she?" clucks the doctor. Hugh, as confused as I am by this diversionary tactic, manages to smile, a little shakily, in agreement.

I am so caught up in this romance, so distracted, that I all but forget the reason for my outburst. The veins in my arms can no longer be used for chemotherapy. Either I must have a catheter implanted to serve as conduit for the chemotherapy—an Adriamycin burn is likely to be next—or some arrangement has to be made with Memorial's surgeon. But instead of discussing these possibilities, Marek murmurs sweet nothings and pinches my cheeks.

The doctor is deliberately sidestepping the issue. His ragtag hospital lacks the technology to install either kind of catheter and he's ashamed of this. A doctor of his eminence buried in a backwater! Still he doesn't want to lose me, even temporarily, to any other establishment. Marek fears for me, but what he fears even more is that I'll leave him for somebody with a slicker setup. He isn't yet quite sure of me.

In Marek's hospital, waiting for the cortisone to heal my hand, life seems an endless, tedious Sunday. I can't bathe as long as I'm tethered to the IV stand, and I feel dusty and cranky. Marek is away in Manhattan; a cultivated man, he has tickets to the opera, plans to take in the Impressionists visiting at the Met. Reluctant to turn my case over to anyone else, he alone has authority to discharge me. Resentful that I must wait until he's had his fill of the city's refinements to resume my life, I'm like a teakettle at the boil. Whistling shrill impatience.

I use whatever powers of persuasion I possess to convince the nurse in charge that I ought to be let go. In my mind, I'm already back at work, back in my gray office blurbing articles, lunching with writers, finding the time somehow for a swim or an hour at my gym. After the nurse discontinues the medication, I step eagerly into the bathtub—ah, hot water, what a blessing! I haven't bathed for over a week. Purposely I walk very quickly when finally we're allowed to leave the hospital as if to say, look at me, how can a person who moves so nimbly possibly be sick?

A few days later, days spent rooting through my closets, taking stock after all these months of what I own, I am, unbelievably, sitting behind my quaint manual typewriter at *Cosmopolitan* back at work for the first time since my surgery in November. A huge azalea plant, dripping pink blossoms, welcomes me home, along with a card from my colleagues, signed in a dozen different inks. But it's not so easy to get back on track. At my first meeting, I speak too loudly and too long, trying to reassert my claim on my job, to make everybody know I'm as fit and bright and brimful with enthusiasm as ever. Long silences greet some of my over-eager remarks.

Homemaking is another challenge. Though I don't like to admit it, the three treatments at Marek's hospital have left me feeling very worn and shadowy. Hugh and I have quit our weekend commute to the country house, drained the pipes, and locked it up. It's struggle enough to keep track of our Manhattan life. The country has been put on hold—it's a luxury we know we can't afford.

I am trying to keep the refrigerator stocked, produce some decent meals. I pretend it's no effort, but it is. In the midst of cooking, I rush to the couch, grabbing a few minutes of precious rest while the burgers sizzle, feel faint with weakness as I stir the marinara sauce. Hugh, who's working part time in a friends antique shop—he needs the flexibility for our Cityside commute—would gladly take over my role in the kitchen, but at this point I'm fixed in my determination that we should live "normally." I have always been the one who cooked.

Shopping for food is even more wearing. In Manhattan there are no shopping malls where you dart into the parking lot and emerge from the supermarket, your cart piled high with groceries for the week. Here, you walk to the stores and you walk back, your arms bulging with the heavy parcels, which you lay down on the sidewalk, gratefully, when you come up against a red light. Shopping in New York is always strenuous. For me, now, its more challenging than an Olympic tryout.

I actually *dress* to go shopping, so determined am I that nobody should mistake me for a person who is sick. Fur coat, high heels with patterned hose. The prosperous matron setting off to feed her household. Normal as anybody. Humming through my chores.

One day I run into Diane Baroni on Broadway, where I'm stopping in at a special little shop that's known for its tomatoes. Fussy me. My, don't you look well, Diane comments, but I know her, out of kindness, to be lying. A close view reveals the flaws in my disguise. I am listing weakly in my heels, rushing wads of Kleenex to my red, runny nose—the cilia that filter irritants in the air have begun to thin, because of chemotherapy—and the headband that holds my wig in place has come askew. You can see a little bald patch just behind one, red, half-frozen ear.

I am trying to pass. Not to be recognized as the invalid, not by Diane, though I trust her. Most of all not by myself. And in some cockeyed way I am succeeding. My life has certainly lost some of its panache. No more expense account dinners. Long, formal meals exhaust me. No more screenings. My day at work and quixotic grocery shop, followed by wavering stints by the stove, are plenty wearing enough. Still, I'm keeping the blood running. And I'm hanging on, however tenuously, to my image of myself. As a woman who functions. Who manages. Who hasn't let disease shake her purchase on the comforting routines of everyday life.

. . .

In spite of my shaky masquerade—here I am, just another over-extended working woman, juggling work at the office and at home—most of my mind is still on my medical problems. I have decided the subcutaneous catheter is probably best for a person who, like me, wishes to stay physically active throughout therapy, and have found out I will need surgery to get one. I make an appointment with a general surgeon at Community Hospital—whatever its other failings, the technology there is up-to-date—and take several days from the office to have the operation. "The catheter won't really be obvious, will it," I plead with Lawson's resident, Dr. Greeley, when we chance to meet. I'm not looking forward to having a Ping-Pong-ball-sized hunk of silicone protrude from my chest. "You *will* see it," says Greeley, wanting me to know the worst now so I don't erupt into tears of disappointment later. My reputation as a difficult patient precedes me.

I myself don't feel at all "difficult." All these doctors are quite lucky, I think, to have a patient as competent as I am. The operation, performed under local anesthetic, doesn't even break my stride. I'm an old pro at surgery. My chest is a little sore after the catheter is implanted, but I'm much heavier than the skeletal Elizabeth, and I don't experience the barely noticeable bump beneath my collarbone as disfiguring.

So equipped, I am prepared for my fateful fourth visit to

Marek's hospital, the one I am already sensing is quite dangerous. It will blast a ragged, gaping hole in the meager fabric of my self-confidence.

. . .

It's now three months into a planned six-month course of treatment, and Marek keeps boosting the scheduled doses of His Drug. Hugh agrees, it's enough to make you nervous, it's enough to make you terrified, never knowing what he's going to do next. One last check, I think, one last check. Let me call Nash. Community Hospital's intimidating oncologist may seem heartless, but at least he follows the usual drill. I'm hoping he'll help me assess the dangers of Marek's treatment, and if they are as formidable as I suspect, allow me to change back to Community Hospital for the remainder of my chemotherapy.

I'm not surprised to find Nash cold and unwelcoming when we meet in a little chamber not customarily used for consultations. Both of us perch on folding chairs, and it's not lost on me that he thinks even ten minutes of his time would be too much for me to take.

I start in, telling Nash that I'm frightened. Marek keeps changing his treatment plan. Also, I'm afraid that he's going to sacrifice the cisplatin, known to be the most effective agent against ovarian cancer, for the much vaguer promise of His Drug. The kidneys can't tolerate both substances in large does. Nash's eyes glow with a reluctant respect when I mention this fear, and I know he's thinking, well, she's not entirely stupid.

Abruptly, Nash asks, why exactly are you here? I thought I might return to Community Hospital for the rest of my therapy, I say. You can't do that! Why not? You've started treatment at Cityside and you've got to finish there. But why, if I think my health, possibly my life, might be in danger there? Because if you don't, says Nash, nobody will know what has become of you.

Aha, here it is again, this queer, and to me horrifying, emphasis on my value as a statistic. Having already been treated by

Marek, I'm no longer a viable subject for Community's research. My blood is boiling as I say with spirit, are you refusing to treat me, Dr. Nash?

At that, the oncologist begins to flip absently through his calendar, looking for an open date. "I suppose we can find something for you," he mumbles. Treating me may be a hassle, but a malpractice suit would be even more annoying, and by checking in with Lawson for monthly pelvic examinations, I've maintained my status as a patient.

I have my dignity however, and decide not to return to Community Hospital. Who wants to go where they're not wanted? Especially in such a deeply vulnerable circumstance. As I leave Nash's office, I know I'm not going back to Community. Not yet. Still, I sense that my situation in Cityside is deteriorating, is hedged about by danger. How much longer, I wonder, will I be staying with the excitable and wildly unpredictable Marek.

· · ·

I'm still looking for a way out, a painless exit from Cityside. I've learned that if you phone doctors very early in the morning, before they're buried by the demands of the day, you frequently get through to them. I phone Alan Thornton at nine A.M., precisely.

Do you have a minute? I ask, quickly identifying myself.

Yes, a minute, but I'm given to understand that's all he has.

The Central Hospital physician has only the cloudiest recollection of our meeting. I begin to explain what's going on at Cityside and that I'm growing wary of Marek, but the doctor quickly cuts me off.

"I'm not here to hold your hand during treatment," Thornton booms. "I am a scientist," he says, resoundingly, "investigating the causes and cures of ovarian cancer. I am not in business to criticize another man's work. Perhaps you should be talking to a psychiatrist." Indeed, perhaps I should. I'm as neurotic as anybody else. Right now, however, it seems more urgent to find someone who can help me assess this course of treatment. Do the possible benefits justify the very substantial risks? Marek's Drug,

I have learned, both through my reading and by observing other patients on his ward, is very damaging to the bone marrow, especially in the huge doses he likes to give. And repeated, precipitous drops in blood counts can be so weakening that the body never fully recovers. I want Thornton to address this issue, but the doctor, occupied with the Great Task of propelling science onward, is unwilling to enlighten me.

It seems I made a fateful turning when I stumbled so confusedly into Cityside. And now there's no going back.

. . .

Hydration begins my marathon fourth treatment, followed by immunotherapy, which is uneventful this time around—no chills and thrills, no uncontrollable hilarity. By the time I meet with my daredevil doctor, I've already been in the hospital several days.

Marek proposes that I take fifty grams of His Drug, and I, as usual, bargain him down. This is better than double the final dose of his original plan. I am growing bolder though. We are intimately connected, Marek and I, and by that queer osmosis through which intimates absorb each other's traits, I've become as ruthless as he in my determination to rout the tumor. The end, a victory over cancer, will justify almost any means.

My impatience plays into this recklessness. I'm sick of the drudgery of treatment, weary of the long haul back and forth from Cityside through the endless urban sprawl, tired of IV stands and nausea and hospital beds that are always a foot too short. I want to put an end to all of this, to knock out the cancer with one bold blow. Marek and I settle for a dose of thirty-six grams, far higher than I ever thought I'd go.

As the nurse mounts the sack filled with treatment fluid, I note that in a more potent concentration, Marek's drug takes on a rich amber hue. Remembering that the twelve-gram dose was colorless, I feel decidely menaced.

The nurse agrees that I may skip the Ativan. Its purpose is to make the nausea bearable, but I've not yet vomited on Marek's drug, and I dread the nightmare-ridden sleep the sedative induces.

Last time, fiery-red lizards kept me company throughout the night.

As Marek's drug drips painlessly into me—my new catheter works perfectly—I spread out magazines and notebooks and settle down to business, writing up article ideas for *Cosmopolitan,* grateful, in this strange and fearful circumstance, for the soothingly habitual task.

As I scribble into notebooks, in my tidy, legible editor's hand, life seems manageable again. I am no longer at the mercy of my own errant, endlessly dividing cells. When Helen phones, I'm pleased to be able to tell her, in my primmest, good-girl voice, that I'm busy working. I anticipate rave reviews, hear the Boss telling Bobbie and the others, why, that Barbara Ann, absolutely nothing gets her down.

We are gossiping contentedly, mainly about the small events of Helen's life—David, her husband, is scheduled for a minor surgery, a temperamental coworker is driving the Boss crazy—when all at once I'm seized by a wave of weakness. In an attempt to steady myself, I begin talking slowly, taking deep, deliberate breaths between words. "This . . . drug . . . it's . . . making . . . me feeble," I tell the Boss in a robotlike monotone, straining for control. I only just manage to put the receiver down before I am spewing vomit. And shivering uncontrollably. Though the spring sunshine pours into my room—it's hot for March, nearly seventy degrees—I'm wracked with chills. Fighting back the surges of nausea, I try to push the suddenly very heavy IV stand toward the toilet. This is what it must be like, I think, to be very, very ancient. Clinging to the handrail in the bathroom, I press the call button, summoning the nurse, who gives me Darvon for the chills and an accompanying high fever.

I sleep and sleep. I feel as if I'm ninety years old. I am approaching my limits now. My body, weakened by these continuous poisonous assaults, can't take much more of Marek's drug.

In this state, I'm hardly capable of real thought, only dim, passive reflections, I feel beleaguered, in danger, all but lost. Who is responsible for my sorry condition? Do I blame Marek? Myself for making the only half-informed decision of taking treatment with him? Or the system for giving me so few and such hazardous choices?

Certainly, I can blame Marek—he tricked me into treatment, promising me Thornton, then failing to deliver. That must have been unethical. And of my compliance in accepting His Drug once he'd snagged me? That move was indeed taken in confusion and in fear. But what cancer patient isn't fearful. And the confusion was hardly particular to me. Nobody knew, nobody could tell me, what path to take to maximize my chances of a cure. The august Shelburne Clinic was striking out with a protocol so toxic they were obliged to cancel it. Standard treatment at Community Hospital, indifferently and impersonally delivered, offered me only the most meager opportunity to survive. I needed something extra, something besides the CAP . . . why not Marek's drug? It wasn't the least plausible choice.

If only I had had more time, more help from an enlightened physician (yes, there was Wirth, but I wasn't his patient, and he was a thousand miles away). If only the system operated more efficiently, if doctors were committed not to keeping patients ignorant but to helping them make informed decisions. If . . . if . . . if! But I was carried forth by the cyclone of cancer into an eerie, treacherous landscape mined with misinformation (a forty percent survival chance, they told me at Community Hospital—a lie!), slippery with ego ("I'll cure you," shouted Marek, and I wanted to believe), and fenced in by rigid medical procedures as forbidding as barbed wire. Perhaps the cyclone can't yet be tamed. But certainly the landscape of cancer treatment could be gentled, made more welcoming.

And so I chose to take my treatment with a gifted renegade, a half-good, half-bad choice, the best choice I was capable of at the time. But now Marek, frustrated because he, the genius, the lion of chemotherapy can't knock out the cancer, refuses to moderate his approach. If three grams of His Drug won't work, he'll give me fifty!

Marek's determination to rout the cancer knows no bounds.

Side effects are not his business. Side effects are common. The patient usually recovers from them, after all. And I am far too weak, too feeble, to lodge a protest. I'm wholly at the mercy of Marek's bold but stubborn—and increasingly reckless—strategies.

. . .

The next night, as my kidneys are cleansed in preparation for the CAP, I'm alert again. I watch enviously as Hugh downs a brandy on the rocks—we keep a bottle of Deauville stashed in the closet —and think, what I wouldn't do for a drink. Jack, the young brain cancer patient, glides effortlessly into our room. Nobody is more agile than he with an IV stand.

Jack brings sad news. Another patient, a woman in her fifties, has just died of lung cancer. Soon her two distraught daughters have also gathered in our room and Hugh is consoling them both with hugs and brandy. The younger and prettier of the girls turns for comfort to Jack, who cradles her in a long embrace. There seems to be more between them than shared grief, and I think, it never pauses, the mating dance, not even in the midst of tragedy.

The mother and husband of the dead woman also stop by and Hugh offers brandy all around. We seem to be hosting a sort of wake. The daughters are guilty, wondering was there something else they might have done, but the woman's mother shudders with relief.

Hugh seems to know this family well—while I'm confined in my room, he socializes in the kitchens and smoking lounge—but to me they're near strangers. I've been preoccupied with my own catastrophe. And though I've made up and put on a fresh turban for our company, I don't really feel equal to this occasion. I offer my condolences but they have a hollow ring.

After the mourning party leaves—this is too much for you, the dead woman's mother kindly tells me, you have problems of your own—I call my brother in Hawaii to recount the events of my day. Tony, too, has recently fallen ill, a victim of postviral fatigue syndrome. Chronically sick though he now is, I think my brother is embarrassed to be suffering from an ailment that seems so trivial, so minor-league compared to cancer. Still, Tony's fatigue makes him unable to travel, unable to be with me, and his humor and affection are available to me only by phone.

I tell my brother about the mourners gathered in our room. "Gee," he says, "you've certainly fallen in with some fast company." I laugh, tee-hee, but don't fail to note there's a touch of hysteria in my voice.

. . .

I try to manage the CAP without Ativan but it's just not possible to cling to consciousness as the world weaves woozily about me. Twenty minutes into the treatment, I'm begging for relief.

As I recover from the chemotherapy and receive Marek's special rescue, which is administered directly afterward, also intravenously, I feel queerly listless. As a rule, I'm wildly impatient to be free of the cursed IV stand. I'm desperate for a bath and a pass that will take Hugh and me out of this dreary hospital into the wonderfully normal world of shopping malls and restaurants. But now, as I nap and wake and nap again, I feel numb and clumsy.

Well, it's been nine days since I was admitted to Memorial. Probably I'll be myself again once they release me. Marek comes by my room, and he, too, seems less full of fight, more subdued than usual. The doctor is afraid he's overreached himself—the chemotherapy I've recently received has never been administered before, my innovative physician made it up as he went along— and nobody can be sure how I'll respond.

I don't know this as I lie limply in my hospital bed. Nor do I know the peculiar listlessness I'm feeling will grow more and more pronounced, as I drift torpidly toward extinction, death's exhausted prey.

More out of habit than conviction, I fight for my immediate release. "Are my blood counts satisfactory?" I ask Marek. "Yes, yes, they seem to be okay." "Let me go, then. I'm sure I'll be fine once I'm out of this hospital." Suddenly, bafflingly, the doctor grows very angry. "You! You are supposed to be *intelligent,*"

Marek spits out the words. "You have the intelligence of a *cleaning woman*," he hisses. The insult hints at my danger, but murkily. I'm given no clear explanation of what is wrong with me. And then he clasps his hands behind his back, and a soldier at parade rest, marches briskly out of my room.

A hand-wringing Newman remains in my room, saying, you must go to a lab tomorrow, have your counts taken. But tomorrow is Saturday. It's routine for cancer patients, even those on much milder therapies than the heroic one Marek has devised, to have weekly blood counts taken. Though I know the chemo savages the bone marrow, which produces blood, I don't realize there are checks on this. I have no idea what Newman is talking about. And in my ignorance I'm reckless. I insist we leave Memorial and we hasten back to the city, where, staggering from fatigue, I go directly to bed.

. . .

I try to tell myself that the physical complaints I'm suffering from are trivial. This strange weariness, a rawness in the throat, and my by now disgracefully runny nose. The cilia are entirely obliterated now, and I've also lost my brows, lashes, even the light fuzz covering my cheeks. Though bald as a plucked chicken and about as vital, I think whatever's wrong here can be fixed right up with exercise and fresh air. I press Hugh to go with me to the park.

Once outside, though, I can barely put one foot in front of the other. The day is dismal—gray and drizzling—and my bag keeps slipping from my shoulder as I reach into it for Kleenex to staunch my wet and blistered nose. We walk around aimlessly for a little while, then flag a cab—I can't make it back to Seventy-Sixth Street on my own.

Our dreary weather continues and I cab to work, where I toy absently with a few manuscripts. Still feeling shadowy, I propose a picnic in Baroni's office to pick up my spirits, only to find that swallowing has become increasingly painful. I leave and lunch alone to spare my companions the discomfort of watching me gag on each bite. The tuna fish I'm eating tastes rough and fiery, like volcanic ash.

At our regular weekly staff meeting, we review the latest issue of the magazine, and though I've read it cover to cover, the contents have blurred in my mind. "Did you have a chance to look at 'Is He In A Marrying Mood?' " Helen asks. "Yes, I think so. Uh, it was, uh, nice," I say, feeling flushed with embarrassment like a student who's neglected her homework.

The next day I have an appointment with Lawson for my regular pelvic exam. Lying in the surgeon's office in a crisp blue paper gown, I'm chilled to the core. I shift my bony body around on the examining table, trying to find a comfortable position, as I wait and wait for my doctor to appear. I'm used to this endless waiting—a noon appointment with Lawson generally takes all afternoon—and so don't even bother to become indignant. Why fuss?

I'm eager to have Lawson do my second operation. There is supposed to be an advantage in having just one surgeon do these multiple operations—presumably, the man already knows his way around your insides. And so have been cultivating Lawson's good will, assuming the part of the good, brave patient and swallowing nearly all my questions. The surgeon will tell me what he wants me to know and no more. I tell myself I'm learning to handle Lawson, as I attempt small talk with him and his retainers —he's always flanked by at least two doctors and a nurse. I tell myself that there is nothing deliberately demeaning in any of this, in being kept waiting naked except for a paper gown for over an hour in a frigid, airless room, or in being examined by a full committee of doctors when you haven't even the usual protection of a modest fluff of pubic hair. And should the surgeon chat idly as he commences his examination about a mutual friend he's met at a party, or a film he's just seen, I don't fault his timing. No, so long as Lawson is amiable, I count the interview a success.

But today I'm too spent to play my usual role. I'm limp as

wet laundry as I hear myself saying, in tones of dismal defeat, "I think I've had enough of Marek's Drug."

"It hurts me to see you suffering like this," says Lawson. "Particularly since Marek's Drug isn't going to do you one bit of good." He has draped his arm affectionately over my shoulder, and I think, with some surprise, why the feebler I am, the better this doctor likes me.

"Can I finish my therapy here at Community then?" I ask.

"Sure you can. Nobody will learn anything from you now" —statistically, I no longer exist—"but we can treat you." And then, shifting to a more confidential tone, "Welcome home!" My next treatment, it is determined, will be taken at Community.

. . .

Back at Seventy-Sixth Street, I phone Marek to see if he can do something for my throat. He asks if I've had my counts checked and I admit I haven't. To tell you the truth, I say, I've been feeling a little pooped. Ah, I knew it, says the doctor, chuckling a little. He sounds glad that he's succeeded at last in hurting me.

Marek says I must come at once to his hospital, but I lag back, insisting I just need something for my throat. Couldn't he call the pharmacy? Come, the doctor insists, take an ambulance, *spend* the eight hundred bucks. Marek sounds as if he's urging me to buy an Armani suit. Whoever heard of anyone calling an ambulance because of a sore throat? I laugh at this idea, put down the phone, and sink into a dreamless sleep.

Hugh is wild with worry when I wake. He's made his own phone call to Marek. Your blood counts are way, way down, Hugh tells me. The rescue wasn't a sufficient antidote to so large a dose of Marek's Drug. Hugh is willing to humor me, but only to a certain point. He won't let me endanger my life. All right, all right, let's drive to Cityside, I finally concede. The idea of spend-ing more days in the hospital is anathema to me. Still, I would dearly love to be rid of this sore throat. Hugh throws a few things into a bag for me and I stumble down the stairs and into the car where I pull my much-worn khaki coat up over my chin—horrible thing, I'm going to burn it the second I'm well—and fall asleep.

As soon as I'm settled in my bed, the G.P. who routinely looks in on Marek's patients pays me a call. She says, "Your color's good, probably your counts are all right." What a fuss over nothing, I think. Next comes the nurse who takes blood from my catheter. Ten minutes later, she's back again in my room. There's something wrong with the way the catheter is functioning, the nurse says. I inquire about my counts but she just hushes me. Don't even think about them, she says. They're far too low to be accurate. We've got to take some blood from your vein. The nurse pricks me several times before she succeeds in filling her syringe. Ouch, ouch, I cry, wondering why this hurts so much more than it would normally.

Here is the nurse again, rushing back into my room, her face whiter than the hospital sheets. The impossible counts are indeed accurate. Marek's megatreatment has so ravaged my bone marrow that the blood it's producing is too thin and watery to sustain life. I have to be transfused immediately. No way, I tell the nurse. I'm not taking any blood from some damn, contaminated Cityside blood bank, I say, thinking about the derelicts that litter the surrounding ghetto neighborhood. It's their heroin-rich blood that they'll be pumping into me. I'll call my friends. I have thousands of friends. They'll come, they'll give me their blood.

Oh, Barbie, Barbie, moans the distraught nurse. You don't understand, there isn't time for that. Blood donations must be screened by the Red Cross before a hospital can transfuse you with them. The process takes several weeks. If I'd wanted my own blood supply—not the worst idea—I'd have needed to set it up well in advance of this emergency.

A sense of urgency and panic surrounds me. Marek's phones from his home to tell me I'm in danger of bleeding to death. My watery blood is all but bereft of platelets, the clotting factor. Without them, even the slightest wound or abrasion is as dangerous as a slit artery in your neck. I'm as vulnerable as a hemophiliac. What can he be saying? I'm completely bewildered. He has never told me that His Drug could be so devastating. I'll sue you if I get hepatitis from the transfusion, I threaten, not really meaning it, but needing to vent my foul temper. This is bound to mean more days in the damn hospital! So sue me tomorrow, says Marek, sounding like a New York cab driver. Just don't bleed to death tonight.

So it begins, round after round of tranfusions, which don't keep me from spiking vertiginous fevers of one hundred and three and one hundred and four degrees. The nurses keep the blood coming, and flowing along with it are rivers of antibiotics. Along with the platelets, my white cells are down in the cellar—the frightened nurse told Hugh she's seen better counts on dead people—and I have no protection against the armies of bacteria, the now-invincible, if invisible predators swarming into me. I sweat and shiver by turns, monitoring my own temperature and ringing boisterously for the night nurse, a steady young man named Bill, whenever it tops one hundred degrees. My fever rises so precipitously that Bill fetches ice blankets to take it down mechanically. Hugh helps out with an almost military precision. When the ice blanket is for a moment mislaid, it is Hugh who tracks it down and covers me with it, never seeming distraught, acting with an ease, a near-nonchalance, that reassures me. Of course, he's more frightened than he's ever been, but this he doesn't let me see. It is because of Hugh's air of quiet competence that I am never really frightened by my collapse, only wildly irritated. I'll be in the hospital *forever* if things go on this way.

What is this? Into my room they wheel a heavy, ponderous machine. It shakes and heaves so vigorously that I think for a moment it must be alive. They suspect pneumonia and have brought the bulky X-ray machine to me. The long trip down to radiation, the bacteria against which I'm now defenseless lurking at every turn, would be too hazardous for me to take. I stagger across the room, pajamas drenched in sweat and ice, so they can be sure my lungs are clear.

By the next morning, the fevers have subsided, though I've been tremendously weakened by them. I'm too wasted to think or read or watch TV. But my anger remains quite lively. When Marek drops by my room, I don't trust myself to speak, afraid if I do I'll erupt into a full-blown rage. You seem mad, the doctor says, pouting in his childlike way. Are you mad about something? Is he crazy? I feel I've been all but murdered. Naturally I'm angry. You're supposed to be the intelligent one, go figure it out, I say.

My friends keep calling—Helen phones several times, and I hear almost daily from Susan and Barbara Lee—but a shaken Carol is the only one who has the time to visit me. They ask her to wear a surgical mask when she's in my room. Everyone who comes close to me, including doctors and nurses, must be muzzled by gauze and plastic. The everyday bacteria that tumble out of their mouths and noses on every exhalation are all as deadly as cholera to me. Carol, whose eyes are ringed in blue and black, looks strangely exotic in her mask, and can hardly speak for nervousness. She's afraid I'm going to die, I think, and am annoyed by her querulousness. Die? I wouldn't dream of it. I'm far too angry.

Hugh has phoned my parents, telling them about the situation, and my father flies into Cityside—my mother, not nearly as vigorous physically as Daddy, isn't up to another trip. The three of us, my father, Hugh, and I, have an easier rapport in my mother's absence. The constancy of Hugh's support earns my father's grudging respect, and anyway, it's mainly my mother who feels, as mothers will, that what she thinks of as failures in my personal life are her failures as well. Daddy has temporarily put aside whatever disappointment he may have in my choice of mate. It's been displaced by more compelling, urgent feelings— his daughter cannot, *will not* die. By the force of his very being he will prevent it.

During the long, shapeless days of my recovery, I distract myself fantasizing about plans for vengeance. I'll sue Marek for malpractice, that's what I'll do. I didn't know that His Drug could have life-threatening consequences. The consent forms I signed are meaningless. Witnesses, I'll need witnesses. One nurse, who'll soon be leaving Memorial, says she'd be happy to testify. I'm not the first one who's been browbeaten into taking enormous quantities of Marek's Drug. The nurse tells me about another woman who spent weeks in isolation recovering from the doctor's mega-treatments.

I hurl my anger at whomever is unfortunate enough to enter my room, except for the nurses, of course. Nurses are my allies in all of this, it is the doctors who'll put your life on the line for a cheap ego thrill, for the pleasure they'll get from stepping onto a podium one day and saying I, *I* discovered the cure for this disease. I don't even spare the tall, beefy Irish priest who wanders innocently by to bestow his blessing. Blessing indeed! I'm shutting this place down, I shout. If you care for your immortal soul, you'll get another job. The poor clergyman backs quickly out of my room, looking sorely aggrieved.

My anger fuels itself until I'm lost in a kind of frenzy. What would be just treatment for a man who, while pretending to heal you, submits your body to poisons so terrible that you tremble at the doors of delirium, and who, what's more, does all this in the service of so insignificant a thing as his career? Poison would be too good for such a man. I think of bloodier punishments. And somewhat maniacally ask Hugh and my father to help me execute them. I'm crazed by a lust for revenge, which startles and shocks my father—his little girl, spoiling for murder, it just isn't possible —but which Hugh takes quite in stride. Unlike my father, Hugh knows my darker side, doesn't idealize me. He knows I can be vindictive. Hurt me and I prepare to strike right back, quickly as a serpent, and as evilly.

Marek knows he's lost me. He's no longer full of bombast, doesn't sail into my room like a clipper ship, shouting terrifying plans for his next treatment. In his presence, my blood-lust loses its strange ferocity. The doctor seems disempowered, a meek, shadowy man, no longer interesting or dangerous.

By slow, creeping inches I'm getting better. After ten days of transfusions and IV antibiotics, I declare myself strong enough for an outing. I think how nice it would be to have a real meal—I've been snacking on stale donuts and takeout burgers—and then perhaps a walk along the river. My muscles are creaky from lack of use. Both Hugh and my father would rather see me safe in the hospital, but as the sun streams through my windows, I'm as stubborn as a child whose heart is set on play.

We're having another heat wave and Cityside's usually empty streets are teeming with sluggish Sunday traffic and brightly dressed pedestrians. We watch them from the open, top deck of the restaurant where I toy with a stingingly sharp bloody Mary. Though the drink hurts my still tender mouth, I drink it all down anyway, intent on the idea of enjoying myself. Downstairs they've set out an elaborate buffet—mountains of crab and spicy fish stews sit alongside the more standard breakfast foods. I fill my tray, an awkward undertaking, since I've got to keep one hand free for Kleenex—my by now blistered nose is running disgracefully—and the tote bag slung across my shoulder feels as if it's filled with rocks. I'm still enormously weak.

The food tastes terrible. I push it this way and that on my plate and then, absurdly, return to the table to fill up again. The food isn't any more palatable on my second trip. I can't conceivably eat.

I look around at the other customers, healthy people enjoying this robust brunch. Here a young mother flirts adoringly with her infant son. I quickly avert my eyes. There two young men, just starting in their careers I'd guess, seem to be talking business. One of them blows smoke rings from the tip of his long cigar. And on a banquette a couple, not much beyond their teens, toy solemnly with each other's hands, rapt with love. I feel left out, painfully singular, hardly part of life at all as I watch these others lost in their separate, satisfied moments.

Despite all my strivings, I belong wholly to my illness now. The enviably normal world to which I clung so stubbornly has no more use for me. I think what my own life might have been like if I'd escaped the blight of this disease. I'm not young, but I'm hardly old. I'm at an age when the long, tunneling years of work might finally have opened into broad vistas of opportunity. With any luck, I might be looking forward to a fulfilling tenure as editor-in-chief of my own magazine. Or I might be watching my child mature. Who'd want me now, sick as I am, for any job of consequence? And who would be foolish enough to give a child over into my care? I am clearly out of the running, hobbled by this cursed cancer. It will be years, if ever, before I'm free of it, and by then I'll be too old and winded to hope to compete.

I take my sorrowful thoughts with me into the ladies' room, where I adjust my no longer fresh-looking wig, and pencil in a smudge of brow. I look thin and sallow and ruined. Without eyebrows and lashes, my face has the same queer, archaic, long-lidded look you see on portraits painted by the old masters. I can hardly believe the eerie reflection the mirror returns. That woman can't be me.

A walk, I'll jostle myself out of this burdensome mood with a walk. Against the protests raised by Hugh and my father, I set a goal for myself. One mile. I'll walk one mile. I'm too ambitious. Though I put one foot ahead of the other with dogged determination, I'm so weak and depleted that I must keep pausing for rest. Even to sit upright exhausts me. I ask Hugh to let me lean against him for support. We sit back to back like bookends on the concrete ledge bordering the river's walkway. I tilt my head up toward the sky and think that for now I must be content with whatever's given me—a touch of summer in April, the pleasure of an unseasonably warm sun against my face.

. . .

Marek is conspicuously absent when we leave Memorial the next day. It's clear that I'm jilting him—why deepen the humiliation with protracted farewells? As for me, I'm chastened. I've learned my limits. The participatory spirit I brought to chemotherapy—I wanted to be a partner in my treatment, and for all his outrageousness, Marek led me to believe I had some say—has, for the moment, quite deserted me. Weakly and with withered confidence, I stagger out to greet my freedom.

It will be months before I understand what happened to me and why. Cancer treatment is complicated, the responsibilities of physicians must be delicately construed. Was I wrong to accept Marek's treatment? Not really. His Drug is effective against ovarian cancer, though rarely enough used. Added to the CAP, it probably gave me a certain, perhaps even a crucial edge in fighting my disease. No, the person wrong here was Marek for proceeding so stubbornly, so recklessly with ever higher and more dangerous doses of His Drug. And for not monitoring me more closely. As for the feeling he gave me that I was a partner in my treatment—a good psychologist, he knew I needed to feel that way—ours was a simulated partnership, never a real one. My ignorance of the hazards of treatment made me Marek's guinea pig, rather than the equal participant I wished to be.

In spite of our wet, gray weather, and against the protestations of Hugh and my father, who want me home, resting, I go to work—I'm eager to rush back to the world of the well, where all is predictable and normal. My father, clucking with worry, keeps asking, are you *sure* you're ready, then, finally realizing he can't restrain me, returns home to my mother in St. Louis. Back at the office, the air of competence I try to fake convinces nobody. I'm vague, unfocused, still pitifully anemic.

Flaccid after so much time in the hospital bed, I go to my gym, where the instructor is flabbergasted by my weakness. The simplest maneuvers take all my strength. The next week I try to swim. My injured hand slaps clumsily into the water, as I force one arm after the other, feebly kicking my feet. I feel chilled and numb.

I phone Dr. Nash to arrange for treatment at Community Hospital, but he's too busy to come on the line and doesn't get back to me. I phone again. Several days later, Nash's nurse returns my call to say that the doctor is very busy, preparing for a conference out of town. He'll try to get back to me when he returns, some two weeks after my treatment should be scheduled. Nash is snubbing me. I suspect he wants me to become so discouraged by his indifference that I'll go someplace else, go away. But I'm not discouraged, I'm angry. Furious, I rip into the nurse. I've been very sick, I say, half out of my mind with rage, I need a *doctor*. Dr. Nash doesn't care if anybody lives or dies, I rant. All that concerns him is the body count at the end of his protocols! Well, I don't think that's fair at *all,* says the nurse with an invisible stomp of her foot. She sounds like the midwestern girls who went to high school with me. She says she'll contact Dr. Lawson's office, see if there's anything they can do.

A few hours later I answer the phone and it's Lawson himself on the line. I am beside myself, belly-up with gratitude, gushing my "so-good-to-hear-from-you's," marveling that he took the time from his busy schedule to call himself. Weak as I am, I need someone to lean on, need to be fortified by a little hope. Tell me, Doc, I say, uncharacteristically—I never ask this boldly about my chances—am I gonna make it?

"Of course," says Lawson. "You don't think I'd let you back in the system if we were just going to have to take care of you while you die."

I put the phone down and stare at it, sorting out my reactions. He wouldn't let me back in the system if I were going to die! What pray, does he do then with those less fortunate than I? Is there no "system" for them? When they scrape feebly at Community Hospital's doors, are they turned brusquely away? Dr. Lawson's answer chills, even as it reassures me.

So it is that, beaten and bedraggled, both my health and my confidence in ruins, I make my way back to Community Hospital. My days as a "human subject" are finished; Marek's great experiment has failed.

I know I'm lucky to be alive.

STRUGGLE

April—August 1987

*A*s I gain strength I plunge headlong back into my life, a buzzsaw of furious energy. At work, I'm light on my feet, quick, efficient. I lunch with all my writers, equip them with fresh assignments, then resolve to attract new talent to the magazine. Helen wonders, do I think Gail Godwin might possibly write for us? Godwin's last novel was on the bestseller list for months and she has another book out this spring—it's sure to be a hit. I write the novelist, whose work I've always admired, and remind her of a long-ago meeting in *Cosmo*'s offices. Probably she's forgotten, but I remember vividly, have been clocking her career and am delighted as can be about her present, much-deserved success. I follow the letter up with a call to her agent, a young man who is very languorous, very British, and what do you know? Gail Godwin is willing to write for us. I scribble a memo to Helen—we've got her. Now that is really a coup!

I maintain my strong, aggressive stride. Every day I either swim dozens of laps or do cartwheels and handstands at my gym. As my blood replenishes itself I grow agile and strong. Rosy from the spring sunshine and plumper every day, I've all but forgotten the frail, sallow woman who clung to her bed in Cityside. That was some other life. Full of optimism, I buy a new light-weight wardrobe—only bright colors, I tell the young salesgirl who helps me shop—and I decide to buy some stocks. I don't for a minute think I won't be around to report my profits to the IRS.

During this happy, charged-up interval—it is now a little over five months since I started chemotherapy—I note with some astonishment that my hair is beginning to grow. First my brows fill in, next a corona of light fuzz surrounds my head. The doctors tell you the hair will come back, but it feels so gone when it's gone. I don't think anyone quite believes them. In the wake of this wondrous regeneration, another miracle occurs. For the first time in the six months since my surgery, I'm moved by a surge of honest sexual appetite.

Hugh and I have been having only infrequent sex during this period. Half my life has been spent in hospitals, and most of the rest of it occupied with the struggle to recuperate. Hugh has been intimidated by my fragility. And I have been shy as a virgin, plunging under the bedclothes to hide my hairless genitals, never not aware of the turban wrapped tightly around my head. In all this time—it's the lengthiest abstinence I can remember—I haven't even touched myself. I'm afraid to test my responsiveness, to find that my deepest fears have come true, that the operation has somehow neutered me.

But now I reach down and discover I am all damp and slippery. I remember my old rhythms and give myself up to them. Soon I'm shuddering with relief, my body emptied of tension. I haven't forgotten how to satisfy myself. The next night I turn to Hugh and discover that, as always, pleasure is sweeter when it's shared.

I have a roommate at Community during my fifth and final hospitalization for the CAP in early April, two weeks behind schedule—I needed the extra time to recover from the debacle at Memorial. She's a woman in her seventies, Jean, who's had a mastectomy and now has a recurrence of her breast cancer on that same site. She's in for surgery and has been told she may lose her arm. Clearly terrified by this prospect, Jean talks and talks—about her son, who will be in for a visit any time now, about her poodle who is affectionate and her daughter-in-law who's not. I hear all about her house on Long Island, including a rundown of the porch furniture. Jesus God, I think, please don't let this woman lose her arm.

When she returns from the O.R., my eyes worriedly scan her sheet-shrouded figure, but I can't really tell if there are any missing parts. Jean's voice is slurred but happy as I hear her tell me, I've kept it, Barbara, they didn't take my arm!

My therapy, administered the next day, after Jean has been switched to another room, arrives late. They give me the Ativan at seven, but the chemo doesn't show up until after three. Another day lost to a fog of sedation and riddled by hunger pangs as well. I'm afraid to eat, since whatever I don't have time to digest will come right up again, a few hours into the therapy. The nurses spend several minutes marveling at the scar from my cisplatin burn—I'm a chapter in their nursing manual come to life—before puncturing the catheter and mounting the IV drugs.

The next morning I wake up feeling fine and when my assistant, Parker, comes by to visit me I ask him to run out for pizza. Carol is there as well, and Hugh, of course. We all of us feast on Sicilian pizza with the works, in the hospital lounge.

There we meet Sarah, who's in for some patch-up surgery and has a sad story to tell. Her hysterectomy, for an endometrial cancer, was botched, and she's since had to have a colostomy. Sarah was married when the cancer was first diagnosed, but her husband left her, she tells us—there's no anger in her voice, she's quiet, reconciled. I notice that Sarah still has a certain faded prettiness as she says, the colostomy, it really isn't all that bad. I'm very clean with myself.

Jesus, I hadn't even thought about that, about a colostomy. Acres of bowel fill the abdominal cavity, where the cancer is, if I still have it—it could be gone, I tell myself, it *feels* as if it's gone, after all. I look at poor, pretty Sarah, proud that she keeps herself so clean, and think how uneasy it makes me, this queer hospital social life, where any minute you can be surprised over pizza by a stranger's shocking tragedy.

Leaving the hospital, I heave a sigh of relief. That's it, I think, or hope rather. I've completed my scheduled course of chemotherapy. No more CAP, no more vomiting, and on my head not just turban and wigs, but a live crop of growing hair. An end to my tribulations.

Of course, none of this is assured. Only if surgery shows that the cancer is gone, defeated, obliterated, will the chemo stop. Otherwise. . . . But I do not care right now to think about that other scenario—a stubborn, unvanquishable cancer. My surgery is now six weeks distant, and I could use a holiday. As it happens, this interval falls just as my class at Vassar approaches an important reunion. Should I go or not? My standard-issue reunion jitters are aggravated by my disease—everybody else will be well and whole, not covered with battle scars, battered by disease.

Still, I am feeling the pull of old school ties very strongly now. Partly this is due to the small blitz of appealing notes and interesting newsclips sent to me by the handful of classmates who know of my illness. But mainly it's because of Vassar's intellectual legacy. My teachers there taught me to do my homework well. Vassar was a rigorous school. I feel it has helped me handle my even more rigorous education as a cancer patient.

Hugh and I decide to go to the reunion, but since we're late buying tickets—the unpredictable consequences of my therapy make it all but impossible for us to plan in advance—we're housed not with our class, but with the good old girls and boys of '38, a hard-partying crowd who drink gin like water and chain-smoke Lucky Strikes. Life's survivors.

On Saturday night of reunion weekend the chapel bells sound the "Salve," summoning us to a big yellow tent on the grounds. The sweet and somber playmates of my youth have loosened up considerably. They aren't dead-serious about themselves or anything else anymore, but they've lost none of their sweetness. A small miracle.

Hugh and I make quite a splash. I dress up for my assigned role as Career Woman—nearly all my classmates have been busy raising children—in floor-length black silk, and Hugh turns out to be the most elegant-looking man at the party. My own career-oriented crowd in Manhattan have always had reservations about Hugh ("but what is it that you *do?*"), but my lightly graying classmates don't need to peg a man to his occupation. Dana Little, class president and firebrand behind this reunion, merely points at Hugh, breaks into her gorgeous, toothy grin, and asks me, "Is all this *yours?*"

Silly to have been apprehensive about this reunion. Almost nobody I wave good-bye to has realized I'm sick. Besides, I'm not the only one with scars to show, though no one boasts of them of course. "At least I got some of what we all thought we were meant to have," says my still shapely friend Helga, as we lounge outside chapel on reunion Sunday, looking over the pretty campus, softened by the light rain and mist. Helga's portion, as a divorced parent, is an attractive, teenaged daughter and a not too badly paid job at a university in Louisiana. Enough to keep her content.

And don't I have some of what was promised as well? Some measure of satisfaction. And hope. I'm delighted we went to the reunion. My classmates and I have survived twenty-odd years of half-missed, half-realized opportunities. No envious comparisons mar our celebration of these journeys.

. . .

The reunion over, I reimmerse myself in work, and in the fast shuffle of office life all but forget my illness. And then about two weeks before my scheduled second surgery, it hits—that I'm still sick, that the cancer may be growing furtively inside me, ravaging my innards, even, as I now realize, blocking the bowel. The impact is staggering—I'm knocked completely off stride. Am I to spend what may be the last days of my life sketching out article ideas and netting writers for *Cosmopolitan*? I turn my attention to more pressing tasks.

A friend, Alice Wheeler, works for a Westchester tabloid, and it's her job to comb the competition for headline-making medical breakthroughs. Alice has been sending me Xeroxes of all her most promising clips. In one, mention is made of an intraperitoneal protocol in Los Angeles, run by a Dr. William Arnold, who claims a seventy percent four-year survival rate with recurrent disease. Survival at the four-year mark is considered tantamount to cure. It is thought that if ovarian cancer does not recur within two years, it is gone forever, vanished. Unlike breast cancer, it doesn't hibernate for lengthy periods, recurring suddenly and virulently a decade after diagnosis. When I call the L.A. physician, I tell the woman who answers that I'm a senior editor with *Cosmopolitan*. This by now is my almost always successful way of getting doctors to come to the phone.

Arnold sounds energetic, approachable. When I tell him that I'm both a writer, researching treatment possibilities for women with ovarian cancer, and a patient suffering from the disease, the doctors says, wow, that's some role you've carved out for yourself! He then explains his protocol: two drugs, VP 16 and cisplatin, used in very high doses and opposed by a neutralizing agent, sodium thiosulfate, thought to protect the kidneys, are introduced through a shunt or catheter, similar to the one I already have in my chest. They circulate directly in the abdominal cavity. The theory is that the cancer is thereby exposed to the drugs in concentrations far higher than the body could tolerate normally. Success rates, Dr. Arnold explains, greatly outstrip those achieved with any other "salvage therapy," that is, treatment given to patients who have failed a first course of platinum-based treatment.

Oh, yes, "salvage therapy." Marek introduced me to the phrase. I recall his voice bouncing off the corridors in Cityside. "There are salvage remissions, but no salvage cures!" he told me once, when trying to scare me into taking some monstrous quantity of His Drug. So-called salvage therapies are almost never successful. The word "salvage" itself suggests the results of such treatment—you rescue whatever you can of life. And usually the pickings, a few months, a year, are slim.

Arnold goes on. I may choose an intraperitoneal protocol at one of three institutions: the Jordan Hospital in Los Angeles where he is located, the Roosevelt Hospital in Pasadena, or possibly, Community Hospital, Arnold isn't sure. He believes Paul Strasser, a talented young oncologist who trained with him, may recently have established a program there.

After thanking the doctor for this information, I shut my notebooks and ponder my dilemma. I want to find out everything I can about intraperitoneal therapy so that should I come to need it, I can make a measured and informed decision and not be rushed into some hasty course of action, as I was after my first surgery. Seeing Strasser would serve this end. But Nash is my oncologist, and given my reputation as a "difficult" patient, I hesitate to ask for an appointment with someone else. I'll just have more doctors hating me.

Beneath my facade of brisk, reportorial competence, I'm shaken. And weary. I'm tired of fighting this unwinnable war against a phalanx of doctors, all armored in their invincible authority. Why must I be so frightened, not just of my disease, but of the doctors who are supposed to be helping me defeat it? I quiet my screaming nerves and steel myself for a visit with Nash.

When I see the oncologist—I make an appointment for within the week—I take care not to waste a moment of his time. Asking about the details of Community Hospital's intraperitoneal protocol, I find out the drugs are given in half the amounts Arnold recommends. The Los Angeles doctor's high-dose protocol is by far the more daring and aggressive therapy. And if this cancer has stubbornly refused to give ground, a daring plan may be all that can save me.

As I'm headed out the door, Nash thinks to offer me a morsel of encouragement, perhaps in return for my having been less trouble than he anticipated. "There's reason to be optimistic," he says. "Neither my physical examinations, nor the CA 125 marker blood test, which indicates the presence of ovarian cancer—show any evidence of tumor at this point."

Optimistic? I stop in my tracks and stare pleadingly at Dr. Nash. I'm in the market for optimism.

But the doctor has already reconsidered this brief moment of generosity. "Of course, neither the marker nor the physical examination is ultimately reliable as a diagnostic tool," he tells me.

Of course, I say.

• • •

In Lawson's office for my presurgical visit, I'm profoundly ill at ease, sure he'll be upset that I talked to Arnold. When I tell him about the Los Angeles protocol, how drug doses are two times higher than those available at Community, he chuckles patronizingly. "I don't think you want any part of that protocol," he says. "Your legs bobble around and you can't feel your scalp." But Lawson has his facts confused. The toxicities he's describing were experienced by patients on a recently-cancelled treatment program offered by the Shelburne Cancer Clinic. I was told bone marrow depression was the only side effect, I say. "No," explains the surgeon. "I'm afraid you're wrong about that. The nerve damage in Los Angeles was very bad, very bad indeed."

I introduce a small but to me important point. During my first operation, Lawson didn't take the cervix, fearing that might cause injury to the bowel. I've been wondering, can I keep my cervix, assuming there's no cancer there, of course? As a magazine editor, I'm familiar with the continuing debate about women's sexual anatomy. Nobody's quite sure what part the cervix plays. Okay, we'll keep the cervix. Lawson is extraordinarily agreeable. Although he thinks my *friend*—he puts heavy emphasis on that word, referring to Hugh, of course—may put undue importance on the role of the cervix during sexual intercourse. I'm not sure my *friend* knows what the cervix *is,* I say. This exchange is taking place in the presence of two other doctors and a nurse, and I'm heating up with embarrassment. As a woman's magazine editor, I read a good deal. Besides, I'm not anxious to lose any more parts of myself to surgery.

My, this isn't nearly as traumatic as I'd feared, I say. You know why it isn't? Lawson asks. No, I don't. I honestly have no idea. Because you've learned to deal with your illness on the level of information. Before, you wouldn't take no for an answer. You're growing up.

There is one last thing—I hesitate, not wanting in any way to interrupt this marvelous rapport—but it's possibly a little awkward to talk about. Would I prefer to speak to him alone? Indeed I would. Lawson's retinue picks up to leave. I find that I'm not entirely, uh, *compatible* with Dr. Nash. "Fine, you can have Strasser." This change is accomplished with astonishing ease. "And by the way," the surgeon adds, "I might tell you that you're not alone."

I'm floored by Lawson's civility. But jaded as I am, I take almost nothing on face value anymore. It's because I'm looking like a winner, I tell myself. That's what's turned Lawson around. Just let me get sick again and I'll see the black side of my surgeon's stormy personality.

. . .

The night before my parents are due in—they want to be with me for this second surgery—I cook and cook. I roast sweet red peppers and slice into an expensive, imported wedge of provolone —delicious with Italian bread. For a main course we'll have either rigatoni with bracciole or chicken breasts cooked the way my family likes them, broiled with butter, parsley, and sherry, and served lukewarm. Hugh and I have already been to the florist's, carrying away armfuls of tall, brightly colored gladiolas, and to the video boutique on Broadway for films. I haven't, in spite of repeated disappointments, given up my fantasy of a family, unified by love, doing battle together against this disease. My preparations are in the service of this fantasy. We are all to be cozy together in my little apartment, eating, talking, watching TV.

"You're going to be fine, I know it," says my mother, soon after arriving. She claims she "senses" these things. In spite of myself I'm irritated. Such baseless reassurances are no help to the cancer patient, they really aren't. I'm tired of my mother's prognostications, her supposed maternal intuition. Doesn't she know that tomorrow I'll be split open, breastbone to groin? I've a right to feel jittery.

At Community Hospital we must wait for hours for my chest X-ray; their machine is down. Then it's up to the day room, where we meet Carol again—without Jimmie, they're on the way to breaking up—and from which I am periodically summoned for laxatives and enemas. Though with every trip to the toilet I grow a little more faint, I nonetheless manage a big bear hug for Courtney. She's perched on the side of my bed, when the nurse—she's so young I mistook her for Courtney's roommate—wraps a blood pressure cuff around my arm.

The traffic in my room is heavy, and includes a visit from the hospital's constantly smiling, buck-toothed priest. To please my mother, I'm still writing "Catholic" under "Religious Preference" on the admission form, though I'm no more inclined to believe in

God than in my mother's much-vaunted intuition. The priest asks why I'm there, and I proceed to tell him in dauntingly technical detail. As he leaves, Courtney and I dissolve into giggles, much amused by the cleric's consternation.

More friends drop by, and the gathering in the hospital takes on the aspect of a party, spirited, exuberant. There is a little sparring about who gets closest to me, guest of honor at this ceremonial occasion. Hugh's influence recedes as everyone clusters around me, including, of course, my parents, who hide their apprehension beneath a stream of constant chatter. My father reminisces about working with the idol of his movie-going youth, Edward G. Robinson. He once directed the late star in a sales film for Anheuser Busch, his agency's client. Robinson was a genius, my father raves, a genius. My mother talks about singing the descant in her church's choir. How the music moves her! To sing professionally is her great, unfulfilled dream.

Hugh plays the wallflower at this queer hospital party. My parents talk mainly to my friends, and Hugh, offended, steps away from the conversation, chatting with other patients and their families, roaming the hospital corridors. Efficient Hugh is also annoyed that my crowd is so noisy, so full of anxiety-driven talk and energy. Let the doctors and patients get on with their work, he mutters impatiently. But I'm as rowdy as anybody, keep hopping out of my hospital bed to check in with the crowd in the day room. Tomorrow will be time enough to deal with the pain and paraphernalia of illness—the catheters and tubes and nurses clutching at your elbow as you weakly push at the IV stand. On my last night of freedom, I'm determined to be gay.

For a minute it does cross my mind that we're behaving the way people sometimes do at a wake. Chattering and laughing. Greeting each other with great shows of conviviality. All but forgetting the nature of the occasion, the impulse to socialize eclipsing grief.

I suspect Hugh misses our quiet intimacy on Marek's ward. At least there was some privacy in the dim, green-gray room, a chance for him to hold my hand. Besides, he's at least as anxious as my parents. I understand the sudden disappearances, the pacing —preoccupied, Hugh is a study in restless motion.

But I don't stop running about long enough to get and give the hug that might reassure us both. I am primping and flirting in my lavender turban and silvery pajamas, the star of the show. Nor am I composed enough to soothe Hugh's bruised feelings. My own adrenaline is soaring. In the morning I will know whether or not the cancer is gone, whether destiny has been good enough to grant me a reprieve.

. . .

We're all still gathered in the dayroom when the loudspeaker unexpectedly pages me. My mother and I hurry back to my room where we're greeted by Dr. Earle, Lawson's supplely-shaped, long-haired, new female fellow. "What's wrong, is there bad news?" I ask. "No, no," says Dr. Earle, "just a little change of plans. Your liver enzymes are abnormally high."

"Shit," I say. "I've got hepatitis non-A, non-B. I am going to sue that son-of-a-bitch." Blood can't be screened for this murky strain of hepatitis. I know at once I've contracted it from transfusions in Marek's hospital. "Now we don't *know* yet that you have hepatitis," says Earle. "Obviously you're an educated woman, but sometimes that's dangerous." She arches an eyebrow. "You can think you know *too* much." My mother's frown is her frantic signal to me that I should quiet down. I know that frown, she's been frowning that way since my childhood, sometimes at an adult who was out of line, but more often at me whenever I broached some forbidden subject, such as how old she was, or how much my father earned.

"Nobody *here*," I quickly reassure Earle, feeling caught out by that frown, "I'm not suing anybody *here*."

"At first I thought you just had a deep tan," Earle continues, "but it must be jaundice. The bilirubin causes that." "It's not jaundice. I *do* have a tan," I say. My nerves are scraped bare. "Listen, right now I'm completely revved, you've got to give me a sedative." Earle rushes off to the nurses' station to write the order.

After everybody is gone, I remain edgy and restless. Sleep eludes me. I dip into my private supply of Valium but keep on waking up anyway. At five in the morning, the hour of the wolf, I wander into the dayroom for a smoke. A young woman is nodding out, lost to an Ativan trance. Another woman, plain-faced, with a lantern jaw, tells me she too has ovarian cancer, she's had six months of chemotherapy, only four more to go. They cancelled the ten-month protocol, you know, I tell her, having learned this from dayroom gossip. What's a protocol? lantern jaw wants to know. The girl on Ativan goes into yet another nod. Four more months of Adriamycin percolating nastily and unnecessarily through her veins. That's a steep price to pay for being so "good" a patient.

Leaving Community Hospital that next morning, I'm famished, exhausted, and as let down as you can be. I'd thought to leave in triumph—no more CAP, no more hospital rooms. Death isn't the hard part, as so many people think. I ponder, with something like longing, other mercifully quick endings. The 747 skidding off the runway, the car gone out of control on an icy hill. No, the hard part of cancer is the waiting; the countdown to D-day, checking days off the calendar as you take the dwindling measure of your life. Outside Community Hospital, a group of protesters, AIDS patients and their supporters, march in a circle, carrying banners that read, "FDA—You Slay Me." I feel the pull of fellow feeling. Their destiny, like mine, has been given over to doctors and to scientists, whose guarded procedures have no respect for the urgencies of their disease. Where are the cancer patients, I wonder, with their placards and their slogans—nobody has been more poorly served than we. My mother pulls at my elbow, as I stare at the AIDS protesters in a trance of sympathy. Hurry up, Barbara, Daddy's found a cab. Our wan little group piles into a taxi. There's not much to do now but to wait.

· · ·

I go back to work the following day, though I've no idea for how long, it could be weeks, or months, before the elevated enzymes are back down to normal. This type of hepatitis is otherwise asymptomatic, but without a healthy liver you can't tolerate anesthetic. Or alcohol. I've been warned that I'd better not drink. Non-A, non-B may become chronic, ending in cirrhosis, and my nightly brandies will help assure this outcome. Terrific; now I have two potentially deadly diseases.

My parents have hastened back to St. Louis. They'd rather not spend money on a hotel, and the apartment can't comfortably hold us all. Hugh and I have Seventy-Sixth Street to ourselves, which makes both of us very happy. With every new crisis, we are welded ever more tightly together. The issues that once divided us now seem far away. Our relationship is very basic now, very stripped-down and essential. I'm not looking around for approbation anymore, don't need hurrah's from family and friends, celebrating my choice of mate. We live now, Hugh and I, on a tight little island, and count only upon each other to make it comfortable and safe. Around us there rage some very angry seas.

My liver and I have been put in the care of Dr. Lansdale, an internist at Community who looks after patients suffering from complications of chemotherapy. I've determined to keep relations with Lansdale as cordial as possible, though we've little enough to talk about except my liver enzymes, which follow an erratic course, falling steeply in the week after my discharge; then shooting right back up. After two weeks of observing these fluctuations, Lansdale advises bed rest. But I feel just *fine,* I protest, sounding like a teenager who's been grounded. The summer— it's early June—is by now upon us, and we're enjoying day after gorgeous day.

I'm back to reading the Merck's, which says there's no scientific basis for restricting the activities of a hepatitis patient. But when I share this intelligence with Lansdale, he's unimpressed. I didn't write the Merck's, nor do I read it, is what he has to say.

I find myself a liver expert and soon I'm reciting my complicated medical history to Dr. Hepatologist, a kindly soul who listens with conscientious concern. The doctor chuckles when I tell him that Lansdale has recommended bed rest. We gave up on that years ago, he says. I mention having quoted from the Merck's. And how did Dr. Lansdale respond? He said he didn't read the Merck's. Well, maybe he should, comments Dr. Hepatologist.

The doctor explains that the worst that can happen is that I'll die from the hepatitis, but that the best and likeliest outcome is complete recovery. Non-A, non-B does have a tendency to linger, however, and it could be several months before my counts are "safe" again. How important is it that I have this operation quickly? I'm not sure, though the strain of waiting is certainly telling on my nerves. Can't I have my surgeon call him? Er, I'd rather not, if he doesn't mind. Dr. Lawson needs to feel totally in charge of my treatment; he won't like being part of a committee.

Meanwhile, I'm feeling unusually high-spirited. Maybe it's not drinking, or perhaps it's all that banked adrenalin, but my body is singing with energy. Now that I have hair—the light fuzz on my head is growing into corkscrews—I start to clown around with my wig, pulling it off in the ladies room and once over lunch in a coffee shop. Now, Barbara Ann, you put your hair back on, chides Diane Baroni. I call my brother, giddily confiding my adventures, telling him I'm back at my gym, swimming a mile each day. Poor Tony can't do any of these things, post-viral fatigue syndrome has him confined to his house. "Your trouble," I say, "is that you don't have enough diseases!"

We're into July by now—seven months since my diagnosis—and nights in the country are magical. We stay up late, luxuriating in the velvety warm air, listening to the serenade raised by the pond full of frogs across the road. I love summer and savor every sunny, sweltering day of it. Who knows if I'll live to see another tangle of climbing roses, or to hear next year's thunder tear apart the skies?

For now I sit still, as Dr. Lansdale has advised, enjoying the

sunshine from a lounge chair set in the raggedy grass of my un-
evenly mowed backyard and watching the dogs dig in the dirt for
the cool. I toy with a four-leaf clover Helen has sent me for luck.
Her mother, dead now for many years, had a gift for finding
them, and the fragile, falling-apart clover I touch so gingerly is
part of her collection. Funny, but I like this gift more than my
gorgeous silk robe or outlandishly expensive Teddy bear. The
clover suggests the grassy smells of Helen's rural girlhood, and
the good luck that has blessed her own life since she left the
country—unschooled, naive, but with "a good head on her shoulders"—to conquer a good part of the world. She's sharing some
part of this luck with me.

We edge further into summer, but however peaceful life may
sometimes seem, I'm still in limbo. And unless I can hurry up this
surgery, that's exactly where I'll stay. Gathering my courage, I
call Lawson. Back to the principal's office again. I tremble as I
dial. "I wonder if there is some danger in delaying this surgery?"
I say. "Sure, but there's more danger in going ahead with it,"
Lawson responds. What numbers is he looking for, where would
he like the enzymes to be? As I understand it—butter wouldn't
melt in my mouth, I sound so innocent—this condition often
becomes chronic. "Not often, sometimes," Lawson says. Would
he be upset if I were to consult a hepatologist—I've no intention
of telling him I've already done so. "Look," says Lawson angrily,
"you do not have a normal liver, and you can blame Marek's
drug. I've known that for some time." Gee—I'm innocence itself,
again—Dr. Earle and Dr. Lansdale both said the hepatitis couldn't
be Marek's Drug, the timing would have been different, that I got
it from the transfusions. "Don't go quoting Earle to me! She's a
trainee! That's where I get into trouble with you. When *you* try
to tell *me* what's medically right." "Could you possibly tell me in
what way my liver is abnormal?" I ask in a near whisper. "No, I
cannot!" "Is it *dangerously* abnormal?" "I don't have time for a
lengthy telephone consultation. If you wish to call my office for
an appointment, you may." And with that, the surgeon passes
the phone off to his secretary. The brutality of Lawson's manner

leaves me reeling. As I hang up, hooting my little barks of laughter, I shout out to Hugh, this you won't believe.

If Lawson's intention had been to punish me for having looked outside Community Hospital for care, he couldn't have done a better job. Like many doctors, he's entirely autocratic, the Big Boss who has his rare moments of graciousness, of leniency, but then peremptorily puts you back in your place. I'd thought to up my chances with Marek, to save my life. But my having gone to Cityside for therapy must have looked to Lawson like the act of a reckless, stupid child. Some discipline is needed here! Who did I think I was, pitting my own judgment against the indisputable authority of Community Hospital. Docility, blind trust, that's what Lawson wants from his patients. He hasn't time for my stubborn, unruly will to survive.

My next call is to Marek. "Oh, you *got* the hepatitis," he says when I describe my situation. Oh, the package *came,* did it? "Lawson says Your Drug damaged my liver," I tell him. Much stung by this accusation, Marek explodes, is spitting bullets, his voice atremble with righteous rage. He's going to call Briggs—that's Community's, physician-in-chief—and have Lawson disciplined. Immediately, I convince him not to make good this threat. I'll really be persona non grata at Community should Lawson hear from Briggs.

"You have hepatitis," Marek continues heatedly, "from the blood. Chemically caused hepatitis, it shows up in a few days. Yours took two months! Frankly I don't understand why you stay there. When you came to Memorial you were full of cancer! You had ascites. You had fluid in the lung. If you're cured, chemotherapy cured you. Forget the surgery—it was chemotherapy." Marek is exasperated, he is irate. He himself has been ill-used by Community, never mind me.

Fiery Marek, still on the periphery of the medical establishment, still desperate to have his genius recognized. I take whatever comfort I can from his reassurances about my liver, but I know that he, too, is blustering out of wounded pride. Any patient who doctor-hops, no matter how good or valid that person's reason, must be prepared for these explosions, must stand up to them. "Proper" behavior would have you live—or die—under a single physician's care. I say go wherever the therapy seems most promising and don't be afraid to change course if it isn't working well enough. Rule-breakers, "difficult" patients, though subject to the tantrums of offended physicians, are often the ones most likely to survive.

After talking to Marek, I don't know whether to laugh or cry. What I should be doing is to steel myself—Lansdale has decided that a "trend" has been established. The enzymes are definitely down. I really think it would be a good idea if you took one more reading before setting up the surgery, I say. There's no need, insists Lansdale. My counts are perfectly normal and he's sure they're going to stay that way. Surgery is set for early August.

At the office, I tap-tap at the typewriter, intent on clearing my desk. "The wolf-bite of emotional devastation can savage the spirit . . . learn these ways to *defang* the beast." A good enough blurb, I decide, so what if the rhythm is a little edgy. Parker delivers a memo from Helen—it's that time of year again, she must delineate the *Cosmo* Girl for advertisers who gather to celebrate our continuing success over lunch at "21." Our contributions are so *tremendously* helpful . . . the Boss doesn't know what she'd do without them.

Uh, oh, I'd completely forgotten the "21" lunch—usually I do up an encyclopedia of notes. I shoot into Helen's office, sure she'll understand. But the Boss is crestfallen when I announce that this year my *Cosmo* Girl notes may be abbreviated. I've just been called to surgery. "But I *count* on you so," she says.

I force my mind into gear. In all these years, I've never missed a deadline, never been late. That evening, when I'm surprised by Hugo, the night watchman, it's past midnight and my wig sits absurdly atop my "in" box. I'm cooling off after my long night's labor. "Tots are *in,*" I've written, "as the *Cosmo* Girl becomes ever more conscious of the remorseless ticking of her biological clock." Helen will have her "21" notes after all. And in a week, I'll be out of limbo at least, though I'm still uncertain what my new address will be.

. . .

Surgery is so strange. You are feeling well and strong but you know that at an appointed time, they'll cut into you with a knife, and you'll wake weak and shuddering with pain, and it will be months before you are yourself again. But you go willingly to this fate—you'd think they'd need handcuffs and a whip to persuade you into your place in the O.R. We're so cool, so rational, so stoical sometimes, gladly suffering these little deaths, so that we still have our life.

The night before I'm to be admitted into the hospital, I prepare for my parents' arrival once again, putting out a cold supper for them, roast of lamb and a lentil salad. I have been disappointed by my mother and father, but I disappointed them, too, and I feel very sorry for them. Ping-Ponging back and forth from St. Louis, determined to see me through this thing. They love me, they're doing their best. When all of this is finished, I'll be a better daughter, not so crabby and nervous, more careful of their feelings. I won't live *for* them though—that proved a terrible mistake—but I'll make them happy in whatever small ways I can. The love between the three of us may be frayed, scraped bare. Still, the fabric holds.

That next morning, as we make our way through the admissions office at Community, yet another of their marvelous machines is down, the one that spits back blood chemistries. As soon as I'm settled on the gynecology floor, I seek out a member of Lawson's team—the new fellow is also a woman, very diminutive, Dr. Steinberg—and say, please, right away, before they start with the cathartics, could you arrange for a reading of my transaminases?

I've again decided to be chic for my company in the dayroom —Hugh and my parents, Carol, one or two other friends—I'm in black silk pajamas, and a black and white silk robe in an Oriental motif. Around my neck I'm wearing a rhinestone necklace, a gift from Hugh—an impudent talisman that I hope will bring luck during surgery, it winks and glitters the word "bitch." I feel it has attitude. Soon Courtney breezes in, bringing toys—balloons, noisemakers, and paddle ball—for our amusement. That's some good loving, says a nurse, as Courtney and I disengage from a long, affectionate hug.

Lawson has arrived, flanked by members of his team. "Do you understand the operation that is to be performed tomorrow?" The surgeon's voice is rich and resonant. I answer primly, as if by rote. Then I take a deep breath. When we spoke on the telephone, you mentioned that my liver had been affected by Marek's drug. Tell me, would this be an appropriate time to ask you to amplify this statement? I'm very diplomatic, Kissinger negotiating with the Red Chinese.

The answer is gobbledygook. I've no idea what Lawson is saying. And neither does Greeley, or so he reluctantly admits when I ask him to explain. So what was Lawson's warning about my damaged liver all about? Could it just have been to browbeat me? I still can't get the hang of that.

My dayroom companions are long gone when I swallow 200 milligrams of Nembutal and drift into an uneasy sleep. Twice I wake up, and with the IV stand dragging after me, struggle to the sink to rinse my pajamas and put on a fresh pair—my bowel control is very weak. It's 5:30 in the morning when the night nurse wakes me up. Time to be weighed, she booms. I was weighed last night, I grumble into my pillow, leave me alone. "Put on this hospital gown," she commands. No way, it's freezing in here! Patient refuses to put on hospital gown, the nurse shouts out into the empty corridor. "And you've got makeup on your face. You better wash it off." It's as if she were addressing a child of four. I get out of bed, pull the IV stand to the sink, clunk-clunk, clunk-clunk, and wash my face. Now get the hell out of here you little twerp. Go back to nursing school! A veteran, I have an old-timer's crustiness.

A few minutes later, a very distracted Dr. Steinberg bustles into my room. "There's something wrong with the enzyme counts," she says. "Shit! Not again! Does that mean Lawson won't be able to operate?" By now I'm fully awake. This can't be happening, this readying myself for surgery at no small psychological cost, only to be canceled again and again. Goddamn Marek and his transfusions. I call my mother. There isn't going to be an operation, I whine, and I am going to strangle the night nurse. Foggily I wander the corridors, my turban askew, my face puffy with weakness and lack of sleep. With clumsy hands, I've put my bitch necklace back on, but it's flopped over, the rhinestones face down. So much for my impudence, my survivor's cheek. Can I have a pill or a smoke or something? I ask Greeley. It is far, far too early to be awake. "I'll be making rounds shortly," says Greeley, brisk and businesslike. After the nurse hands me ten milligrams of Valium, I sink into a shallow, sludgy sleep.

I open one gluey eye and see that Lawson is standing beside my bed, looking unusually fit and well. "Hi, Dr. Lawson," I say. "This is very frustrating, you know." "For me, too" replies the surgeon. "I have a schedule, as well." "I asked Lansdale to test the enzymes again, but he said there was a 'trend,' " I say, without bitterness, just reporting the news of the day. "I know, he told me." Bye, bye, Dr. Lawson. I bunch the pillows into a ball and bury my head in it.

It's a little later, and I'm more fully awake when Lansdale dashes in. He's very quick, very light on his feet, as if stepping in and out of buckets of hot water. "You must have passed a gallstone," Lansdale says. "That's the only thing that would make your enzymes jump this way." Oh, yes, a gallstone. What a wonderful idea! Maybe I can still have my operation. Dr. Lansdale wonders whether I've been having any pain in the upper abdomen. Well, I did have a tiny cramp while swimming. It isn't looking good for gallstones. Lansdale rushes out of my room.

A sonogram has been arranged to search out the guilty gallstone. I sleep right through it. Back in my room again a defeated Lansdale tells me my enzyme counts haven't changed, that there's no gallstone, and I can be discharged as soon as I catch up with Dr. Lawson.

My parents have arrived, as has Hugh, who's efficiently packing up my things, all business, his way of coping with apprehension and disappointment. Next, Lawson shows up and treats us all to a little speech. "My job is to see to it that the ovarian cancer doesn't determine how long you live," announces the surgeon. "Your job is to go to bed and treat yourself like an invalid." How about moderate exercise, I plead, moderate exercise is supposed to be good for you. "Have you heard the expression DGMC?" No, can't say that I have. "It means Don't Give Me Crap." Lawson is so awkward. Talking this way is, I understand, my surgeon's way of being friendly. Anyway I intend to ignore him. I've decided that Dr. Hepatologist and the Merck are right. How fast the ezymes right themselves has nothing to do with my level of activity.

"The ovarian cancer is something we may be able to cure. I don't want this new condition to develop into a chronic disease that we can't handle," the surgeon concludes, squaring his shoulders as the mantle of his authority gives an invisible twitch.

As we leave Community Hospital, I'm totally at odds with myself. It's a fine midsummer's day, the sky's as clear as laundry blueing. It's a day to drive to the ocean and watch the breakers roll, or to sprawl in the backyard of my house in the mountains and soak up the sun. What a waste of life, I tell Hugh, as we rattle over the potholes toward home. What a tragic, useless waste!

· · ·

I'm back at work again, for however long nobody can be sure. My poor parents, nerves drawn tighter than a drum, have left for St. Louis. I swing as best as I'm able into my old rhythms, ignoring Lawson's admonition that I treat myself like an invalid. I need this constant stream of activity—it helps me forget I may still be dangerously sick.

At my swimming club I no longer bother changing in the locked bathroom stalls. I've enough hair now not to be concerned about people staring. If anyone notices the scant fuzz on top of my head, she'll probably just think I'm a little old for such a funky cut. One woman does appear to be studying me, however; she's young, pretty, there's nothing rude or hostile in her interest. The woman asks, "When did you stop chemotherapy?" A couple of months ago, I say, surprised, and, as if in response to that, the young woman lets her bra slip to her waist, displaying two amply proportioned breasts. "Four years for me," she announces, "and look . . . I just had reconstructive surgery." Her breasts, each with its own, spreading, pale-brown nipple, look identical. You'd never guess they weren't both God's work.

"I'm Diana," says the woman, who then tells me that she's pregnant. She seems full of happiness. Her boyfriend, now her husband, had been with her only a few months when her breast cancer was first diagnosed. To her surprise he didn't run, stayed loyally by her side throughout surgery and chemotherapy. I think about Sarah, desolate, pretty Sarah from the day room, and wish every woman with cancer the good luck of having a mate like mine and Diana's. Cancer, I have learned, affects couples in one of two ways. Often the partner who's well abandons the sick mate —love just isn't strong enough to hold. But in other cases, the pair draws closer together, feelings are deepened by this urgent new need.

As I step into my thongs, preparing to go upstairs to the pool, Diana takes my arm. "Feel that?" she says, pressing with her fingers, "that's energy."

I've come a long way since my days in Marek's hospital, when I kept myself so separate from the other patients—theirs was a club to which I didn't wish to belong. Now I'm stirred by a sense of camaraderie. Just try, just keep on trying, Diana seems to be telling me. I made it, so can you!

. . .

Weekends during this strange hiatus are spent soaking up sunshine as we visit all our favorite country spots. One Sunday afternoon we meet Barbara Lee and her family, her husband Douglas, daughter Kate, at Colgate Lake, mountain-ringed, deep, pristinely cold, and all but black. This lake doesn't have roped-off bathing areas—there's nothing to stop you from stroking all the way to its far, densely wooded shore. Hugh and Douglas bait Kate's hook for fishing, while Barbara Lee swims after me as I glide through the water, stopping now and then to float on my back when she falls too far behind, staring peacefully up at the wispy clouds drifting slowly in the sky, the only sound the splash-splash Barbara makes as she catches up.

Later, back at the house, Barbara snaps picture after picture of me, turbanless in a bright pink swimming suit, says my meager quarter-inch of hair makes me look "gamine," and "sophisticated." Barbara knows I need a little bit more loving attention than usual and gladly gives it, but without seeming to baby or to pity me.

We spread out on blankets in the backyard, talking animatedly as we look past a clothesline pinned with laundry fluttering idly in the easy summer breeze at the meadow and the mountains. Barbara laughs at my imitations of Marek's rantings or Lawson's pedantry—by now they're quite practiced—and listens intently, and she has always listened, as I talk about the details of my treatment. She makes me feel like some bold traveler, just returned from a faraway land and full of news about her unlikely adventures.

Is Barbara stretching her resources? She has sometimes talked me down from panic, up from despair. Am I stretching mine? Beating back my fears by reveling mindlessly in the pleasures of a summer's day, somehow I'm not surprised by Barbara's generosity. And a stretch, she makes me feel, is nothing less than she would ever have expected from me.

· · ·

I am coasting, resting, gathering stamina for the trials that still lie ahead. Any day now I could be called for surgery. As I prepare for the operation, I think I must call Dick Wirth. What I do after this surgery will be crucial. I urgently require his advice.

As always, the Atlanta physician is very patient with me, very clear about how I should proceed. If no cancer is found, I will be in luck, one of the fortunate seven to ten percent. If only microscopic or invisible cancer is present, I should have the abdominal catheter implanted and remain at the hospital for their standard six-month protocol of intraperitoneal treatment.

There's a third likelihood, though. I might have macroscopic, visible cancer and, in that case, I should visit Wirth in Atlanta immediately, to be evaluated for a possible autologous bone marrow transplant. The doctor doesn't think I'll be cured of macroscopic cancer by any therapy less radical than this. He explains this procedure, which I have difficulty understanding. Once I understand, I've even more trouble accepting it.

During autologous bone marrow transplant, a portion of the bone marrow is taken from your body—it's extracted from the base of the spine under local anesthetic—and frozen. Then you're submitted to huge doses of chemotherapeutic drugs. Normally, they'd kill you, but the frozen marrow constitutes a kind of rescue. You're put into isolation and transfused with it; for the next thirty days you're alone, in an atmosphere of surgical sterility, waiting for the stem cells to reproduce. The physical plant of your body is then operating again, though not at optimal capacity— you can expect a lengthy malaise, feelings of great weakness, before you're fully recuperated.

Not everybody does recuperate, of course. Fifteen to twenty-five percent of patients who receive an autologous bone marrow transplant don't make it through. They die of the treatment. Or so the doctor is obliged to tell me.

Wirth is giving me his best advice. I know that. But such advice, such a treatment. Irrationally, I feel Wirth is somehow responsible for my needing so drastic a procedure. Extract and freeze the deepest essences of me? Hating the cancer, right now not even liking the good doctor Wirth very much, I think, no way! No way! Go find yourself some other guinea pig.

· · ·

Finally, the transaminases have quieted and, having once again welcomed my parents to New York, I enter Community Hospital for another try at surgery. As I settle into my room, I'm subdued, as are my sprinkling of visitors—nobody has strength enough anymore to make a party. Ruled by a strong tide of anxiety, I wonder, will they cancel me yet again? That would hardly seem likely, but then the saga of this operation has been crowded with twists and turns that strain belief.

I am Lawson's second surgery for the day, not the best post position. Up at dawn, alone, alert and awash in apprehension, I wait for a sedative which doesn't come until after eleven. The drug I'm given is quite mild. I watch the hands on the clock sweep toward noon and one and two, when at last I'm wheeled through the cool, cavernous corridors surrounding the O.R. For some reason they leave me parked outside an operating theater with what seems a lifeless body on the gurney next to me. The body nods awake. It belongs to another patient in a trance of sedation, a good-looking young man who tells me he's to be operated on for colon cancer—they won't know for six weeks whether or not the colostomy he's scheduled to have will be reversible, he adds. We chat some more—I'm very grateful for the company. Then somebody comes to wheel my charming new friend away.

I'm still conscious when rolled into the O.R., conscious and very, very chilly—I'm dressed only in a blue paper gown. I say hello to Dr. Greeley and tell him he looks roguish in his surgical mask. Propped on my elbows, I crane my head around the room, looking for Lawson, looking for the chief. As the surgeon approaches, I plunge abruptly into a heavy, artificial sleep. An anesthetist must have surprised me with a needle, but as I tip over into the darkness, I don't feel a thing.

In the recovery room, I call, "doctor, doctor!" Nobody answers. Then I'm suddenly back in my own room, queerly, vividly alert, surprised that there is so little pain. A thick, gauzy bandage covers my left side where the catheter has been implanted, making me feel like an awkwardly wrapped parcel. It tells me that I'll need the intraperitoneal therapy, that my hopes are smashed. The cancer is still with me. I register first Hugh and my parents, then Lawson and his team. The surgeon tells me that they found and removed a one and one-half centimeter growth from the "stump" of the cervix. I recoil from the ugly word. But they couldn't resect the five millimeter strands of tumor dispersed throughout the peritoneum. Lawson says they're as thin as a dime, as thin as strands of tinsel. I imagine my belly festooned with cancer, shining with the glittering strands.

That's macroscopic cancer, I cry out, cancer you can see. Wirth's warning is emblazoned on my mind. Lawson doesn't know what I'm getting so excited about. Thirty days in sterile isolation, every organ in my body scorched by chemotherapy, twenty-five percent mortality, that's what I'm excited about. My mother tells me not to worry, I have the catheter now, I'm going to be just fine. With some effort, I manage not to become annoyed by her reassurances. Remember, try to remember, she's talking to herself, not me.

The next day I am still, astonishingly, free of serious pain but I've spiked quite a high fever and can't stop sobbing. A tube slithers through my nose down past the esophagus through the coiled bowel to the very pit of my abdomen. It brings up an endless stream of mud-colored bile. The back of my throat is so clotted with phlegm that I fear I'll choke. Lawson instructs me to use the spirometer, but I ignore him, and take to the halls, trailing my IV stand behind me, drowning in bile and phlegm and tears. I find Dr. Lansdale and demand a sedative, which I'm finally given after an interview with the hospital shrink. I want an end to consciousness, to scramble back into the darkness, to be at least temporarily free of the stupendous weight of my disappointment.

I can't believe it! I have fought harder for my cure than I have for anything else in life. I have battled and battled. And yet here I am, exhausted and defeated, statistically a no-hoper now, eager for my only relief, the dark cocoon of sleep.

VICTORY

August 1987—May 1988

I face the recuperative period after surgery, during which I must relearn my independence, restore my strength, with a fragile and depleted spirit. The first operation left me feeling weaker than this by far, but then I was sustained, at least at the beginning, by the expectation that I would be cured. My hopes for recovery are by now quite thin and worn. I've survived two surgeries, months of chemotherapy, the sudden, surprising collapse in Marek's hospital when my blood ran thin as water, and a long bout with hepatitis, only to find myself in an even weaker position than I was when I began this strange odyssey. In the course of this, my unexpected education as a cancer patient, I've been obliged to live with even higher levels of anxiety.

Against a strong, pulling tide of despair, I pit my own persistence. Within a day or two of surgery, as soon as I'm strong enough to sit upright, I am rifling through my notebooks, reverting, however mechanically, to the problem-solving mode that has sustained me throughout this illness. There must be something, something in these notebooks that can help me! I flip from page to page, looking for the jottings I made the day I spoke to William Arnold, the Los Angeles doctor experimenting with high-dose intraperitoneal therapy, the promising new treatment mentioned in the news clip Alice Wheeler sent to me when I was still uncertain about what the outcome of my operation would be. The minute I look into these notebooks, I am beginning my long fight back to recovery. Cancer is an unpredictable disease, and I, a survivor, am learning to roll with the blows it so unexpectedly delivers. My hopes have been destroyed. Now I must learn to hope again.

Why, this isn't so bad, I think with some surprise, as I find my place in the notebooks and remember that Arnold is claiming a cure rate of seventy percent for patients like me, those with advanced disease who've failed a first course of chemotherapy. No other doctor, no paper published in a medical journal would put my chances anywhere near that high. Data on my group is scant; little has been published. We're not the most promising subjects for research since so few of us survive. But the popular press has picked up on Arnold's flashy numbers in a "Miracle Cure Brings Hope to the Hopeless" sort of way. Doctors or members of their teams will sometimes leak news to a reporter before they're willing to present it to their peers. Word of Arnold's protocol has surfaced in just this underground fashion.

I find, amazingly, that I am gathering momentum. Let me call Dick Wirth, I think. But when I reach the Atlanta physician, he tells me that Arnold's projections are wildly, baselessly optimistic. According to Wirth, who doesn't look to the *Cleveland Enquirer* to keep up, Arnold's therapy is forty percent effective, fifty percent of the time. I wonder how this can be, two top doctors telling me such different things? I am, in spite of my vulnerability, my turbulent emotions, *interested* by this phenomenal discrepancy. Promising to be down to see him within the next two weeks, I put in a call to Strasser, now my oncologist by Lawson's generous decree, and the man Arnold suggested I see when we spoke on the phone in April. Maybe Strasser can help me make my way through this welter of confusing, contradictory information. I'm in a fun house of doctors, going dizzily from mirror to mirror— you'll die, one doctor says. Oh no, says another, you'll live. You'll live.

My nurse is giving me a sponge bath when I'm surprised by two visitors at once—Helen and Lawson. The Boss steps gracefully aside as my surgeon approaches. Surely you two know each other, I trill politely. No, Helen says, our acquaintance has been over the phone. This disease really stretches your social skills, I think, as I twist around, naked beneath the sheets.

At last, after a wait of several days, I'm finally visited by the elusive Strasser, whom I've called and called, but who seemed not to want to see me. I ask him, which is better—the protocol at Community Hospital or the one Arnold runs in L.A.? "We don't know," he says. "Since you know so much about ovarian cancer, you should also know that." Who knows most about ovarian cancer in this country? I ask extravagantly. I want to talk to him. If no consensus exists among these warring camps of doctors, I'll go to the top of the line. Except there apears to be no top to this eroded pyramid. "I'm afraid I can't tell you that either," says Strasser, rocking slightly on his heels. If I'm not mistaken, the man is enjoying himself. Putting an impertinent patient in her place. One-upping him, I report what I've recently been told by Wirth. This takes Strasser by surprise. Wirth says *that!* Wirth thinks *that!* The doctor seems frankly astonished. I can see him rushing back to his colleagues—that Wirth, he's really something, he'll say.

The politics of research seems to be what really fascinates Strasser. If only my problems intrigued him equally. With no guidance from my new oncologist, I'm on my own, left to point my shaking finger at one or another of these wildly different and decidedly menacing therapies.

Leaving the hospital after this, my third and finally completed try at surgery, I'm overwhelmed by grief and confusion. I've talked to three top men of research, Strasser, Arnold, and Wirth, about what to do next, and among them there is no consensus, none!

Before I got this disease I imagined that cancer doctors worked together in a feverish rush, communicating their discoveries with urgent, urgent haste—wait twenty minutes and who knew how many more might die? The facts are more prosaic. I'm begining to realize that cancer research operates like any other industry. The doctors and their tight little teams are narrowly focused on their own therapies. Like businessmen, they keep their eyes pinned closely to the bottom line. Some play their chips shrewdly, waiting for the optimal moment to make a presentation or to publish formally. Others, the fast movers, the players, make aggressive claims for their treatments. And in the hustle for funding and for glory, a particular scientist's good and valuable work can easily get buried, lost. Studies are published that dispute the claims of other studies. And so it goes, on and on. Full cooperation among researchers is honored only as an ideal. What seems to go on is an endless duel for prominence, a fast and intricate shuffle, as first one doctor and then another takes the lead.

And what of me, two times gutted, poisoned nearly to death? I can't possibly wait for these jousting doctors to agree. I have to act now. Though trembling with apprehension, and without any clear direction, I must somehow decide what my next move should be.

Within a day or two, the family piles into our Toyota and heads for the country. Hugh drives, with me beside him, and my parents jammed uncomfortably into the back seat, the two dogs panting over their shoulders, eager for the cool of the mountains. I'm wearing a dress Hugh, who knows my tastes and shops for me whenever I'm not able, brought me from Banana Republic— a long, loose, tan shift. Pressure on my abdomen is still quite uncomfortable, and I can't stand any constraint. I've hardly eaten in the last ten days, my appetite ruined by apprehension and my digestive system overwhelmed by the strains of surgery. We plan to be in the country only a week; by then I hope to be strong enough to visit Wirth in Atlanta, and on the way home, to check out treatment possibilities at the Shelburne Cancer Clinic.

Once arrived in the country, I try to keep very still. Not to jostle my bruised body, my damaged soul. Hugh moves a lounge chair for me down among the locust trees that stand tall around our tumbling-down old barn. The crumbling wood is embraced by a teeming tangle of vines and berry bushes. Diane Baroni brought me Milan Kundera's *The Unbearable Lightness of Being* while I was still in the hospital, and I'm surprised to find that this cool, detached book compels my attention. Is it because Kundera writes, however ironically, about the big issues of freedom and survival? Or is it, rather, the book's strange philosophical overlay, the idea conveyed by the novelist that life is no better than a dress rehearsal, that we haven't an opportunity to come fully into our characters because we're allowed only one quick run-through and will never know the shape our lives might have assumed had we taken some other path?

The idea of other lives, other paths, reverberates powerfully in my mind. I've been obliged to take a narrow, dangerous road and have all but forgotten the vagabond innocence that I once enjoyed, the rich sense of possibilities that was mine before the earth-splitting eruption of my disease sent me scrambling, helter-skelter, among the ruins, scavenging, surviving, amid the shattered landscape of my life.

And shattered it certainly is. If I've any doubt of this, I've but to consult my strained, tension-ridden relationship with my parents. The quiet I'm carefully cultivating, seated so peaceably among my locust trees, is not to be. My mother and father, at least as disappointed by the outcome of my surgery as I am myself, haven't the strength to feign the necessary pleasantries. They ignore Hugh, and are unexpectedly surly with me. Possessively, worriedly, they've taken charge of my cure, but they're not equal to it. My father hasn't the strength to help me from place to place and so it is always to Hugh that I turn for assistance, which turns Daddy's face sour with jealousy. My mother is too exhausted to cook, and my father doesn't know how. It is indeed Daddy's improbable cooking that occasions an ugly scene.

The quarrel appears to be about a chicken leg, though of course it is really about life and death and all the ways we have all let each other down. I have requested that Daddy broil one. Okay my father says, he will boil one up, in some spaghetti sauce. No, broiled, I object, please broil it. And I can't digest spaghetti sauce! And then my anxious, worried father explodes. I am picky. I am demanding. I'm not nice to him, not nice to my mother, not even nice to the *dogs!* Don't I realize how much he and my mother are suffering. Why their sufferings are *worse* than mine. I don't care, I cry. I don't have it *in* me to worry about you now. It's all I can do to stay alive! We're two warring camps again—my mother and father, Hugh and I, hiding at opposite ends of the house, the yard. For several days, we barely speak.

In spite of such unpleasant eruptions, I regain strength much faster than I did after my first surgery and within the week feel well enough to travel. Hugh and I leave the car with my parents and fly to Atlanta to see Dr. Wirth. I am eager to meet the physi-

cian who has so far only been a disembodied voice on the telephone, but on whose judgment I have come to rely. Out of our
scraps of conversation I've put together a picture in my mind of a
man of caring and brilliance. Now I'll finally see how close this
portrait is to reality.

Wirth turns out to be younger than I'd expected—somewhere
in his late thirties, I suspect—a pleasant-looking man, scholarly
and mild in clear-rimmed spectacles. He seems indeed a man of
gentle spirit. But what he says is harsh and bruising. Wirth is even
less optimistic about my chances with intraperitoneal therapy in
person than he was on the phone. He says the odds of achieving a
cure with Arnold's high-dose therapy are under five percent, no,
less than one percent, if I want the truth.

Wirth's attractive female associate, Dr. Faber, concurs emphatically, brushing Arnold's work away with a brisk wave of
her hand. "If he had something, don't you think he'd *publish?*"
she says impatiently. I don't like the sense of competition, the
one-upmanship her manner suggests. She's so young—just past
thirty, I'd guess—so aggressive. At best, an enthusiast, I think; at
worst, a careerist. I am, however, devastated by Wirth's more
neutrally delivered judgment. I've the clear sense of him as a
responsible man, a man of ethics. This is no posturing, ego-driven
Marek, pushing His Treatment above all others. What he's telling
me, I'm sure, is the truth as he knows it, and given his position
and my own assessment of his character, such knowledge as he
has is not easy to discount.

Before committing myself to the Los Angeles protocol, Wirth
warns, I should be sure to get *real* numbers from Arnold, not
projections drawn from "Life Table Analysis." How many actual
women were treated? How many cured? Is this some kind of
veiled warning? Is Wirth suggesting that Arnold is distorting his
data, inflating cure statistics, with some kind of complicated computer assist?

With the transplant, Wirth goes on, my chances would be
much better, close to fifty percent, in his estimate, *if* I live

through it, of course. This treatment is very radical, he's obligated to remind me, and not every patient survives her "cure"!

How many women with my disease have had the transplant? I inquire. Here, in Atlanta, only one, Wirth says. "And she's doing brilliantly," adds Dr. Faber, with breathless enthusiasm. "She's been out there for a year now, beating all the odds. She's back at work again, she's healthy!" Just one, I think, what can they possibly know from one woman? and she's only survived a year. That's far too early to pronounce anybody cured. You have, er, a rather small research population, I say, and Wirth is obliged to agree. The technique has so far been mainly used with advanced breast cancer patients, he explains. But success rates with them have been extremely promising. About fifty percent of patients who've received the transplant—and these are women who had no chance of cure at all with other therapies—are still alive, Wirth tells me.

What would you advise if your mother or sister were in my situation, I ask, a standard "smart patient" question, since it invites the doctor down from his pedestal and encourages him to consider your predicament in human terms. "I really can't answer that," Wirth tells me. "You can't make this sort of decision for another person. It would depend on how much she was willing to risk, or to endure, in order to get well." And if it were you? I persist. "If it were me, and I wanted to be around three or four years down the road, helping people, I'd have the transplant," he says.

I'm impressed by the way Wirth has answered my question. The absence of glibness, of easy promises. I am more than ever persuaded of the man's integrity. "If I wanted to be around, three or four years down the road, helping people . . ." The words lodge in my mind, though they hardly cheer me.

The doctor checks me over, examining lungs, heart, and reflexes, sending blood chemistries to the lab—only the strong may be considered candidates for autologous bone marrow transplant —and he finds me in surprisingly good condition. When I tell him

I plan to check out treatment options at the Shelburne Cancer Clinic before making a decision, the woman who's been ushering me back and forth from waiting lounges to examining rooms says, Oh, I used to work at the Shelburne, you'll like it there, it's *very* nice. She reminds me of the Welcome Wagon ladies who greeted my family when we first moved to the Middle West. She has the same jaw-cracking smile, the relentless good cheer. Yes, I'm sure, I say sarcastically. First a little trip to Wilson to contemplate having all my bone marrow removed, then a drop in at the Shelburne. This is a regular walk among the lily pads.

Wirth tells me he thinks I'm strong enough to survive the transplant and urges me to make my decision soon. Once again, as after my first operation, I have little time in which to consider my options. I must embark on one path or another quickly. After leaving Wilson, Hugh and I rent a car, planning to break up the long drive to D.C. with what we hope will be a restful stop on the Del Mar peninsula. Even at this emotional nadir, we're still trying to grab at pleasure, to take a recess from this school of nightmares in which we've found ourselves enrolled.

We find a lonesome-looking shoreside motel at Cape Charles, and with flagging spirits, settle in. Whatever optimism and energy I've brought to fighting the cancer is exhausted now, and my reservoir of hope is parched and dry. Wirth's evaluation of my chances with intraperitoneal therapy has devastated me, and the prospect of the transplant—so relatively unproven, so dangerous—leaves me faint with terror. Right now, I'm convinced that I'm probably going to die of this disease. For the first time I think about *how* the cancer gets you—does it stop the bowel so you starve and bloat with gassy pain? Cause the liver to fail until you're skinny and yellow with the slow poisoning? I look out at the ocean through a blurry film of tears, not "sorry for myself" exactly, just enormously regretful that I may not have so many more chances to watch waves break on the shore. As the sun sets, Hugh and I huddle together in an abandoned rowboat—I hold onto him as tightly as a fearful, wretched child. I feel infinitely sad. And small.

As we drive into Washington the next day—we plan to stay with Hugh's brother Irving and his sister-in-law Mosella—my mood lightens considerably. We're moved now by a sense of purpose. Who knows but that this may be the place where our goal is finally achieved? I'm practically buoyant by the time we're inside the huge, impressive private facility, marveling at how smoothly it runs. What a wonderful place. The two of us feel rather foolish for not having come here before—why the Shelburne is *Mecca,* more streamlined by far than Community Hospital, showing up Memorial as the pathetic backwater it surely must have been. What a fool I was to go slumming there!

When I'm examined, however, I shift gear yet again, back into anger and the beginning of dull despair. The young Irish doctor who takes my history, here because opportunities for research in his country are so meager, seems barely out of his teens. And the sour-faced woman physician who sees me next gives me a most reluctant rundown of available protocols. I may be treated intraperitoneally with an Adriamycin analogue, but in that case must expect severe abdominal pain, possible heart damage, and a number of other discouraging side effects. Success rates with this drug are pitifully small, though the damage it does is quite devastating —a leukemia patient on Marek's ward, I will later find out, dies from complications of this drug, which is no longer used, not even experimentally. Or I might try something called an "immunotoxin conjugate"—nobody has signed up for this treatment program yet, so both results and side effects are unknown. Last, I may opt for intraperitoneal interleukin II, assisted by lymphocyte-activated killer cells, whatever they may be, but once again, the side effects, which include blood pressure so drastically lowered that patients have found themselves confined to intensive care, are dire.

Tell me, I sputter at Sourface, irritation getting the better of tact, why would anybody consent to be treated on *any* of these protocols? They don't work. They make you sicker than you are already. What would be the point? "Well, some people think they might work," she says sullenly. She seems quite impatient with me. People don't generally come to the Shelburne Clinic just to

check the menu, she explains, they come to be treated, with assignment to the various protocols made randomly. Terrific; they
don't even let you pick your poison here.

Before leaving the clinic, I visit its library and take away a
stack of research papers, which I read back at Irving and Moe's.
There's little enough in the way of good news here—Wirth seems
to be right. "Most patients who fail to respond completely to a
first round of chemotherapy are destined to die of their disease,"
one paper reads. I ponder the paucity of adverbs here. No "tragi-
cally," or "sadly," not even an "unfortunately"—just the facts
baldly stated. Fail chemotherapy and you die. The only possibly
bright note: Arnold's name pops up repeatedly as the author of
the clinical trials that had the most promising results. Whatever
Wirth may have been suggesting about him, the man has, it
seems, done excellent work. It's right here in black and white. I
mark these studies in red ink.

I'm about to be visited by a major depression, but it's arrival
is delayed by a brief fit of outrage. Nobody's interested in practic-
ing medicine at the Shelburne, I tell Hugh and Irving and Moe.
Nobody's trying to *cure* anybody. What you have here, at the top
echelons, are the smart boys of research, all in a dead heat, racing
for the Big Breakthrough, competing for the Nobel prize. God-
dam glory-seekers, that's what they are!

Later, when I'm on the phone to my parents, I can no longer
keep the depression at bay. My voice is thin and hollow when I
say Wirth is probably my only hope. Right now, I don't think I
have much chance without an autologous bone marrow transplant.

I'm still physically frail and psychologically at my absolutely
lowest ebb, when more out of conscientiousness than real interest
or hope, I phone William Arnold in Los Angeles. I flick on my
tape recorder, along with its telephone attachment, because I no
longer trust myself to remember the arcane details of yet another
esoteric treatment. Skipping my usual round of apologies, I press
through to the crux of my problem. I've just been to see Dr.

Wirth at Wilson Medical Center, I tell Arnold, and he says I have a less than one percent chance of making it with your therapy.

This seems not to concern Arnold at all. "Well, Dick doesn't really know what we're up to here," he explains breezily. Dick? "Yes, we were classmates in med school." Why doesn't Dr. Wirth know what you're doing, I want to know. "Because I haven't told him . . . frankly, we're engaged in something of an intellectual competition."

My reaction to Arnold's words are intense and wildly confused. "Intellectual competition?" He can't be serious—does he think cancer is some kind of game? See how clever I am; I've just taken your queen? I'm boiling over with anger. But at the same time I'm breathless with hope. Wirth doesn't know, because he hasn't been told, about Arnold's good results. Maybe I won't be forced to go through an autologous bone marrow transplant after all. My palms are moist as I grip the telephone receiver, telling myself, be prudent, go slowly.

I keep firmly in mind Wirth's caution that I get Arnold to give me real numbers, not projections. And already the L.A. doctor has begun to talk in a way I don't understand. "According to Life Table Analysis . . ." he is saying. I can't understand Life Table Analysis. I never studied statistics, I object. I need to know how many *real women* have survived at the two- and three- and four-year marks.

"Let me extrapolate from the curve," says Arnold patiently. "It's very important that you be comfortable with these numbers. All the women that were going to die, and that was twenty-five percent, had the opportunity to do so within the first twenty-five months."

Some "opportunity," I think.

"And after that we've seen no recurrences at all."

Arnold adds that he'll be happy to Federal Express me a copy of his most recent paper, soon to be published, which gives success rates for this and other clinical trails he's inaugurated over the past six years. I will be reading the paper in advance of Arnold's competitors and peers. "What you must realize," the doctor tells me excitedly, "is that you're tapping into information not yet available to the medical community."

I'm stunned by this remark. If this is life-saving data, why *isn't* it yet available to the medical community? I'd have thought doctors were morally obliged to share such information quickly. But I'm becoming fast disabused of this naive assumption. It is up to the individual research physician to decide when his results are conclusive enough to share. Thus the ignorance of the honorable Wirth. If information does not reach the medical journals, no scientist, no matter how highly placed, can know of its existence. Just a little quirk in the system, a quirk that helps put thousands of men and women, who might have been saved, through the agony of death-by-cancer.

Keeping my outrage to myself, I ask next about the side effects of the therapy. They're quite mild, says the doctor. Myelosuppression—bone marrow depression—is modest, and the neurotoxicity so slight they haven't been able to measure it clinically. I can expect nausea on the day of treatment and mild-to-moderate hair loss. And though doses of cisplatin are very high, damage to the kidneys is next to nil. They're protected by the sodium thiosulphate.

There's nothing here I can't live with. I go from wretchedness to buoyant hope within the five minutes I've chatted with Arnold on the phone. The misgivings Wirth has planted in my mind— that Arnold's numbers have been manipulated—are lightly rooted weeds. Quickly I dispatch them so they won't crowd and choke my newly seeded hopes.

I have now only to make that difficult but necessary leap of faith that will commit me to the experimental treatment. I want to have intraperitoneal therapy where they do it best and have the most successful track record, I say without hesitation, waves of hope washing away the gritty fear. The prospect of death has turned me decisive; shilly-shally, settle for half-measures, and you die.

"Welcome to Los Angeles then," says Dr. Arnold, a note of

genuine enthusiasm in his voice. He tells me how to book a bed and advises me to hurry—the sooner I have therapy, the safer I'll be. A minute later I'm on the phone to Wirth, saying I've decided to go on the L.A. protocol after all. When I tell him about Arnold's soon-to-be-published paper, he seems less persuaded than he was before about the ultimate uselessness of intraperitoneal therapy. "Let me ask you this, Dr. Wirth," I say, double-checking, and again I marvel at the words that come next, their balanced objectivity, "Have you the reasonable expectation that your treatment is more effective than anything else currently available in this country?" Wirth's equivocal answer is what secures my decision to sign up for Arnold's protocol. "I'm afraid that's the reporter coming out in you," he says. So . . . he isn't sure his treatment is the best, won't say so for the record. I'm right to be going to Los Angeles, I'm sure of it.

I'm at Seventy-Sixth Street when I make these calls, and just after finishing them, I phone my parents who are still in the country. Their relief that I'm no longer contemplating the transplant is stupendous, and they're heartened by the note of hope in my voice. My father says he wants to be the one to come with me to Los Angeles, and after a quick consultation with Hugh, we agree this will be our plan. It will be good for your father to have some time alone with you, Hugh says. He understands how distraught Daddy is, and hopes that coming with me to Los Angeles will ease his unhappiness.

Am I wrong, or are the warring camps beginning to put aside their arms, aiming at a truce, if an uneasy one, built upon their shared concern for me?

· · ·

Flying to Los Angeles with my father beside me, his hand resting protectively over mine, I am flushed with a sense of adventure, giddy with hope. Have cancer, will travel, I think, as amazed by the steps I am taking to defeat this disease as I am by the strange circumstances that continue to beset me. I am about to challenge the terrible numbers martialed against me by batallions of doctors, preparing to launch yet another vigorous campaign against my disease.

And it will be a campaign of breathless speed and intensity as for the next six months I rush back and forth from New York to Los Angeles, my emotions ricocheting more wildly than sniper fire with every good or bad report. I will rocket to almost manic highs as the conviction mounts that I will surely, surely be cured, and then plummet into the abyss as my hopes are periodically shot down. What will keep my emotions from running entirely out of control is the stabilizing routine of work—I'm to be on the job for most of this period—and the never wavering support of those who love me.

When I meet William Arnold in my room at Jordan Hospital, I congratulate myself on my choice of physician. Arnold is young, about my age, lean and athletic-looking, with hair the color and texture of steel wool. His face is alive with intelligence, and he moves crisply, decisively. I'm less delighted with the consent form he produces for my signature. It states, in prose that's murderously clear, that even if I'm disabled or die as a result of the therapy, neither he nor the hospital is to be held accountable. I'm reminded that this is no pretend war being waged around me. The weapons being brought to bear are real and powerful, and they can turn quite treacherously against the very individual they're intended to protect. Frightened, I ask the doctor once again to run through the side effects of the therapy, and when he speaks in a considered way about mild hair loss and slight neurological impairment, I think, what am I waiting for? This isn't the autologous bone marrow transplant I was considering until very recently. Arnold promises me they haven't lost a patient to the therapy yet, and, convincing myself that this is a mere formality, I put my signature to the forbidding document.

Soon afterward, I meet another personable young man, Bruce Dolan, the physician's assistant who is coordinating the protocol. I warm to Bruce immediately, though I can't yet know that he is destined to become both my very good friend and my strong ally in what remains of this long and difficult war. Bruce will supply me with intelligence from the front, telling me how the women on the protocol are really faring, intelligence Arnold, as our commander-in-chief, feels no reason to share.

I'm not so brave a soldier, though, as to be entirely unafraid of this new treatment. Some very high doses of some extremely toxic drugs will be circulating directly in my abdomen, and I can't quite believe what the doctor has told me, that there will be no pain. He's right though; I don't feel a thing. The routine at Jordan Hospital is very much the same as it was when the drugs were administered intravenously. First, hydration, followed by a healthy dose of Ativan—it causes me to lapse into the familiar nightmare-ridden sleep to which I've already lost so many days. Just as before, I come awake six to a dozen times to vomit. The only difference is that now after treatment I'm so bloated I can't zip up my jeans. The gentle young nurse—she looks like a flower —attempts to drain the treatment fluid from my abdomen, but enough remains so I look about four months pregnant.

After discharge, my father and I take a hotel room for several days, until I'm strong enough to travel. We spend the time peaceably lazing by the pool, and since it's now seven weeks since surgery, I go for a swim. Slouching toward the pool, clutching at my hurting, bloated abdomen, I suppose I must look ill and rather pathetic, but I know myself to be gaining strength. After ten or so lengths, I hoist myself awkwardly out of the water, completely spent. Still, I'm pleased by the achievement.

We fly back to New York by way of St. Louis, where I say good-bye to my father, who is hugely relieved that I seem to be back on course again and hopeful. He'll rejoin my mother, who left for home the day before we flew to Los Angeles. It's early September by now, and I feel that familiar surge of crisp, end-of-summer energy. Back to school! Within the week, I've returned to work, feeling upbeat and positive. I take on my share of the line editing, catch up with my regular writers, and try and succeed in attracting some lively new contributors. I want to be sure I deserve the raise I'm about to ask for, and receive. The Boss doesn't even attempt to counter my argument that though out for nearly half the past year, I've still done well for the magazine. I can point to some fifty articles commissioned and bought, a decent enough record even for someone who hadn't been sick. I'm queerly determined about this raise, needing the money, to be sure, but more important, wanting to be acknowledged as a fully active staff member, unwilling to be written off, dismissed. A woman without a future.

Arnold has told me I'll need a Manhattan oncologist to care for me between treatments and recommends I try Ezra Greenspan, who, I'll eventually come to think, deserves his reputation as among the finest oncologists in the country. At this point, I'm expecting only routine checkups from Greenspan, and for him to provide access to a New York hospital should I come to need one. I don't realize that I'm dealing with one of the giants of modern medicine, a man whose pioneering research in the sixties helped usher in the world of modern chemotherapy, and whose skill in private practice keeps the many patients in his care alive and flourishing long years after they were supposedly destined to succumb to difficult and in some cases "incurable" cancers. Once again, I have happily, if all but accidentally, bounded to the top of the line.

After a short wait in Greenspan's Fifth Avenue office, my name is called, and I'm greeted by an expensively tailored man in his late sixties, who is hobbled by a pronounced limp. Greenspan's manner is impatient, bordering on gruff, and he talks fast and emphatically. Put aside the good clothes and the precise reasoning behind his rough, staccato style, and you might be talking to an old-time New York cabbie. He has the same gestures, the same surly, urban impatience.

The doctor gets straight to business. "Dr. Arnold told me all about you," Greenspan says, "how bright you are, how inquisitive you are, and how well you are. Is it all true?" Well, I'm the only patient I ever heard of who referred herself to a protocol, I say, with my most confident grin. Dr. Greenspan just harrumphs. "Your platelets are down, they're at 87,000, have they ever gone that low before?" I'm not sure, I say, Marek never bothered with weekly counts. "Oh, oh, you were treated by Marek, were you?" Greenspan's small, raisinlike black eyes seem to double in size as they flare with curiosity. I tell Greenspan about the steep drop in my counts that led to the eleven-day stay at Memorial. I wasn't such a smart patient then, I say. "Marek gave you His Drug at the same *time* as the CAP," says Greenspan, evidently surprised, and quickly assessing the damage this might have been expected to do. Yes, we got all the way up to thirty-six grams. The grim look on Greenspan's face seems to corroborate my sense that I was lucky to writhe out of Marek's grasp.

In the examining room, I meet Dr. Greenspan's Australian-born nurse, Heather Canning, who's tough and spiky as a cactus. She tells me she's survived two cancers, an endometrial malignancy and a rare form of leukemia. Heather was a nurse in Vietnam, where she was heavily exposed to Agent Orange, the likely cause of both diseases. "Patients complain about losing their hair," she tells me. "I say, look at me. *Mine* grew back. It came in a different color, mind, and it's a bloody pain. I never had to blonde it up before."

Heather's husband, a prominent journalist, left her shortly after the first cancer was diagnosed. Another one of those men who couldn't take the strain. Then, ironically, while Heather continues to flourish, he died of the combined effects of a heart attack and ulcers last year. I can't know this yet, but what I am keenly aware of is Heather's spirit and cheek, marks of a survivor.

After Heather draws blood from my catheter, Dr. Greenspan quickly examines me. "You'll be around a long time," he says. "The question isn't if you'll survive, but how long." I don't understand what he means. And how long is long? "Five years, seven years, even ten years," he says munificently. How about twenty-five years, I suggest, still the same stubborn bickerer I was when Marek treated me. I'm after a cure, I say.

"Ah, that's another matter. A cure is a reasonable aspiration, but it's one not everybody can achieve."

It is a mark, I think, of my growing sophistication as a patient that this assertion heartens me. When I first fell ill, so qualified a statement would have distressed me badly. I wanted to be told at the outset that there was no cancer, and failing that, assured the malignancy could be cured. But having been burned by Marek, who failed to deliver on his extravagent promises, disappointed by surgery, I like Greenspan's cautious optimism—it seems the only intelligent outlook.

· · ·

I'm not expecting to go bald. Hair loss on the protocol, Arnold has told me, is mild to moderate. Most patients keep a head of hair throughout the treatment and don't need a wig. So late one night, about two weeks after my first treatment, I visit the bathroom and am astonished to find my panties littered with scraps of pubic hair. I'm also surprised and a little alarmed by the way my scalp feels, sore all over, pulsing with a queer sort of ache. Not wanting to bother Arnold with such mild symptoms, I phone Bruce Dolan, whose verdict is more or less what I'd expected. "Odd that you're losing the pubic hair first," Dolan says. "As a rule, that's the last to go. But if you're having scalp pain, I'd say you're definitely in for some hair loss."

More and more hair comes out. It is beginning to look as if I'll be completely bald again, but though this is certainly distressing, I'm not nearly as wretched as I was the first time around. The hair comes back, I know that now, and besides I've dealt with baldness before and know I can do it again. The loss is temporary. I'm practiced in coping with the inconvenience.

Still, I'm more upset than I want to admit with William Arnold. My new Dream Doctor has begun to show some flaws. Arnold told me hair loss would be slight, and yet three weeks later, I'm well on my way to baldness. I can't help but wonder, are there other, perhaps more serious side effects of the therapy that Arnold hasn't bothered to mention to me?

· · ·

On my second trip to California, in October, Hugh and I build in a short pretreatment stay by the sea. And by so doing, give our cross-country medical commute the aspect of a much needed holiday. This is the first time we have been away together since our trip to Jamaica last winter, and although the purpose of our trip, chemotherapy, is hardly romantic, we feel like honeymooners. Dazed and warmed with pleasure, we read and relax, baking under still summerlike skies, and now that my body is pretty well healed, we remember again how our bodies fit together in love.

Then it's on to Jordan Hospital where Dr. Arnold tells me he's too busy in the lab to serve as the attending physician on my case and explains that a woman doctor, Melissa Eaton, will look in on me when I come in for treatment. Okay, whatever, I say, though I'm secretly quite disappointed. I wanted us to be tight, a team.

Bruce Dolan, who's ordinarily very cheerful, seems a bit disheartened when he comes in to open my catheter. I wonder what's wrong and he tells me he's just had bad news. A woman on the protocol has died, someone he was very fond of. I assume it was the cancer, but Dolan says no, she failed to survive an intestinal obstruction. Lesions from therapy caused her death. Lesions? What lesions? This is the first time I've heard about lesions. Dolan explains that as the chemicals circulate in the abdomen, they cause internal scarring, which may become severe enough to eventually block the bowel. Food can't pass through the clogged innards, and if the condition isn't corrected by surgery, the patient dies. "Morbidity" is the word doctors use to describe such a serious, though not necessarily fatal, complication. There is a "risk of morbidity," that is, a risk of death.

My hair is entirely gone by now, and I am subject to possibly lethal intestinal damage, a hazard against which I have not been specifically warned. It's only five weeks since I chose Arnold as my savior and already I'm treading on swampy, uncertain ground. What next? I'm disturbed and frightened that I was apprised of neither the side effects nor the risks of this therapy.

Nor is the woman recently dead after a bowel obstruction the protocol's only loss. Two other patients—they both completed therapy before Dolan came to work here—have also succumbed, this time to the cancer itself. Their demise, Dolan explains, has "significantly raised our hazard function."

"Hazard function" is another of those interestingly neutered scientific phrases—it means "risk of death" as well.

I've been keeping so busy, planning, arranging, learning about my disease, that I've tamed the sense of my danger, contained it. Now it returns, however, with a loud and savage roar. I haven't by my cleverness quite outwitted death. It may still, I realize with sinking heart, be out there waiting for me.

. . .

Home again, I have cause for yet another grievance against William Arnold. Ezra Greenspan has given me a paper of his to read, the subject, BCG, an effective immunotherapeutic agent without toxicity. You could benefit from this stuff, you really could, he says. So read! Greenspan sounds like a short-order cook and not the genius he very likely is. BCG, I find out, is eleven percent effective against ovarian malignancies, and not wanting to waste a single percentage point in my battle against the disease, I decide to do as Greenspan says, and receive the immunotherapy, which is administered by injection, like a vaccine.

By this time, however, I've come to understand the very rigid guidelines that govern research protocols. Treatment must be absolutely uniform. A set of specific drugs in fixed quantities is administered and then the follow-up data—cures, remissions, deaths—are duly recorded. And Arnold is *not* testing the efficacy of BCG. Never mind that the eleven percent edge it would provide will help me substantially toward cure. The integrity of Arnold's data is paramount; for me to take the BCG might violate the controls of his experiment.

Reluctant to ask Arnold if he'll allow the immunotherapy, which is nontoxic—no side effects at all—I call Dolan instead. He says he thinks Arnold would be obliged to drop me from his research population if I were given BCG—I wouldn't be counted in his published data—but he's pretty sure the Los Angeles doctor would continue to treat me. Fortified by Dolan's words—he's also said that if he had cancer BCG would be the first thing he'd get—I call Arnold and am surprised and disappointed by his response. Oh, don't let Ezra talk you into that, he says dismissively, and then, more firmly, that if I insist on receiving the immunotherapy I'll have to go elsewhere for treatment.

Hey, Dr. Arnold, I object, that's putting *your* protocol ahead of *my* life. No, says the doctor, it's simply that we have to be able to sort out the various toxicities. I don't point out that Greenspan has told me there is no toxicity. Couldn't you er, footnote me? I plead. I've learned from my bit of reading that anomalies in the patient population are sometimes dealt with this way. But Arnold's icy "I don't think so" is delivered with an air of finality. Here we have it again: Research comes first; patient welfare a tardy second. That's the scientific way.

At the office, I skip through my latest bank statement and note that our already ransacked savings will be almost entirely depleted by the time I finish this cross-country commute. How to reconcile our need to economize with my determination that we should build "up" time into each of our trips to Los Angeles? More than ever before in my life, I am living in the present, afraid to project into the now uncertain future, wanting to wrest as much pleasure as I can from the moment, and wanting, too, to take the dread out of the long months of chemotherapy, the laborious hospital stays. Depression is always there, lurking just below the level of consciousness, and I have to fight hard to keep it submerged. Creating intervals of pleasure is my only way of doing this.

With our needs, both financial and emotional, in mind, I come up with a plan. If I were to write a travel piece on Palm Springs, we'd be able to secure press discounts on lodging there and so would be able to afford a few days of rest in the desert with every trip to the West Coast. Helen agrees to this plan, and I begin loosely mapping our itinerary, happily anticipating a winter punctuated by the desert's reliable sunshine and wide sparkling skies.

In all, I will spend about twelve thousand dollars in illness-related expenses, travel and so forth, during the two years that I'm sick—my medical insurance covers the really big bills—not a pittance, but not a fortune either. I will come to consider the money expended to keep my spirits from collapsing, to afford relief from the tedium and anxiety of disease, very well spent indeed.

. . .

Our schedule for my third treatment has been set—Hugh and I will spend several days in the sun in Palm Springs, then hop a plane for Los Angeles and treatment, followed by a weekend of rest before flying back to New York. I work double time at the office to make up the week I'll be away.

I am very much looking forward to the time Hugh and I will spend together in Palm Springs. Some couples are no good when they travel. Their life together depends on their shared obligations as parents, property owners, boosters of each other's careers. When temporarily deprived of these arrangements, they fall to bickering, grow irritable with each other, at odds. For Hugh and me the opposite has always been true. It was in the ambitious city where my achievements so outdistanced Hugh's that we fell short. Left to ourselves in the country, we always came together again. And when traveling, we're at our best, buddies, good friends, happy on the road.

The Desert Princess, where we're staying in Palm Springs, is marvelous, a jewel of a hotel inlaid on the desert floor, with views of the rugged Chocolate Hills and the snow-topped peak of Mount San Jacinto. Lazy days by the pool are followed by late nights around the piano in the hotel lounge. An afternoon's shopping has supplied me with a small but colorful wardrobe of lightweight pastels—apricot, salmon, baby blue—and I feel glamorous and gay. Perhaps I delude myself, but I don't think anybody has the slightest idea I'm sick.

We set aside a day to drive to Los Angeles. I've arranged to see a doctor there, Phil Goodridge, whose name appeared almost as frequently as William Arnold's in the papers I took away with me from the Shelburne. I feel no sense of urgency about the visit with Goodridge, but as we're going to be in the area, I think, why not? I don't want to leave any stone unturned.

As the day approaches, though, both Hugh and I are reluctant to relinquish our holiday mood, and so plan a route that will make the outing seem vacationlike and less of a chore. We'll zip into L.A. on the freeway, then take a leisurely, scenic route back, down the coastline to San Juan Capistrano, where we'll tour the mission and have an early supper before turning inland into the grassy foothills that wind upward towards the rugged San Bernardino range.

How is it possible that bad news can still take me by surprise? What Phil Goodridge tells me blasts my holiday mood to pieces and has me edging back toward the black pit of despair. Goodridge savagely attacks Arnold's data—the patient population in Los Angeles is mixed and includes women with microscopic disease who could be expected to last four years without *any* form of therapy, he tells me. Arnold's cure rate of seventy percent is wildly inflated, with real successes closer to the five to fifteen percent mark. Given my particular cell type, Goodridge would give me only the five percent, with just two years before the cancer could be expected to run out of control. As for Greenspan's BCG, he thinks I'm deluded to expect any help there. The studies which heralded it have been discredited, he says. Nor does, he, Goodridge, have anything better to offer me. I'm stuck with two years, with a measly five percent, unless I want to try autologous bone marrow transplant. I might be one of the rare individuals who could benefit from it. Goodridge is quite civil, friendly even, as he tells me all this, as he smashes my hopes to pieces with this well-considered critique of his colleague's achievement.

As Hugh and I begin the drive south to San Juan Capistrano, I'm sunk again in misery. The mission is shut tight by the time we arrive, as is the little town that bears its name. All we can find open is a sleazy bar, where I quickly down three gin and tonics. Outside it, in a public phone, with traffic whizzing by, I make a phone call to Bruce Dolan, asking in a rambling, desperate way about cell types, about cure rates of one to five percent. Bruce tries to reassure me, but I'm too panicky and confused to absorb what he says. Goodridge is an expert, as famous as Arnold. Perhaps he's right, *probably* he's right. I've been a fool to think the Jordan Hospital protocol would work. Then in the fading but still beautiful early evening light, we begin to climb into the mountains just above Palm Springs, and as we follow the wildly curving road, I toy with thoughts of suicide. It would be so easy just to let the car swing wide on one of these steep, swooping curves. In my mind, I see it rolling over and over, a somersaulting fireball, landing finally in the deep green cushion of a ravine. One little movement of the wrist, a slight unsteadiness on the steering wheel, and this life, to which I've been clinging so tenaciously, would finally be finished. Over at last.

When we arrive back at the Princess, where memories of the lovely days we've passed so recently seem ghostly and cruelly mocking, I decide to phone Greenspan. Maybe he can help assuage my fears, lift this deadening despair. Surprisingly, for his is a frantically busy office, I'm put through to the doctor right away. "That Goodridge, he sounds very pedantic to me," says the Manhattan oncologist when I explain what I was told in L.A. "You know what the word means, 'pedantic'?" Of course I do, I say, in a dull, spiritless voice. "That's a priori reasoning. I myself would give you a fifty percent chance to make it all the way out to the ten-year mark if we continue with the immunotherapy." But Goodridge says the BCG doesn't work. I say that the study that established its efficacy has been discredited. "Not discredited," says Greenspan, "just not repeated. There's a difference. Look, there's no doubt in my mind that it's going to do you a lot of good." I immediately adjust my mind's picture of Goodridge. He's just another of the impatient young Turks of research. Probably Greenspan knows as much; maybe he knows even more.

I tell Greenspan about my hope, so far shared only with Hugh, that I'll soon be well enough to adopt a child. "That's a tough decision," Greenspan says. "I feel for you, I really do." It's tough all right. Goodridge gives me just two years, and even if I get the decade Greenspan is hoping for, that's still not nearly long enough to raise a child. Besides, each day, month, and year of that decade will be awash in this fearful uncertainty. I'm not giving up my hope for a child yet, not for a while, but clearly any attempt to adopt must be postponed until my future is more secure.

After finishing with Greenspan, I'm quieter, though still hugely exhausted by the day's unexpected emotional turbulence. Relief issuing from every pore, I climb into bed with Hugh, and hugging him tightly, sink into a heavy, dreamless sleep.

. . .

The next day, we've a balloon trip scheduled at sunrise, and it is amazingly easy, while floating high up in the air, over a rather mundane vista of miniature swimming pools alongside midget condos and roadways dotted with tiny cars, to put Phil Good-ridge's grim prognosis out of my mind. Through the day my mood lifts, gradually but steadily, like the kerosene-powered bal-loon, and by that night, as we feast at the Princess on grilled wild turkey and pumpkin mousse, I'm in the clouds.

The next day we attempt a doubles tennis clinic, and though Hugh, whose game is reasonably strong, performs well enough, I'm all over the court, thrown off balance by the speedy pace and unfamiliar strokes. Then, suddenly, splat, I'm face down on the asphalt. I've rolled my ankle on a tennis ball. The tennis pro assists me off the court, and puts me in a folding chair, where I sit, my injured ankle wrapped in ice, telling Hugh, who rushes to my side, not to bother, I'll be all right, to keep on playing. But soon it's clear that this is a really bad sprain, and I'm wheelchaired into the car and to the Palm Springs Trauma Center, where the ankle is set in a soft cast and I'm supplied with a pair of crutches.

I'm definitely not too agile on crutches. At the airport I inch over the tarmac, slow as an earthworm, and by the time we arrive at the hospital in Los Angeles, it looks as if a wheelchair is going to be my preferred mode of transport for the next several days. Actually, we need two wheelchairs, one for me and the other for our heaped-high holiday gear, which includes tennis racquets, tripods and cameras, as well as Hugh's golf clubs. We make quite a spectacle, wheelchairing up to the eleventh floor, where a grinning Bruce Dolan is moved to remark, "Hey kids, I think La Costa's south!"

My stay in the hospital is a particularly arduous one, since I must manage the ever present IV stand with the use of only one leg, but by the time I'm ready to leave, the ankle has nearly healed. I need only a cane when we step into a cab. I forget the altogether bearable pain right away. What remains in my mind is the comical picture of Hugh and me rolling onto an oncology ward with our festive-looking wheelchair. It would seem the Chemotherapy Kid has made her return.

· · ·

Hugh and I have discovered a pretty suburb of Los Angeles and are particularly drawn to a stretch of cliffside coast where the water seeps into broad sandy coves, and the rocks a few hundred yards out are littered with seals. We check into a hotel there while I recuperate from chemotherapy and nurse my ankle sprain. Bruce Dolan drops by to visit and brings with him a young, blonde, brilliantly beautiful California girl. Alexandra Scotti. A voluptuous thirty year old—she's all juicy curves—who seems to ooze health and vitality, Alexandra has been grappling with neuroblastoma, an invariably fatal juvenile cancer, for the past thirteen years.

Nobody lasts more than two years with neuroblastoma, nobody. Alexandra, alive and even glowing after eight surgeries, repeated courses of chemotherapy, is, like Heather Canning, an amazing anomaly.

Alexandra's story comes tumbling out at me. She's gabby, unguarded, and, a small-town girl at heart, eager for my supposedly worldly *Cosmopolitan* editor's point of view. Alexandra married young, just out of her teens, and now she "loves" but isn't "in love" with her husband, Jeff, she tells me as we stroll the cliffs —Hugh and Bruce are back at the hotel bar—watching a gentle winter sun tease silvery lights from the placid slate-gray surf.

216

She'd wanted to model, but Jeff didn't think much of that, and anyway, the same year she was invited to New York to be the new Black Velvet girl, a tumor sprang up, near her aorta, and she nearly died of a heart attack.

Neuroblastoma is a weirdly fascinating disease, it doesn't invade any one organ, as most cancers do. Rather, a series of contained malignancies keep on coming, exploding in the body, here, there, everywhere. This is not, as a rule, a survivable experience.

The doctors told Alexandra not to get pregnant, said she'd never live to see her child's third birthday, but she went ahead anyway—would I like to see a picture? Her daughter Elise is eight now. She just learned to ride a two-wheeler this very morning! But what Alexandra really wants to talk about is the husband she's not "in love with" anymore, and the lover she's come to prefer. Alexandra wants to leave Jeff, but can't. Any minute the cancer could come back and he'd say she couldn't take care of Elise. She'd lose her child. Besides, this new guy, well he likes her pretty well right now, but if she ever got sick again he'd probably freak. You know how guys are.

I offer no advice. Neither my role as cancer patient, nor as *Cosmo* editor, has equipped me to tell a girl cheated of her youth by cancer, how to conduct her life. But I'm drawn to Alexandra, drawn by her valor, her amazing spirit, drawn on this pretty California morning to another woman who has an even deadlier disease than I do.

Carol once said to me, you know you're amazing. If I had your disease I'd just turn my head to the wall. I'm not sure Carol's right, about herself, that is, but I know that this, this not turning my head to the wall, has helped preserve my life. Just as it is helping Alexandra preserve hers. People like to think it's mind over matter when you beat disease. It's not though. You might better call it a certain stubborn persistence, you might better call it love of life, you might even like to call it courage, if you're talking about Alexandra Scotti, my compatriot, my friend.

. . .

Arnold's timetable calls for me to have a CAT scan in December between my fourth and fifth treatments, but therapy has been scheduled for just after Christmas, and I find myself reluctant to make an appointment with Greenspan's radiologist. Goodridge came close to devastating my Thanksgiving and I so much want a calm and happy Christmas. Greenspan is out of town, and as I tell myself and Bruce Dolan, who calls to nudge me, so is every-body else. It just isn't feasible to schedule the scan until after the holiday. Bruce isn't at all impressed by this line of reasoning. "I can't help but feel that if there were a little more motivation here, you'd arrange something," he says. His words makes me realize exactly how frightened I am of this latest scan.

Gathering courage I call and schedule the X-rays. I warm to the radiologist, Peter Hill, immediately. He's quite young, in his early thirties, modest and kindly in manner, extraordinarily com-petent. Radiologists routinely let technicians administer scans, which they later interpret. If the pictures taken aren't complete enough, you're called back into the office to chug-a-lug more glasses of barium and to slide in and out of the giant X-ray ma-chine for most of yet another day. But Peter Hill takes his own pictures, instructing you to shift this way and that on the scanner, to be sure his views of your insides are sufficiently panoramic. It's an impressive performance.

Back in the office the next day, I try to put the CAT scan out of my mind, focusing on work. And on Christmas which, moved by a strong sense of community, I am determined this year to celebrate. I only seem self-sufficient, I think—I would have been long lost were it not for my powerful support system. The co-workers who covered for me when needed, my good, good friends, Helen, Hugh, my parents—I couldn't have survived without them. At Christmas you tend to review your life, sum up its accomplishments, see where you fell short. And if some-times in the darkest moments of this disease, I've been tempted to think, I did *nothing,* am worth *nothing,* now I'm easier on myself. No, I didn't make enough of my relationship with Hugh, didn't start a family, but if I had done nothing, been nothing, then how is it that I'm now drawing so much in return? "You've lived very generously," Hugh has told me, whenever I've grown down on myself, belittled my accomplishments. And now, this Christmas, I'm tempted to believe he's right.

. . .

I'm in the midst of arranging our upcoming stay in Palm Springs —we'll have a little longer than usual, owing to the holiday— when Parker tells me Bruce Dolan is on the line. Peter Hill has sent him the films from my scan. "If it's something depressing, don't tell me," I say glibly to Bruce, still in my happy Christmas mood. The long pause on the other end of the line promises bad news, and suddenly I'm very, very frightened of what Bruce is going to say. He tells me that the L.A. radiologist sees several pockets of possibly malignant fluid in my abdomen, an enlarged lymph node in the vicinity of the pancreas, and a small cyst, about as big as a dime, on the liver. What all this suggests, he reluctantly explains—I can feel him shrinking away from the phone—is a cancer that's run out of control, no longer held in check by the shield of chemotherapy. I'm to come to Los Angeles for biopsies but should expect to be treated only if the results of these are negative. Why wouldn't I be treated anyway? I ask. "Because frankly it would be cruel to continue with the therapy if you have persistent disease," says Bruce Dolan, and the pity I hear in his voice is loathsome to me. It's the kind of pity reserved for someone who no longer has even the smallest chance.

Immediately, I forget how much I like Bruce. He's not a doctor, I think, and he's entirely unequipped to be drawing these conclusions. He's just a glorified *nurse,* for Christ's sake, and he's also a tactless pseudo-intelligent would-be scientist *oaf!* I'm hating the messenger again, of course. With all due respect, Bruce, you are not a doctor, I say. I'd like to hear this from William Arnold.

Panicked, I put in a call to Peter Hill who comes promptly to the phone. The rule among radiologists is never to talk to patients, to let all bad, or even good, news come from the referring doctor. Peter, who responds deeply to people's fears and needs, who wants so much for everybody to be well, breaks this rule routinely. "There's cause for concern, but there's also good reason for hope," he says. "Ordinarily, when we see fluid in the abdomen we think bad things." Peter Hill can't say the word "cancer," and always substitutes the phrase "bad things," which I find endearing. "But your abdomen is nothing like the normal person's. You've had two surgeries and four courses of intraperitoneal therapy. The fluid is just where we'd expect to find it if fluid from treatment had been insufficiently drained. And what they're interpreting as nodularity, I myself think is just a loop of bowel. The cyst on the liver is all but certainly benign." You're good, aren't you, Dr. Hill, I say, you're very, very good. "I can't say that about myself." But you are, aren't you, you're the best. "I'm pretty good," Hill modestly concedes.

Arnold calls me that evening at home. "Admittedly, I'm compulsive," he says, "but there was enough that was funny about the scan for me to want to see biopsies before we proceed."

It looks as if I'm to spend another Christmas wholly preoccupied by my disease. There's an eighty percent chance that the cancer is spreading, Bruce Dolan has told me. If I'm to believe him, odds are strong that I won't survive to see another holiday.

Our Palm Springs Christmas is blighted by worry over this latest scan. We're settled into La Quinta, an aristocratic resort in a lovely mountain setting. But the beauty of the place feels like salt in a wound. It's queerly cold outside, the air brisk and keen and breezy, yet the hot desert sunshine is equally piercing. A tangerine tree is just outside our room, and as I sit beneath it, bundled into my warmup suit, I marvel that I can feel so bereft of hope and happiness in so appealing a place. Heavy with dread, I don't budge from our patio.

Hugh doesn't make any but the most passing attempt to distract me. He appreciates the weight of my worry, knows I will come out of this at my own pace. Hugh respects my moods, however extreme they may sometimes be. Throughout the course of this illness I've been sorrowful, spiteful, explosively angry. Yes, I've had my long stretches of good cheer, even certain moments which some might call "brave." But my emotions have also been difficult, stormy, and Hugh has moved through their thrashing wake with admirable steadiness. How would I have coped without him? I would have collapsed beneath the burden of my own turbulent feelings without his arm so firmly locked in mine. My anchor. And sometimes, my only comfort.

And so I sit beneath my tangerine tree, utterly disconsolate, with Hugh quietly beside me. What can I do, I wonder, to defeat this sadness, shake free from this evil spell? Knowing there is nothing to be lost—I can hardly feel worse—I decide to phone Heather Canning, Greenspan's nurse. Back in wintery New York, Heather is making soup for her man friend when she takes my call. When I tell her about Dolan's edict, that it would be "cruel" to treat me if I were to have progressive disease, Heather tells me to put this right out of my mind. "If the cancer stops responding, you simply find some other, more effective combination of drugs," she explains, adding that she herself was given only a two percent chance to make it to five years, and a zero percent chance of getting all the way out to ten. "Statistically, I don't exist," Heather says. All at once, I'm calm again, the black dread, spilled like ink into my mind, is whited out, erased. I remember Peter Hill saying there was "every reason for hope," and as I recall those words and breathe in the sharp, pellucid desert air, my mind suddenly shifts back into gear.

Feeling light and unburdened, Hugh and I decide to spend the rest of the day on top of Mount San Jacinto. And what a day it is, crisp and sharp and shimmering. The sunlit green of the pines is luminous against the bluest sky I've ever seen, and the thick carpet of snow on the ground untroubled by so much as a footfall. Warmed by the penetrating sun and moved by the radiance all around us, Hugh and I strip down to our T-shirts and fall into a happy embrace.

How blessed I am, I think as I hold Hugh close to me, to be enjoying this intoxicating day. It reminds me, and I do sometimes need such reminders, of how very much I still want to live.

. . .

The day after Christmas Hugh and I leave La Quinta and drive to Los Angeles, settling into a rather dingy motel by the sea. We'll stay here until the biopsies have been completed and I'm admitted into the hospital for treatment. As I confirm arrangements for these procedures with Bruce Dolan, the anxiety I've put on hold escapes as hostility. How angry I am at all these young Turks of research with their impeccable computerized programs so often without any real understanding of the healing arts!

Dolan has told me about a new treatment for ovarian cancer underway at a California university. It is what is called a "phase one trial," and involves an immunological agent, or "biologic response modifier," of doubtful efficacy. Both Greenspan and Dolan have told me the stuff doesn't work. In fact, phase one trials conducted to establish not the potency of the drugs employed but their toxicity almost never work, in spite of their often having damaging side effects. Why, I've asked Bruce Dolan, do patients sign on for these protocols? According to Bruce, patients recruited for phase one trials are given a heavily edited version of the truth. They're told that not all of the side effects of treatment are known but will, it is hoped, be manageable, that the drug being tested has shown enormous promise in the laboratory, and that, right now, nothing better is available for their disease. Bruce has told me that the manageable side effects are sometimes devastating, and that the treatment may not prolong lives by so much as a single day.

The phase one protocol has as its aim not cure—for many patients, the doctors know their medicine isn't going to work— but the garnering of potentially interesting data. Patients on these protocols are being used as guinea pigs. Better, I should think, not to let yourself be so used. Better yet, to seek out treatment from a gifted backyard oncologist like Ezra Greenspan, who, unrestrained by the rigidities of protocols, can prolong or possibly even save the lives of so-called "terminal" patients through imaginative and flexible use of known anticancer agents. The only difficulty here: it is the rare backyard that shelters so bold and gifted a talent.

I myself am on a much more promising "phase two trial"; toxicities have been established; what's being tested now is effectiveness. Should Arnold's projected numbers prove out, it will become a "phase three," or standard, treatment, though given the laborious schedule research follows, that can't be expected to happen for several years. In the meantime, of course, science must continue on its forward march, and immunotherapy is the coming thing. Protocols involving biologic response modifiers are easily and handsomely funded. And however unhelpful these phase one trials may be to patients, to scientific research, as it is structured today, they are essential. As Ezra Greenspan points out: "Probably fewer than five percent of patients are helped on phase one trials. But this is not to say we could do without them. Phase one protocols are the starting point. Without them we'd never move along to the more sophisticated treatments that do have a curative effect."

Again, I'm in the CAT scan room. The fluid in my pelvis, easily withdrawn and quickly analyzed, has been shown to be harmless, but it still remains for the doctors to sample tissue from the hard-to-reach cyst on my liver. This hospital, I remind myself as my anxiety over the coming biopsy begins to swell, has the best interventional radiologists in the country, perhaps the world. Still, I am annoyed that they are continuing with the biopsy at all—Peter Hill didn't think it was necessary and neither do the radiologists. They look frankly worried, and Dolan has told me that they regard the awkward procedure as difficult and not without risk.

Arnold comes by as I lounge sullenly on the CAT scanner, dressed in my blue paper robe, waiting for the radiologists to begin. My mood is edgy. "Look," says Dr. Arnold, in an apparent effort to pacify me, "it's entirely possible the cyst isn't malignant. After seeing the tests we ran on the fluid, I myself would put the chances of that at less than ten percent. But if it were to be cancer, it's the kind of growth we can zap immediately with radiation." I find this a persuasive argument, and as Arnold leaves, try to quiet my nerves by wisecracking rather feebly. Watch that sciatic nerve, I tell the radiologists, who plan to enter from the back, I hear it's delicate. The resident preparing for the procedure shows a face that's tight and gray. I stop this ridiculous patter as the intern positions the needle and, painlessly, precisely, plunges it into my liver. What an exciting life we patients lead!

We're soon told that the biopsy is negative. The malignancy hasn't spread. I have to remain in the hospital for several hours, though, so as not to further jostle my bruised insides, and Hugh, after showering me with hugs and gleeful declarations—"I knew it would be all right, pussycat!"—goes out for enough quiche so that most of the radiology department gets a taste.

Late that afternoon I'm slated to see Arnold. I find myself quiet and not particularly friendly—think of what the man has just put me through, declaring me all but dead, and on Christmas Eve!—as I ask about Dolan's adhesions. The doctor admits that they have been known to cause small bowel obstructions, "a factor related to morbidity," but these can be dealt with surgically, "usually without a colostomy." Though he dismisses the danger rather lightly, bowel obstructions are grievous events that sometimes lead to death.

Next, I ask the doctor about the deaths Dolan has told me about, and wonder if he's been obliged to revise his "hazard function." Arnold admits that he has indeed done that: survival is no longer at the seventy percent mark, but has dropped to fifty-seven percent. One more death and survival rates will dip down to about thirty percent, that's how small Arnold's group of subjects is. I'm beginning to understand the severe, built-in limitations of formal research. The patient cohort typically available to research doctors is very small, largely because of problems of recruitment, and the resulting data often inconclusive. But this is the only sort of data deemed acceptable by the research community. Ezra Greenspan has dealt with many more ovarian patients than Arnold, and I suspect with greater success, but the information he's amassed, the fruit of a long lifetime of labor, has been collected "anecdotally." As far as organized science is concerned, it doesn't exist.

Many of Greenspan's ovarian patients, who would be given virtually no chance at major cancer treatment centers, have been brought into remissions so long-lasting—approaching the ten-year mark—they might well be taken for cures. Greenspan uses hormones and immunotherapy to enhance the effects of known anticancer agents. When one drug stops working, he brings another stronger or different one into play. It's a tinkerer's approach, more flexible than the rigidly set treatment plans used at cancer centers like Community Hospital or Jordan Hospital, and often more effective. But there is no mechanism through which information gleaned from individually tailored therapy can be incorporated by the world of formal research. This is a great loss, because such inspired tinkering yields provocative data about effective new drug combinations, and is, besides, often the best or only way to keep a dangerous malignancy at bay.

Entering Jordan Hospital that night for my fifth treatment, I feel curiously exhausted. I'm weak, chilled, and slightly feverish. But Eaton, quite a shadowy figure to me—she's always rushing home early to tend to her family—determines that I'm fit for treatment. The next morning, as I wrench free from the Ativan, the groggy, exhausted feeling still hasn't lifted, and as the day wears on, I begin to suffer as well from abdominal cramps, which grow steadily more severe. I ring for Eaton, who is, typically, unavailable, and the intern who drops by to tap casually at my stomach says not to worry, it's probaby just gas. I doubt this, since I feel no pressure to expel any gas, but when the nurse starts collecting my things, saying I'm free to go, I can think of nothing much to do but stagger out.

Back at our motel, the pains grow worse. When Barbara Lee calls to see how I'm doing—no matter how crammed her schedule, Barbara always, always calls—I mumble something about the pain. Well, you generally have pain don't you, says Barbara, sounding cheerful, optimistic, and as if preparing for a nice long chat. Not like this, too much pain, can't talk. My voice is weak and watery as I return the telephone to its cradle and ask Hugh to run out and get a thermometer. It registers 102 degrees. After phoning Arnold and getting a telephone diagnosis of peritonitis, I slide awkwardly into a cab, groggy with pain and severely bloated. It's back to the hospital again. I feel like Job.

There, a culture from the fluid drawn from my catheter is taken. It will confirm whether I have bacterial peritonitis, with the biopsy the likely culprit. I'm instructed to take nothing by mouth, and am transfused with IV antibiotics. So it is that I spend New Year's Eve sucking ice cubes as I lie spent, ill, parched, and hurting on a hospital bed at Jordan. Hang on, I tell myself, hang on, by New Year's next year, you are finally going to have something to celebrate!

· · ·

Back home in New York, I'm still very weak and foggy, and Hugh is desperately worried—"Get to Greenspan fast," he admonishes, and since he's not usually an alarmist, I attend to this advice right away. Feeling vague and disoriented, I drag myself into Greenspan's office where blood counts and chemistries are taken. Greenspan is appalled by the results of both series of tests. Though my counts are nowhere near the nadir to which they plummeted after Marek's megatreatment, they have dipped to quite an alarming low, and the chemistries reveal abnormal liver enzymes which Greenspan thinks may now be chronically elevated. Adding to my discomfort, I have a terrible cold. "Look," Greenspan says, "you take a vacation from that protocol, two weeks at least. I don't care what they're telling you in Los Angeles, that's my advice." Greenspan doesn't give a damn if he offends Arnold, I realize, and I know this to be unusual among doctors. This magnificent indifference to a fellow physician's feelings feeds my admiration for Greenspan—he cares more about his patients than about professional solidarity. Greenspan also tells me to stay home from work, if I can possibly get away with it. "There's a very real advantage to your not walking around on the streets right now." I don't mind the postponement of my treatment, but don't want to be absent from the office. Not after having been away for two full weeks. I resolve to work half days instead.

For a while, this routine works well enough, but I seem to be getting worse, not better—the fatigue is becoming incapacitating—and one Monday in mid-January, I haven't the strength to go into the office at all. I phone Parker and ask him to type up a brief memo to Helen explaining that for the next day or two, I'll be working at home, and that she should call me there if she needs me. Parker phones back saying Helen has thanked him for his note, and that he should tell me not to worry about *Cosmo,* but to concentrate on regaining my strength.

For reasons that are not wholly mysterious—I am very sensitive to any hint that I am not in control of my work—I am suddenly furious. What does Helen think I have, sniffles, a headache? I phone the Boss and say she might like to know that yesterday I put in ten hours, even though extremely sick. Not worry about *Cosmo?* What is she talking about? I worry about *Cosmo* all the time! "There is absolutely no satisfying you, Barbara Ann," Helen tells me. "I know you work like a demon when you're able, and if yesterday was a day you were able, that's fine." Uh, oh, I say, don't be mad. I don't want you to be mad. "And I am not going to be yelled at for trying to be nice, Just know that I love you," Helen says summarily. And with that, she hangs up the phone, leaving me feeling chagrined.

The next day, back at work, I wander into Helen's office trying to mend this ridiculous rift. But the Boss is in Phoenix, delivering a speech. I canvass my office friends, saying don't you think Helen should have known how hard I'm working. Uh, I think she *did* know, say the office friends, looking at me like I'm slightly crazy. The next day, when Helen is back, I visit her office again. I asked six different people, am I right, I say, and they all told me, no you're not right, you're crazy. "Well, then, I'm talking to a crazy woman," Helen laughs. "But that's all right, so long as you know you're crazy."

I'm hardly alone in feeling that my professional identity is under siege. Cancer patients feel, quite rightly, that employers and coworkers no longer respect their competence. In fact, my long tenure at *Cosmopolitan* and my friendship with Helen Brown makes me one of the lucky ones. Both my boss and the corporation for which we both work have been extremely loyal to me. Most cancer patients aren't nearly this fortunate. Those with blue-collar jobs are often let go shortly after getting sick and made to assume the cost of their own medical benefits. Even solidly middle-class employees have difficulties. Perhaps they're not fired outright, but they are stigmatized, given no further pay raises or promotions. Lacking the leverage good health bestows, they feel both frozen in their jobs and ill-equipped to seek out new employment. Though as well positioned, practically, as a person can be, I share the typical cancer patient's insecurity. I, too, feel disempowered, hobbled by my disease.

. . .

Our sixth and last stay in Palm Springs is quiet and lovely, and it seems at first as if the chemotherapy that follows will also be uneventful. But once again, we're back at the beach motel for only a few hours before my temperature starts to climb and I experience the abdominal pains I now know accompany peritonitis. I check back into the hospital for intravenous antibiotics, which are so slow in coming—it's Presidents' weekend, the staff is skeletal—that I'm obliged to stay awake, ringing for tardy doctors, until four and five in the morning. Are these long, wretched stretches of dead time in the hospital never to end? After fifteen months of treatment, I feel as if I've been sick forever.

A few days later, after the pain has eased and the fever lifted, Melissa Eaton is in my room, come to say good-bye, to discharge me from the protocol. "We recommend that you have a third-look laparotomy in six weeks," she says, extending her hand in farewell. Eaton is referring to the look-see operation which will confirm that the cancer is no longer present. I'll think about it, I say, but right now would you mind arranging for me to have one more course of IV antibiotics? Eaton gives me a stony stare—she doesn't like me telling her how to do her job—but I don't mind. I don't want to return home only to find that I'm still sick with peritonitis.

I pay very little attention to Eaton's recommendation. Within reasonable limits, I now trust myself to make my own medical decisions. I've been weakened by this protocol, particularly so during the last two months. My counts are way down, the two bouts of peritonitis have exhausted me, and I have begun to suffer from a loss of sensation in my hands and feet. Neuropathy, caused by cisplatin, Arnold and Greenspan agree, and Greenspan adds, you're lucky it isn't worse.

I have other reasons to resist Eaton's suggestion. Bruce Dolan has told me that at the last international conference on intraperitoneal therapy, back in November, Arnold came under attack. Paul Strasser, his turncoat protégé, sent a representative who accused Arnold of underreporting neurotoxicities. More significantly, Dr. Chris Webb, the surgeon who'd been operating on most of Arnold's patients, protested the use of the third-look operation as a research tool. He holds it carries with it formidable dangers. After two surgeries and six courses of therapy, the peritoneum becomes so scarred that a third look puts patients at significant risk of a bowel obstruction. Webb now refuses to do the operation as a routine part of the protocol and will consent to operate only if he is personally persuaded that to do so will be safe. Dolan, whose loosely held loyalties to Arnold have by now all but completely collapsed, has told me flatly that he doesn't think I should have the surgery.

I trust Dolan. He's not one of those technocrats of research, trained to maintain distance from his troublesome human "subjects." Still, I'm not so sure I want to decline the surgery; without this operation I'll never know whether or not I've been cured, never be able to fully put this disease behind me. I decide to wait and see what Greenspan thinks.

The next time I'm in Greenspan's office, for my monthly pelvic exam, the doctor brings up the subject of my possible upcoming surgery. "Now, we've got to talk about this operation," he barks impatiently. I've got my spies, I tell him—Arnold is under the gun for underreporting toxicities, and Webb is on his back for recommending impossible laparotomies. Greenspan hoots at this intelligence. He doesn't mind my smart-aleck ways. They want me to get a CAT scan right away, and to have the operation in six weeks. But I don't see any reason to rush into it. I want to wait for a couple of months, build strength.

"That's smart, very smart," says Greenspan approvingly. The real question, though, is do I have this operation at all, I say. Greenspan appears to think I should. We talk a little about surgeons, and I tell Greenspan about the way Webb handles this operation. He doesn't proceed unless it is entirely safe to do so, simply sewing the patient back up again if he finds too scarred and vulnerable an abdomen, not wanting to cause further intestinal injury. At this, Greenspan steps back, his eyes alive with attention and respect. "Ah," he says, "a man of high ethics." Then, abruptly, "I think you should go to Los Angeles for the surgery."

Greenspan gives this advice on the run, doesn't go into the reasons behind it. He's off to see his next patient. I conclude that he thinks the West Coast surgeon's extremely cautious approach is medically the most correct. But I'm frustrated that he hasn't given me more time. I'm always hungering for information, never satisfied with the little scraps of it I get. I am, however, far more seasoned now than when I began therapy. Now I expect less from doctors. Greenspan is busy, he's overextended, I tell myself. There are others who need him more than I.

. . .

At work, I'm contacted by a friend, a publicist who has just heard about my medical problems and who insists that I read a book,

The Healing Brain, by Robert Ornstein and David Sobel. It helped him put an end to a long, crippling siege of back trouble, and he's sure it will also help me. He'll messenger the book over right away. So it is that I come to dip into another of what I've begun to call my "magical medical books." And although my antagonism to this sort of reading has been mounting throughout the months of my illness, I try to keep an open mind.

The authors, who wield a sophisticated vocabulary, argue that the so-called "placebo effect" ought to be used as a "powerful medical intervention." Though I myself find it difficult to believe in a placebo effect that is more than very mild and fleeting, I'll admit that it exists and could conceivably have medical uses. But when the authors announce that "small yellow pills seem to work well for depression, while large blue pills have a better effect as sedatives," they begin to lose me. I wait to toss the book to the floor, however, until they describe the case of a woman with an inoperable uterine cancer. Say the authors: the power of "expectant faith . . . caused her to experience a decrease in swelling and fluid in her abdomen, and an increase in appetite. . . . Within five days she was able to return home from the hospital, and *although she died about three months later as expected* (italics mine), she was able to lead quite an active and comfortable life until her death." My, my, jogging in the evening followed by paté and rack of lamb right to the end, eh?

The trend towards self-healing began with Norman Cousins who made the "placebo effect" part of the culture's vocabulary in *Anatomy of an Illness,* the story of how he supposedly cured himself of a usually fatal degenerative disease by staying out of the hospital (where his blood was frequently and, he argues, weakeningly taken). Instead, he was visited by his doctor (the power of whose ministrations are discounted) in a hotel room where he watched Marx Brothers movies (it was his own laughter, he strongly suggests, that cured him). A careful reading of his book reveals that the man just got lucky—in no important sense did he really heal himself. It is a predictable irony that Cousins, a respected and otherwise moderate intellectual, became a national institution only after he loosed this ridiculous fiction upon the world, a world that prefers to believe that all misfortune, disease, poverty are the results of a lapse of will and can be remedied by vigorous self-assertion.

The legacy of Cousins lives, and not just in *The Healing Brain*. One has but to consider the enormous success of Dr. Bernie Segal's bestselling handbook of lore and superstition, *Love, Medicine & Miracles*. Or to look on the cover of *Life* magazine and see a smiling, triumphant picture of the now deceased Gilda Radner, under a banner headline that reads "Healing With Heart and Mind." It is reported that Gilda has held her ovarian cancer at bay with a strong assist from The Wellness Center, a support group that carried on "joke fests" and has Norman Cousins as its honorary chair. How many people have to die before the gullible public will cease believing that the grizzliest of viruses and the most aggressive of malignancies can be defeated by the magical powers of laughter and love?

This belief would be merely silly and sentimental were it not also dangerous. Along with Cousins, the party most to blame for the magical belief that the mind can heal the body is Dr. Carl Simonton who developed "imaging," a visualization technique that supposedly cures cancer. The trouble with imaging, quite apart from the fact that it is unreasonable to expect it to work, is that Simonton and his disciples are stern taskmasters. If the patient fails to achieve a cure, it is because he didn't try hard enough, didn't sufficiently purge himself of the negative emotions that led to the cancer in the first place. Guilt is added to the burden of pain and sadness the cancer victim already has to bear. While Simonton doesn't argue that visualization should serve in place of medical treatment, he is frequently misunderstood by patients already querulous about "invasive" surgeries and "toxic" or "poisonous" chemicals as meaning exactly that. More than a few curable cancers have gone untreated while patients foolishly imagined they could defeat their disease through the force of mind alone.

That night for comfort I reread a favorite book, first discovered when I was being treated by Marek, Susan Sontag's *Illness as*

Metaphor. Sontag, herself a survivor of what might have been a fatal breast cancer, argues that twentieth-century myths about cancer are as backward and ungrounded as those that surrounded tuberculosis in the last century. Just as the romance of TB failed to survive discovery of its cause and cure—a villainous microbe but one by no means attracted, as people believed in the last century, by an ethereal temperament—so, too, will today's anti-romantic mythology surrounding cancer, which holds that it strikes only those who are cold, unloving, and emotionally blocked, crumble into dust when science finally defeats this disease. In the meantime, she points out, we have the partial cures offered by the advancing sciences of chemo- and immunotherapy, and these are certainly more effective than trying to exorcise non-existent emotional bogeymen.

No support group can substitute for timely and effective medical treatment. Nor should the unlucky patient who doesn't respond to therapy ever be blamed for the deadly progress of his or her disease.

. . .

I read through the journals I've been keeping ever since last January, when I'd recovered sufficiently from the shock of discovery to begin keeping a record of the perilous adventure on which I'd embarked. When I find the portions that deal with Goodridge and Wirth, and remember that both of them have said that my chance of cure is under five and maybe under one percent, I find myself sliding into a depression. Though others have discounted this view as too negative, it's difficult to put aside entirely the dread of their grim prognosis once instilled in me. Having the time to think, to ponder, isn't necessarily so fortunate. I was happier when my every moment was occupied, either with work or the logistics of my cross-country commute. Easter is approaching. The sense it brings of new beginnings only deepens my distress. I cry when Carol, who loves holidays, brings me some painted Easter eggs, and I cry some more after Barbara Lee describes the Easter basket she has put together for her daughter Kate. I think, nostalgia running in my mind like a dirge, about chocolate bunnies and Easter outfits—I always had a light woolen coat in some birthday-cake pastel, shiny Mary Jane's, a hat with flowers bunched about its rim, and though I generally either sweltered or froze in my pretty, promising new clothes, I always thought I looked wonderful. Lost in these feelings, I recall how innocent my life was in the old thoughtless days before I became so sick. I'd phone my mother every Friday afternoon, and she would always feign surprise at the call, saying, "Hello, Baba!" using her baby name for me. Now she never calls me "Baba" when we talk, and our subject isn't parties or new dresses or goings on at *Cosmo,* as it used to be, but rather what Greenspan said to me, and have I gotten my CAT scan yet, and when do I think I'll be going in for surgery?

I talk these feelings over with Barbara Lee, who, for the past year and a half, has never failed me as a confidante. I've begun longing for my childhood, I tell my friend, or even for the normal knockabout ease, the casual aimlessness I felt when cancer was still a disease that happened to old people, other people, certainly not to me. Barbara is visiting my house in the mountains, and as we talk, we're walking through a big, still-barren pasture toward the woods and the brook, just beyond their border, which is high now with spring rain. You can hear it lightly rushing behind a tall stand of pines. Somehow we always take this route, pausing at the edge of the woods to sit back on our haunches, smoke a cigarette, and listen to the brook, whenever either of us has anything important to say.

Barbara tells me about a friend of hers who gave birth to a grievously deformed child. The tragedy was even worse than it might have been, because the child lingered for nearly a year. When Barbara's friend finally lost her daughter, she went through a deep depression and hasn't come out of it yet. "She says that she and her husband will never be happy again in the old way," says Barbara Lee. "I guess that's what happens when the fabric of life is irrevocably rent."

I wonder, was it luck that brought me Barbara Lee as the companion of my youth who would always stay close to me. Or did I do something smart when I saw her rush of straight blonde hair and long, slim legs hurrying through the *Cosmo* corridors, and thought, that one, that one will be my friend? Barbara Lee understands what I'm going through. Her intelligence—and compassion—are as welcome as the coming spring.

. . .

A call comes from Alexandra Scotti. Her speech is fast, her voice pitched high, either in excitement or in fear, I can't tell which. "The cancer's back," she tells me. Oh shit, I say. Shit, shit, shit! "I know it's horrible, but Barbara, I have to tell you, it almost doesn't matter. I've just had the most wonderful *time* in the past few months. Even if I die, at least I'll have had these months." Alexandra, who's been in and out of the E.R. six times in the past three weeks for pain, has left her husband, and is now juggling a small brass band of boyfriends. I hear about each of them, their virtues, their possible flaws, what do I think? Which one sounds the best to me? Usually she wouldn't be unfaithful—"I'm basically monogamous"—but frankly, right now, she's trying to keep them all, she can't tell which of them is going to "freak" when he realizes how sick she's become. Alexandra's talking a mile a minute, girl talk, boyfriend talk, and then, almost as an afterthought, tells me she'll be having a radical new experimental treatment, injections of radioactive isotopes targeted to destroy the tumor without damaging healthy tissue. "My doctor—and, Barbara, this is the good thing, I *love* the doctor I have—he says it will just get the cancer, zap!" Alexandra's treatment has to await the construction of a special lead-lined chamber. For several days she'll be as hot as an atomic bomb.

"Even if it doesn't get the cancer"—Alexandra knows no treatment is ever likely to cure her entirely—"I'm still glad I did what I did. I've had more fun in the past three months than in my entire life. And Barbara, I never said anything, but you know, sex with Jeff, it never was that good." Alexandra's sex life apparently has greatly improved with the advent of the boyfriends. Finally, in spite of her great danger, Alexandra has broken free.

Full of bravado, Alexandra says she plans a trip to Europe—"I've never been, and if I die of a heart attack or something while I'm there, well that will be okay"—and also wants to visit me in New York. She's never been East, longs to shop at Blooming-dale's, see all the plays. I say, come Alexandra, come, I'll spring for half the ticket and you won't spend a penny while you're here. We make arrangements for her to visit, which we'll end up post-poning—first she's too sick, then while she's preparing to go to San Francisco for the new treatment, I'm in the hospital for my third surgery. But I want to spend a week of my life with Alex-andra Scotti, girlish, full of hope in the face of death, determined to have as much of love and pleasure as she can.

I think of the moaners I've known through the years, the gripers, the sourpusses, who take to their beds because a boss is edgy, a boyfriend neglectful, a child a strain. And inevitably, I compare them to Alexandra, so full of gusto, so uncontaminated by bitterness. I can't help but wonder why those who have a fuller plate don't share her marvelous appetite for life.

. . .

In my office, I sit in a pool of late April sunshine—it's now exactly a year since I collapsed in Marek's hospital—and compose a short but quite careful and concise letter to Greenspan, working on it nearly all day. He never gives me quite enough time, and now that I realize how many faults riddle the Los Angeles protocol and how very iffy Arnold's cure statistics actually are, I've begun to think about what may very well be the next campaign in the long battle of my illness. What will I do if the operation isn't "clean," if, during surgery, they find I still have the disease? I've raised this question with Greenspan before and he's said in that case we'll switch to "Greenspan's special crossover therapy," a combination of known cytotoxic drugs, given in reasonably small, homeo-pathic amounts. Side effects are minimal, Greenspan has promised, the therapy is given in the office, and it keeps people in remission for years. But when I ask, how about thirty-five years, the doctor demurs. "Well, that's another thing," he says. Greenspan isn't making any promises he won't be able to keep.

Foggy about what exactly to expect from "Greenspan crossover therapy," I ask in my letter whether it's true that remissions are sometimes of indefinite duration. I also ask if any women have died while on the therapy. Greenspan doesn't answer my letter, though—I've asked him to call me during one of his rare quiet moments—a lapse that hardly surprises me. He has too many patients, not enough time. But I've kept a copy and bring it with me on my next visit.

"You're putting on weight," Greenspan says, when after several hours spent in the waiting and examining rooms he finally gets to me. "But it's not unbecoming." And then to Heather, "She's good-looking *and* intelligent. That's what's rare, the combination. The only trouble is she talks too much." But then Greenspan thinks better of this observation. To me, "Actually you don't talk too much. You're a good listener. You're just too intense!" "Wouldn't you be intense in my situation?" I ask. "Yes, yes, I didn't mean it as a criticism." "I wrote you a letter," I comment, seeing in Greenspan's informality evidence of a good mood and the possible opportunity to clear up my confusion. "Yeah, you wrote me a *long, long* letter, asking me to look into my crystal ball and tell you how long you're going to live." "No I didn't, Dr. Greenspan, I wrote you quite a short letter with very specific questions that you don't need a crystal ball to answer." Noting that the doctor is still smiling, I proceed to take the letter out of my briefcase and wave it in the doctor's face. "Shall I read you my questions?" I continue. "Maybe I should have put a box beside each of them so you could check yes or no." My tone is good-natured, and indeed the atmosphere in the examining room is quite relaxed. Heather seems to be enjoying the way I'm putting Greenspan on the spot, and Greenspan is jovial as well. In this rushed and hectic office, I've begun to feel like family. He reads my letter, as if for the first time, pausing to appreciate the phrasing. I have written that I need to "rehearse psychologically" for a negative outcome to the operation. "I like that," says Greenspan, " 'rehearse psychologically,' that's nice." "Now, the questions," I say, and read directly from my letter. "Am I correct in my understanding that remissions sometimes last indefinitely?" "Yeah, yeah, I told you that a million times. Especially if the patient is immunocompetent." Greenspan arches his brows promisingly. He's given me tests that show my immune system to be in good working order. Okay, next question, "Have you lost a significant number of patients on the therapy?" "We lose ovarian patients all the time." What am I, a nincompoop, don't I know that this malignancy is often fatal? "That's not my question. Have you lost them while they were on the therapy?" Greenspan scratches his head and turns for help to Heather. "Heather, has anyone died since we added the actinomycin-D?" "I can't think of anyone," Heather answers, after a short pause. "Fine," I say, "you've answered my question."

But Greenspan isn't ready to let the subject go. "The real question," he says, "is how many women are on crossover therapy. Do the profession a favor. Call the chief ovarian chemotherapist at M. D. Anderson, Sloane Kettering, and Dana Farber. Ask each of them what they're doing with their platinum failures after second look. What formal or informal protocols are they recommending?" I surmise that Greenspan thinks these protocols aren't doing patients a great deal of good.

Too eminent to be worried about peer reviews and other constraints that keep doctors from talking about their fellow physicians' mistakes, Greenspan doesn't hesitate to take a critical stance. Or to share his misgivings with me. Many, many women are dying, Greenspan says, who might be alive were doctors less rigid and less conventional in their choice of therapy.

As I leave Greenspan's, and rush back to work, I'm growing more and more elated. *Nobody has died on Greenspan's crossover therapy.* If the operation shows continuing disease, I won't have to be poisoned to death on a phase-one protocol. Once again, it is hope, beautiful hope, that rules me.

· · ·

In my office, I phone Dr. Webb in Los Angeles to discuss my upcoming surgery. "I understand that there may be risks associated with this operation above and beyond those involved with any major abdominal surgery," I say. "Yes," replies Dr. Webb, who seems patient and very gentlemanly. "It can lead to bowel obstruction, which may need to be corrected by a succession of progressively more delicate surgeries." "I don't want to sound neurotic," I say, "but I really don't want to be maimed." Dolan has told me of a woman, so damaged by therapy and repeated surgeries that she now takes all her sustenance through a tube. "That's doesn't sound at all neurotic to me," says Dr. Webb, who proceeds to tell me what I've already learned from Bruce Dolan, that he takes a very conservative approach to this surgery. "I don't want to leave the patient with problems she didn't have before," he says. "If I encounter large amounts of scar tissue, working around them becomes a formidable undertaking. There is the risk of developing further scar tissue that would greatly increase the chance of intestinal obstruction. And in that case, I can't proceed with a thorough third look." "So I've been given to understand," I say.

"You may have had some contact with Dr. Arnold while you were out here?" offers Dr. Webb, his tone is deceptively conversational. "Yes." "And you may know he holds a somewhat different view?" "I'm familiar with Dr. Arnold's point of view," I say—it's to operate, no matter what —"and I understand why he holds it." I don't elaborate, don't complain. "Fine," says Webb, the note of relief in his voice clearly audible. He doesn't want to have to discuss his differences with Arnold, doesn't want to compromise a colleague. "But given your approach," I say, "the dangers would be minimal. Is that correct?" "Yes, that's true, but the predictive quality of information yielded by the operation might be very poor." "I understand that," I say, "and am willing to sacrifice a more certain prognosis for the sake of my safety."

I tell Webb about my plans, if the results of the operation are not good. "My reasoning now," I say, "is to stay away from any phase one protocols, on the grounds that they're very toxic and rarely effective." "I'd go along with that," says Chris Webb. "I'd stay with what's proved." "I would not," for example, "submit to an autologous bone marrow transplant," I go on. "That stuff is for when your back is really against the wall," Chris Webb says.

The doctor tells me that recurrences do happen even when no disease is found, and that two years isn't any longer, as once was thought, the home-free mark. The disease may recur at five years or even at ten. That's a long time, longer than I knew, to wonder if the cancer may still be prowling evilly inside me. I've no choice but to live with this ambivalence. We set a date. He's to do the surgery on the morning of May 3. As I hang up the phone, I think about my early encounters with Don Lawson, how fraught they were with tension and confusion, how miserably powerless and alone they made me feel. And I know that with Chris Webb, I've been lucky enough to find a surgeon as amiable, ethical, and communicative as he is skilled. I'm in good hands here, I know it. It's not just "instinct" that tells me so—my instincts in the past have led me very wrong—but rather knowledge, hard-won. Webb has criticized a fellow professional in order that patients be better served, and this is a rare and selfless action for a physician to take. In the tightly knit community of doctors, the Hippocratic oath— Do no harm—has been turned on its head. What it now most often means is do no harm to your fellow doctors.

Since I'm having the surgery in Los Angeles, I'll be obliged to stay there three weeks; Webb doesn't want me to travel until I'm well on the way to recovery. I make arrangements at an oceanside hotel, booking a small suite for Hugh and me and a studio for my father, who is determined to be with me. My mother, enormously fatigued by the strains of my disease, will stay at home. The reasonably priced hotel isn't at all fancy, but it's airier than the rather dingy motel where we've been staying and has pretty balconies overlooking the sea. I'm determined that we will all three be happy there, no matter what the results of my operation may be.

In my room at Jordan Hospital, Chris Webb comes to see me. The surgeon is of medium height, spare, erect with the bearing of a soldier or tennis player; his posture as he straddles a straight-backed chair is relaxed and casual. Evidently, Lawson's formal visits of state are not to be repeated here. "I'm going to give you a little quiz," Webb tells me. "I'd like you to repeat what we discussed last time we talked on the phone." And I, the excellent student, who may by now be nearing graduation day, give him an accurate recounting of everything he's previously told me. Webb seems pleased with this recitation.

The intern who examines me next finds me in astonishingly good shape. I'm lean, but no longer skinny, and still tan from our last visit to Palm Springs. As he tests my heart, lungs, reflexes, and muscle tone, he smiles and remarks, "Are you *sure* you're the same woman I've been reading about in this chart?" My surgery won't be for two more days, and in preparation for it, I'm put on a liquid diet. This makes the emptying of the bowel far less violent and humiliating than it was before my previous surgeries. Nor is my modesty thrust brutally aside by those who tend to me. Indeed, the nurse who gives me one or two light enemas seems so embarrassed she can't manage to insert the tip of the bag. Maybe it would be easier for me to do that, I suggest, and so give myself the enema. I'm also asked, just before surgery, whether I wish to make use of an experimental device through which patients are able to regulate the flow of morphine into their veins. Here, pain-killers are put directly in the sack that feeds the IV. Why, of course, I think, there never was a need for those painful morphine injections at Community Hospital, the ones that were so rigidly scheduled I had to beg for them. And though I decline the device, worried by its experimental nature, I'm impressed and pleased that so much thought has been given to patient comfort. When the time for the operation grows near, I'm wheeled without sedation directly to the O.R., where—what kindness!—I'm wrapped in blankets just out of an electric warmer.

And so I come to realize that it is possible to conduct a surgery without dehumanizing the patient. Here there are no nurses screaming at me to wash my face, no freezing, aimless journeyings around the O.R., which left me feeling like a piece of meat. Before the surgeon enters, a mask is placed over my mouth, and as I breathe deeply from it, I slide into an easy sleep.

The next thing I recall is waking in the recovery room, where —another pleasant surprise—I'm breathing clearly, there's no tube in my nose, Webb didn't think it was necessary. My surgeon walks over to the gurney where I'm resting comfortably, looking pleased. I know the pathology report won't be available for several days and wonder if it would be appropriate to ask about the outcome of the surgery before he's heard from the lab. Any hunches? I can't help but ask. "No hunches," says Dr. Webb, "but I do have very optimistic expectations." I realize that he's certain I no longer have the disease. The nurses are gathered around my gurney, come to congratulate me, and when the path reports do arrive, it is as Webb expected. No visible or microscopic evidence of disease.

. . .

And so it comes, my moment of victory, amidst the noise and disorder of the recovery room. This time there is no terrible pain to blunt the impact of my surgeon's words. I hear, I understand. Yet my reaction to this news is quiet, strangely so. Is it because I cannot believe that this, my long-worked-for goal, into which I've poured such hope, such desperate, desperate energy, has finally come to pass? Do I feel that this, like the nightmare of the cancer itself, is also a waking dream? Never did I fully believe that I might die, and now I can't believe I'll live.

But my reactions are muted for another reason as well. I know that this, like every triumph over cancer, is a conditional victory. The disease may still return. And by now, my perception of life and health is quite different from what it was before. I feel my purchase on both is very loose, very tentative. I know now that the world is full of frightful accidents. And have found I'm not exempt from them.

And so I don't bring down the hospital with jubilant cries of triumph. Instead, I savor this reprieve in the privacy of my soul, and in my love for Daddy and Hugh. Quietly I rejoice, and in this, my limited and never fully expected happiness, I, who have been agnostic through the whole of this illness, finally offer up a prayer.

I phone my mother and Tony who, of course, are jubilant, and Helen who also sounds excited and happy, and then proceed to call all the friends who've stood by me so steadfastly. Susan, a fatalist, is almost as surprised as she is pleased by my news, while sunny, optimistic Barbara Lee is delighted but altogether unastonished, and Carol is just plain giddy with happiness. "Oh my God, I can't believe it! You're well, you're well!" she raves exuberantly. Dear Parker, who has been spared most of the dreadful details of this illness, sobs with happiness and relief, which moves—and also surprises—me. I thought he was too young, too much a part of the world that doesn't yet believe in aging or death, to appreciate my danger. I underestimated him. All along he knew.

Some flowers come, just a trickle of them, not a rush. I've had too many operations, too many hospitalizations, to expect or even want a stream of tribute. Barbara Lee, restricted by her tight freelancer's budget, sends a modest bouquet. Helen dispatches a plant. A dozen roses, sent by a writer friend who has learned of my good news from the grapevine, is accompanied by a simple but eloquent note: "Congratulations on a great victory." We will easily be able to transport these few offerings to our rooms by the sea.

My recovery in the hospital is painless and uneventful—there is a passing light fever, some slight discomfort as I use the spirometer—and within the week I'm discharged. As I'm packing to leave, Bill Arnold drops by to see me. He is wreathed in smiles, his clasped hands upraised in a ringside gesture of victory. We knocked it out, this cancer, it's flat on the floor. Whatever my misgivings about his protocol, I'm happy to see him. I guess we did it, I say, returning his smile, I guess we won.

Back at the hotel, I'm pleased to note that there's no longer any rivalry between Daddy and Hugh about who is better able to care for me. If not exactly friends, they've come to feel a sort of comradeship, having both been in the foxholes with me for so long. The detritus of past bitterness thrown up, I now realize, by their disappointment, their fear, is easily carried away in the quick, clear rush of our shared happiness. By the end of the third postsurgical week, I'm finally strong enough to sit up at the table, and the three of us take Bruce Dolan, that other foxhole buddy, out to dinner to celebrate.

Just before leaving Los Angeles, I have a last conference with Chris Webb. He is obliged to remind me that though the results of the operation were entirely negative, there is still a twenty to thirty percent chance of recurrence, a statistic with which I'm already familiar. That word, "recurrence," is misleading, suggesting as it does that the cancer has gone away but then returns. In truth, the "recurrent" cancer is one that has been partially dissuaded but not entirely defeated by chemotherapy. Some malignant cells, unseen by the surgeon's eye, missed even by the microscope—there are billions of cells in your abdomen, you can't possibly biopsy them all—remain, and as the years pass they regain their vigor, their killing edge, which has been temporarily blunted by chemotherapy. Those with recurrent cancers, and not just of the ovaries—many cancers share this ability to hibernate—have never really been cured at all, and it is possible, of course, that I will be one of them.

Then Chris Webb adds to my store of knowledge in a way I don't expect. "We're in uncharted territory here," the surgeon says. "This is the first time people have been exposed to the cisplatin in such high doses. It can drive the cancer so far underground that late recurrences, at the five- or even the ten-year mark, take place on sites rarely seen before—the lungs, the liver, even the brain." Like some monster mutant virus, the neoplasm finds its slow but deadly way to outwit even the most massive doses of the most potent drugs. From deep within I'm shaken by a terrible deep shudder. I have seen up close, at Marek's hospital, what happens when malignant cells crowd and derange the brain. For a moment I can't find air to breathe.

The stifling fear gives way after a moment or two to a need for discussion, for analysis, to the need to *know* that has marked me from the beginning of this illness. There are still some loose ends here; they need wrapping up. Panic gives way to my good student's need for summary and review.

I don't think patients should be used as guinea pigs, I tell Webb, after giving him a brief account of my misadventures with Marek. Even experimental treatment ought to aim, as its first and most essential goal, at cure. Out of tact, I neglect to mention that Arnold, too, has sometimes made me feel more like a bit of possibly promising data than like a patient to be healed. At the words, "guinea pig," Webb steps back. "I've begun to feel that way myself," he says. "That's one of the reasons I'm leaving the academic world." Webb will soon be moving into semiretirement in another state. "I'm ready to do what your Dr. Greenspan is doing, to take the best of what's available and just use it."

Wanting to test my own perceptions against Webb's surer knowledge of this disease, needing a knowledgeable perspective from which to view my experience, I tell the surgeon about some of the other difficulties I've had with doctors. At Community Hospital they said I had a forty percent chance to make it, I say, and Webb agrees this estimate was wildly optimistic. "More like ten percent, I'm afraid," he volunteers. Next I tell him about Wirth and Goodridge both putting my chances of cure on this protocol at under one percent. "I don't see how they possibly could have said that," comments Webb, mumbling something about doctors and their hobbyhorses. "Did they offer you anything better?" "Autologous bone marrow transplant," I reply. Webb shakes his head in disbelief. "Did they tell you about the mortality associated with that, the dangers?" "Wirth said it was my only hope," I say.

I myself will soon conclude that it's something less innocent than hobbyhorses that makes for such confusion. Weeks later, still trying to round out my view, I will call Wirth and find that after studying the results of Arnold's published work, he has reversed his judgment of it. And for this I don't blame Wirth, but rather a system that permits rivalries between doctors to flourish and is so very slow to circulate life-saving information. Wirth gave me his best advice at the time. He couldn't have yet known the value of Arnold's work.

Does Webb think I'd be irresponsible to adopt a child, assuming I could put my hands on one, of course? Adoption won't be easy, given my age and medical history. "Not as long as you have another parent," Webb says. I've nothing to fear there. Hugh would be fully involved should we succeed in adopting. "You should maintain the attitude that you're just fine now," my surgeon continues. "Try not to dwell on the idea of recurrence. Your worrying won't make any difference."

Webb reminds me to check in every month or so with Dr. Greenspan, and to have regular CAT scans. It will never quite be over, I'm reminded, the tension, the waiting for verdicts that still may overturn my life. Poised at the frayed edges of my uneasy peace there still glitters a sharp and treacherous sword of Damocles. When I finally say good-bye to the surgeon, who shares with his patients as much of the truth about their disease as they can bear, and who does his best to cure them, I realize that I've rarely met so fine a man.

Back at the hotel, I take pen and notebooks with me to the pool and begin to write. Still a little bit in limbo, perhaps never to regain the lost paradise where I dwelled when still a stranger to my own mortality, I feel I must record this perilous experience. What drives me, I think, is the same impulse that compels the combat soldier, back from fighting, to carve out a memoir of his war, to tell those who've had the good fortune never to have left the safety of home about the heroism and horror, about the riotous confusion and sheer unearthly strangeness, of the killing fields.

EPILOGUE

*I*n November, I began to suffer from intestinal symptoms, diagnosed by Dr. Greenspan as a partial blockage. I went on a low-residue diet and we waited. For the next eight weeks, I was subject to violent bouts of vomiting, throwing up food, bile, and, most alarmingly, fecal matter. By Thanksgiving, I was unable to keep even water down and was admitted into Central Hospital in New York. Greenspan feared the obstruction was becoming acute.

At the hospital, they sank a mercury-filled Miller–Abbot tube down through my nose and esophagus into the bottom of my abdomen. This unpleasant procedure sometimes eases an obstruction. I was given nothing by mouth and made to wait for a week, sometimes watching my clamoring insides on closed-circuit TV.

After a week, it was determined that the obstruction was acute and the decision was made to operate. A top Central Hospital gynecological oncologist stood by, looking for evidence of recurrence, while an accomplished bowel surgeon attached the portion of the small bowel directly above the obstruction to the colon. No evidence of cancer was found and the operation, called an anastomosis, was deemed a success.

I remained in the hospital two more weeks, sustained mainly by intravenous feeding. I still couldn't eat. I believed I'd rally when I returned home, but my condition worsened precipitously after discharge. Still unable to eat, or to eliminate normally, I couldn't maintain the level of nutrition that had been supplied by the IV. I also began to suffer from relentless gas pains, which couldn't be relieved by opiates. Whatever I took to ease the pain would also put the bowel to sleep, causing me to vomit up whatever small sustenance I'd been able to take. In the two months that followed, months of constant pain and near starvation, I lost thirty pounds. I thought, *now* I know what cancer can do. I didn't think I'd have the strength and stamina to get through this unimaginably difficult period. Physically, this, not any of the experiences I had had earlier, was the toughest part of my ordeal. Though he never said as much, I believe Greenspan shared my doubts that I'd have the strength to pull through.

Then, one day in late February 1989, the gas pains suddenly abated and I was again able to eat. Apparently, my much-abused bowels had been in cramp and the spasm had unaccountably vanished. Though my nutritional status stayed borderline and I remained very feeble, Hugh and I were able to go to Palm Springs, where I began to eat hugely, making up an enormous caloric deficit, and to regain my strength.

The bowel obstruction could be traced to several factors: the multiple operations—I'd had three in two years; the intraperitoneal therapy; the presence of a foreign object, the catheter in my abdomen, which was removed during my fourth and last surgery. Most likely it occurred because of some combination of the above. My treatment had indeed defeated the cancer, but it very nearly also got the best of me.

. . .

What conclusions have I drawn from my long and perilous adventure? That the ethics of cancer researchers are badly frayed? Yes. That life-saving therapies are buried by bureaucratic inefficiency and lost to internecine rivalries among physicians? Again, yes. Patients' needs often come a distant second to the hunger for funding and prestige.

I was obliged to witness, firsthand, the murderously slow and confusing progress of formal research. I stumbled upon Arnold's promising data in *advance* of the medical community, signing on for the Los Angeles protocol against the advice of several highly credentialed physicians. In the absence of any consensus about how my malignancy might be best treated, I had to become a student of my disease, checking one therapy against another, shopping for my cure and, ultimately, the arbiter of my own treatment.

I am hardly alone in having been made to bear this responsibility. Self-education, accompanied by advocacy, is frequently the only way the cancer patient can survive. But what of those who lack the resources, physical, financial, or emotional, to investigate the latest therapies, or to travel, if necessary, to benefit from them. Often they succumb to their disease. According to Dr. Ezra Greenspan, Chairman and Medical Director of the Chemotherapy Foundation in New York, no fewer than 60,000 cancer patients die needlessly each year as the result of outdated or inappropriate treatment.

Dr. Vincent De Vita, formerly director of the National Cancer Institute and subsequently physician-in-chief at Manhattan's Memorial-Sloan-Kettering Cancer Center, has also criticized the backwardness of our nation's oncologists, commenting publicly on their widespread failure to use the most effective treatments. Dr. De Vita blames this failure on ignorance—many physicians simply do not keep up with advances in research—and on economics. Specialists treating a cancer patient will often recommend their own specialty even if other treatments are superior.

To help remedy the tragic, avoidable loss of life caused by negligent and self-serving doctors, the NCI has established a patient hotline (1-800-4-CANCER) which offers information about the latest, most promising therapies. Dr. De Vita has also advised patients to be sure their private oncologist uses the Physicians Desk Query (PDQ), a full, computerized listing of state-of-the-art treatments available nationwide.

Hotlines and computer banks will often lead the cancer patient into the world of experimental therapy, where the latest research makes its debut. But while survival outside this world may be impossible, surviving within it can also be a treacherous ordeal. Some experimental therapies, particularly those totally unproven protocols known as phase one trials, are not only cripplingly toxic, they offer virtually no shot at cure. Patients on these trials are being used as guinea pigs. I had the good sense, or maybe just the good luck, to steer clear of them.

But even the relatively conservative treatments to which I did submit were far more hazardous than I knew. Marek did not tell me about all the dangers of His Drug; William Arnold was remarkably reticent about the possibility of adhesions in my abdomen, adhesions which did in fact bring me near death. In theory, the research physician is obliged to apprise a patient fully of the side effects of treatment. This certainly was not my experience.

Given the rigors and the hazards of my approach, would I advise other people in predicaments similar to mine to do as I did, to rely on self-education and advocacy in tracking down their cure? My answer would have to be yes. Experimental therapies can be dangerous, to be sure, but cancer itself is more dangerous still.

Ideally, your physician should check out treatment options, including experimental therapies, for you. In practice, however, many doctors will decline to undertake such a search. In that case, I'd advise launching your own inquiries. The NCI's cancer hotline is your best source of information. At your request, staffers manning the line will conduct a computer search of the approximately one thousand clinical trials testing new therapies underway throughout the country, and provide you with a computer print-out of those pertaining to your particular malignancy. The print-outs contain only bare-bones information, and your next step would be to phone the doctor coordinating the trial to inquire more closely about duration of therapy, success rates, and side effects. To take advantage of these trials you must, as a rule, be prepared to commute for therapy, and though travel can be an expensive and time-consuming prospect—insurance covers actual treatment costs—it's one you may well want to consider, if your survival chances with standard treatments are poor.

In selecting a clinical trial, however, I cannot overstate the need for caution. In their zeal to recruit subjects for research, doctors may underplay the hazards and overstate the benefits of a particular therapy.

I can only submit that you take whatever lessons you can from my own experience: be wary of self-serving doctors, ask careful questions and insist they be completely answered, then hope and pray that a measure of good luck accompanies your choice!

It is in any case good operating procedure, even with a more common and more easily cured cancer than I had, to visit one of the nation's twenty-five comprehensive cancer centers or twenty-one clinical cancer research centers, for an evaluation and consultation before committing yourself to a particular therapy. These institutions, funded by the NCI, are well known either for research or patient care or both. Although you may not need to participate in a clinical trial, you *will* need timely and expert treatment, and a consultation at a major cancer center can help assure that this is what your doctor is prescribing. A listing of these centers is available through the NCI hotline.

As you might judge from my experience, the road to the best and timeliest therapies for cancer is not an easy one. It is studded with pitfalls and mined with unexpected dangers. One can't help but think that there ought to be a better way. And perhaps one day soon there will be. Efforts are now ongoing to launch a cancer patients' lobby. More and more AIDS victims are surviving their disease because the gay population has mobilized into an organized political force. The time is past due for cancer patients to follow their lead.

The most crucial issue in the treatment of cancer is one of accountability. Right now, nobody monitors the ordinary oncologist to be sure he recommends the most effective therapy. Nobody polices our research institutions to assure that new, life-saving data is promptly shared and utilized. And nobody checks our research scientists to see to it that they are honest and humane in their treatment of human subjects. In addressing these problems, a patients' lobby could help usher in an era when responsible, state-of-the-art treatment is easily available to everyone stricken by this disease.

For now though, each cancer patient still stands alone. And for many of us, to take aggressive action in our own behalf provides not just our best but our *only* chance at cure.

AFTERWORD

by Ezra M. Greenspan
Chairman and Medical Director
The Chemotherapy Foundation

In May 1990, Barbara Creaturo developed signs of intestinal obstruction, this time confined to the lower bowel near the pelvis. CAT scans and clinical examination showed relatively localized recurrent cancer masses. I urged her to accept a simple but permanent colostomy which would allow treatment with a promising new secondary chemotherapy then being developed. She opted instead for an aggressive surgical tour de force performed by a highly skilled surgeon at New York's Mount Sinai Hospital. This forthright decision, optimistically approached, was in conformance with her usual intellectual and emotional life style. However, multiple futile attempts to revise and bypass the involved area of cancer eventuated in a downhill course over the next four months. Late in October 1990, while in full possession of her faculties, she signed a Do Not Resuscitate order one week before her death at Doctors Hospital, New York, while under the merciful calming influence of morphine. Her bravery and realism will always be remembered by family, friends, and physicians!

. . .

Recent developments have highlighted the pressing need for political action in the field of new cancer treatments. AIDS activists have shown how aggressive, unrelenting pressure on the National Institutes of Health, Congress, and the FDA can force early release of drugs for life threatening illness. Dr. Vincent De Vita, before resigning his position as head of the National Cancer Institute in May 1988, bypassed the FDA and NCI committees by issuing a nationwide Cancer Alert simultaneously to the media, the medical profession, and the public. The Alert indicated that years of extra disease-free survival could be available if thousands of women were given chemohormonal therapy for high-risk node-negative breast cancer. Dissemination of this life-saving information through the usual medical journals would have led to a delay of several years and much needless loss of life. Dr. De Vita's action underlines the critical need for swift release of clinical research data.

Already, lobbying efforts by affected cancer patients have had fruitful results. The womens' health advocacy movement has been responsible for pushing the medical profession, particularly surgeons, into accepting lumpectomy and breast perservation in selected breast cancer cases. Mammography has been made available through political efforts primarily, and not through the profession per se. However, the progress of formal clinical research as it exists today in this country, and the approval and release of new cancer drugs, continue to be frighteningly slow. Two new major drugs, carboplatin and mitoxantrone, which improve the quality of life and reduce the risk of unnecessary toxicity for patients with ovarian cancers, lymphomas, and other tumors, were released during Barbara Creaturo's illness, but after at least five years of unnecessary delays. In December 1990, hexamethylmelamine (Hexalen®) was finally approved for ovarian cancer after more than fourteen years of study at Mount Sinai Hospital. As the fourth drug in a combination of cisplatin, Adriamycin, and Cytoxan, known as CHAP or HCAP, it will provide additional years of quality life for ovarian cancer patients. Unfortunately,

Barbara Creaturo never was treated with this combination even though data indicating the improved survival was known for a number of years, but not emphasized, within the oncology community. Clinically useful secondary and tertiary protocols of treatment for ovarian cancer after platinum failure are still not clearly formulated by and for the profession. The need for immune stimulation in ovarian cancer patients, as indicated by my studies showing that good immune competence in patients as a result of previous recovery from tuberculosis resulted in unexpected long-term cures in both ovarian and breast cancer, has never been followed up. The antituberculosis vaccine, BCG, was finally approved in June 1990 for treatment of bladder cancer by local instillation, although it had been known to have beneficial effects for almost two decades for other cancers, including ovarian cancer.

Unrealistic FDA requirements in the past for proposed new drugs for life threatening illness have steadily driven the cost of drug development to astronomical heights, leaving the United States well behind Europe and Japan in the treatment of cancer. Because of the arbitrary FDA standards, physicians are forced to wait for as long as five to fifteen years because of an unrealistic twenty percent survival difference *required* to permit publication of data on effective, well-studied agents with government approval. As a result, chemotherapists in this country all too often draft hackneyed or highly toxic protocols which draw off much needed research funds and energy and are predictably of little use to patients suffering from first failure of "approved treatments."

A cancer patients' movement can reverse these trends. The year 1990 was marked by the release of the immune stimulant levamisole, to be used in combination with fluorouracil in the chemotherapy of colon cancer. This agent was known for twenty years, and numerous studies have been made in Europe and in the United States indicating this area of application, which was never permissible until now. Favorable results in the ten to fifteen percent range were admittedly possible with this agent, and would represent a potential saving of many thousands of lives. Yet lev-amisole was only released by an almost coincidental interpretation of two conflicting studies.

The victims of ovarian cancer should look forward to increasingly better treatment results with combination and sequential chemotherapy, and the combined use of immunotherapy including levamisole and BCG. There is ample evidence to indicate that an improved immune status, together with an improved cytotoxic antitumor effect of chemotherapy, can increase survival and even cure ovarian cancer in a significant number of patients.

In a democratic society pressure through active cancer patient advocacy could prove crucial in saving many thousands of lives in the future. Physicians, who are too often poorly served by our slow-moving research institutions, need the political impact of cancer patients' insistence on active, innovative, and progressive responsibility by decision makers in government.

A recently formed advocacy group known as the Cancer Patients Action Alliance (CAN ACT)* is now actively pursuing these goals. The fact that the members of this group are predominantly survivors of ovarian and breast cancer increases the effectiveness of their efforts. The informed lay person must become the catalyst in the complex, frustrating, but increasingly successful battle against cancer. Better treatments are useless if they are not available and applied. Cancer patient advocacy is an urgent necessity to achieve increasingly successful control of cancer.

As a result of the steady improvement in chemotherapy, the five-year survival after a diagnosis of ovarian cancer, which was five percent in 1960, had increased to fifteen percent by 1975. With earlier and better surgery, survival increased to twenty percent by 1980. In the decade of the 80's, the five-year survival increased to thirty-five to forty-five percent. At least twenty percent of patients are now disease-free and apparently cured after five years. With further improvements in patient education and earlier diag-

* CAN ACT is located at 26 College Place, Brooklyn, NY 11201.

hope that immunological stimulants and biomodulators will facil-
itate this great leap forward.

. . .

Dr. Ezra M. Greenspan is Clinical Professor of Medicine (Oncology) at the Mount Sinai School of Medicine in New York. The
Chemotherapy Foundation, a non-profit organization located at
183 Madison Avenue, New York, NY 10015, provides grants for
innovative cancer research programs at major medical institutions
in the New York metropolitan area.